T0400022

LONGITUDINAL STUDIES OF SECOND LANGUAGE LEARNING

Longitudinal Studies of Second Language Learning: Quantitative Methods and Outcomes provides a how-to guide to choosing, using, and understanding quantitative longitudinal research and sampling methods in second and foreign language learning.

This volume will provide readers with exemplary longitudinal studies of language learning outcomes, as well as an overview of widely used methods of data analysis. Readers will understand how long-term data collection processes are organized and archived, and how the data are managed over time prior to analysis. Each of the chapters provide applied researchers with examples of how language learning outcomes gathered over time can be organized into data sets useful for insightful descriptive and inferential analyses of learning outcomes.

As the only edited volume that focuses on longitudinal data analysis specifically for a second language acquisition (SLA)/applied linguistics readership, this will be an invaluable resource for advanced students and researchers of SLA, applied linguistics, assessment, and education.

Steven J. Ross (PhD, University of Hawai'i at Mānoa) is Professor of Second Language Acquisition at the University of Maryland, where he teaches research methods, language assessment, and second language acquisition. He has served on the editorial boards of the *TESOL Quarterly*, *Applied Linguistics*, *Language Testing*, *Language Assessment Quarterly*, and *Language Learning*. He is co-author of *Research Methods for Applied Language Studies* (Keith Richards, Steven Ross, and Paul Seedhouse). His chapter, "Mixed Methods in L2 Pragmatics Research," was previously published in the *Routledge Handbook of Second Language Acquisition and Pragmatics*. He also has a chapter entitled "Claims, Evidence, and Interference in Performance Assessment", published in the *Routledge Handbook of Language Testing*.

Megan C. Masters (PhD, University of Maryland College Park) is Affiliate Faculty with the Second Language Acquisition program and Director of Academic Technology Experience, where she oversees large-scale research programs related to second language learning, program evaluation, learning analytics, teaching, testing, and assessment.

SECOND LANGUAGE ACQUISITION RESEARCH SERIES

Susan M. Gass and Alison Mackey, Series Editors
Kimberly L. Geeslin, Associate Editor

The Second Language Acquisition Research Series presents and explores issues bearing directly on theory construction and/or research methods in the study of second language acquisition. Its titles (both authored and edited volumes) provide thorough and timely overviews of high-interest topics, and include key discussions of existing research findings and their implications. A special emphasis of the series is reflected in the volumes dealing with specific data collection methods or instruments. Each of these volumes addresses the kinds of research questions for which the method/instrument is best suited, offers extended description of its use, and outlines the problems associated with its use. The volumes in this series will be invaluable to students and scholars alike, and perfect for use in courses on research methodology and in individual research.

Questionnaires in Second Language Research
Construction, Administration, and Processing, Third Edition
Zoltán Dörnyei and Jean-Marc Dewaele

Longitudinal Studies of Second Language Learning
Quantitative Methods and Outcomes
Edited by Steven J. Ross and Megan C. Masters

Researching Creativity in Second Language Acquisition
Ashleigh Pipes

For more information about this series, please visit: www.routledge.com/Second-Language-Acquisition-Research-Series/book-series/LEASLARS

LONGITUDINAL STUDIES OF SECOND LANGUAGE LEARNING

Quantitative Methods and Outcomes

Edited by Steven J. Ross and Megan C. Masters

Routledge
Taylor & Francis Group

NEW YORK AND LONDON

Cover image: Getty Images

First published 2023
by Routledge
605 Third Avenue, New York, NY 10158

and by Routledge
4 Park Square, Milton Park, Abingdon, Oxon, OX14 4RN

Routledge is an imprint of the Taylor & Francis Group, an informa business

© 2023 selection and editorial matter, Steven J. Ross and Megan C. Masters; individual chapters, the contributors

The right of Steven J. Ross and Megan C. Masters to be identified as the authors of the editorial material, and of the authors for their individual chapters, has been asserted in accordance with sections 77 and 78 of the Copyright, Designs and Patents Act 1988.

All rights reserved. No part of this book may be reprinted or reproduced or utilized in any form or by any electronic, mechanical, or other means, now known or hereafter invented, including photocopying and recording, or in any information storage or retrieval system, without permission in writing from the publishers.

Trademark notice: Product or corporate names may be trademarks or registered trademarks, and are used only for identification and explanation without intent to infringe.

Library of Congress Cataloging-in-Publication Data
Names: Ross, Steven, 1951– editor. | Masters, Megan C., editor.
Title: Longitudinal studies of second language learning : quantitative methods and outcomes / edited by Steven J. Ross, Megan C. Masters.
Description: New York, NY : Routledge, 2023. |
Series: Second language acquisition research series |
Includes bibliographical references and index. | Identifiers: LCCN 2022025504 |
Subjects: LCSH: Second language acquisition–Research–Methodology. |
Second language acquisition–Longitudinal studies. | LCGFT: Essays.
Classification: LCC P118.2 .L669 2023 | DDC 401/.930721–dc23/eng/20220527
LC record available at https://lccn.loc.gov/2022025504

ISBN: 978-0-367-54159-0 (hbk)
ISBN: 978-0-367-54158-3 (pbk)
ISBN: 978-1-003-08793-9 (ebk)

DOI: 10.4324/9781003087939

Typeset in Bembo
by Newgen Publishing UK

Access the Support Material: www.routledge.com/9780367541583

CONTENTS

CONTRIBUTORS

Amber N. Bloomfield (PhD, Northwestern University) is a senior data scientist at American Institutes for Research (AIR). Her primary interests are applying data science methods to explore, explain, and understand data, using machine learning, statistics, and visualization. Previously, she has worked as a data scientist in institutional research for University of Maryland and as a research fellow with the Maryland Longitudinal Data System Center. In addition, Dr. Bloomfield led government-sponsored research projects supporting second language training and testing activities and the adoption of new technology solutions as a research scientist at the Center for Advanced Study of Language at University of Maryland.

Martyn K. Clark (PhD, University of Hawaiʻi at Mānoa) is a data scientist with the Academic Technology Experience group at the University of Maryland's Division of Information Technology. Dr. Clark has a background in second language acquisition and has previously worked as a research scientist at the Center for Advanced Study of Language and as Assessment Director at the Center for Applied Second Language Studies.

Daniel R. Isbell (PhD, Michigan State University) is an Assistant Professor in the Department of Second Language Studies at the University of Hawaiʻi at Mānoa where he teaches courses in language assessment and quantitative research methods. In addition to conducting research on language testing, he has experience developing and administering local and large-scale language tests. He currently serves on the editorial boards of the journals *Language Testing* and *TESOL Quarterly*.

Beth Mackey (MAs, Mary Washington University and the University of Maryland Baltimore County) is a PhD candidate in Second Language Acquisition at the University of Maryland College Park. She recently retired following a career with the US Government, where she worked primarily in language training and language testing. Her research interests include language aptitude and language assessment.

Atsuko Nishitani (EdD, Temple University) is a Professor at the Center for General Education at Kyoto Sangyo University in Japan, where she developed a new English as a foreign language (EFL) program for non-English majors. She served as the Deputy Director and oversaw the program from 2013 to 2017. She received her EdD from Temple University and MA in teaching English to speakers of other languages (TESOL) from Brigham Young University. Formerly she taught English as a second language and Japanese courses at universities in the United States. She has also co-authored several Test of English for International Communication (TOEIC) textbooks for college students.

Leslie N. Ono (EdD, Temple University) is an Associate Professor in the School of Policy Studies at Kwansei Gakuin University, where she teaches courses on research methods, academic writing, intercultural communication, and global Englishes. She also teaches undergraduate research seminars, providing instruction and advising on junior and senior thesis research projects. From 2009 to 2018 she served as the Director of the school's English language program.

Xiaowan Zhang (PhD, Michigan State University) is the test development manager at MetaMetrics where she is responsible for the development, delivery, and validation of their language tests. While at Michigan State University, she taught second language acquisition, teaching methods, and pedagogical grammar to TESOL undergraduates. She holds a master's degree in TESOL from the University of Illinois at Urbana-Champaign.

Qi Zheng (PhD, University of Maryland College Park) has research interests situated in the fields of second language testing and assessment, second language phonological and lexical processing, language variation, and language aptitude. She also holds a master's degree in Evaluation, Measurement, and Statistics from the University of Maryland.

INTRODUCTION

Longitudinal Design and Analyses in Second Language Research

Steven J. Ross and Megan C. Masters

In the domains of second language acquisition and applied linguistics, intervention studies with a pre-test, intervention, with or without controls, and a post-test have been the most commonly appearing design in the research literature. The duration of the intervention has served to differentiate studies that are essentially short-term from those that could arguably be called *longitudinal*. As language learning is inherently a gradual and cumulative process, the rarity of actual longitudinal studies has been seen as a consistent short-coming in second language acquisition and applied linguistics research. Two state-of-the-art summaries of longitudinal research (Ortega and Iberri-Shea, 2005; Barkaoui, 2014), appearing a decade apart, noted the infrequency of authentically longitudinal studies. A recent search of the literature suggests that the situation has changed little. As much language learning research is done in academic settings where access to study participants is often limited to less than two contiguous semesters, the research literature on both naturalistic exposure and intervention studies has tended to feature short-term laboratory-based studies and proof-of-concept interventions. These short-term studies increase the risk of unstable, inauthentic, and difficult-to-replicate outcomes. Our aim in this volume is to feature mainly large-scale studies that have been conducted at institutions with consistent multi-year archiving of language learning outcomes using standardized measures. Through the systematic examination of outcomes measures over time, researchers can develop unique insights into patterns of change that may have otherwise gone unnoticed. To this end, we will provide an overview of analysis methods useful in assessing the durability and validity of assessment policies, programmatic interventions, and the impacts of institutional policy changes.

DOI: 10.4324/9781003087939-1

Second language learning is inherently a multi-year process involving sustained contact and interaction with a speech community, or in a program of foreign language study organized around a curriculum. Immigrants and long-term residents are typically exposed to massive amounts of contact with a language through media, community, and educational interactions. Foreign language learning often begins in adolescence in compulsory curricula, which may continue into tertiary foreign language requirements. A subset of foreign language learners opt for more advanced instruction, and may augment formal instruction with study-abroad experiences of varying lengths. Assuming that successful language learning is a cumulative transitional process of converting declarative knowledge into procedural actions, especially in instructed second language acquisition and foreign language learning contexts, or a gradual process of restructuring an interlanguage based on both explicit learning and implicit induction of form–function relationships, it becomes ever more obvious that second language learning is a longitudinal process.

Much research on second language learning has focused on identifying the specific features of what is learned or acquired. The majority of research on language learning has been essentially structural, focusing on morphology, syntax, phonology, lexical size, and the mental lexicon of second language learners. A subset of research has, in contrast, focused on the acquisition of functional abilities rather than on specific linguistic structures. A focus on functional abilities might, for instance, entail a tally of can-do competencies, performances such as monologue narratives, descriptions, reports of facts, or role-played speech acts such as requests, complaints, or refusals. The research methodology for documenting the acquisition of both structural and functional aspects of second language learning has been as varied as the phenomena studied.

Analysis of structural or lexical acquisition is often based on cross-sectional samples involving experimental or quasi-experimental designs. Short-term learning experiments performed in laboratory settings often involve newer technologies, such as priming, followed by reaction time measures, eye tracking, or event-related processing measurements. Analyses of functional abilities are less feasibly measured with such technologies. When considering how longitudinal studies can be designed, it is certainly the case that newer technologies could be incorporated into repeated sampling of the same individuals over time. While this is a possibility, most quantitative longitudinal studies have tended to use more conventional measures of language proficiency rather than either narrowly defined structural or functional criteria. The use of aggregated test scores on standardized tests has the advantage of comparability with other research using the same outcomes. The tradeoff inherent in the use of gross measures, rather than narrowly defined measures, is essentially in the specificity of claims about what actually has been acquired over time. Minute analyses of interactional competences, for instance, can be documented with micro-analyses of interactions on repeated occasions with the same individual. Here the advantage is specificity of detail rather than generalizability. In contrast, group- or cohort-level analyses of gains in proficiency as measured with standardized instruments make comparison across languages, contexts, and cohorts more likely to be generalizable if the same sets of factors reappear as having a systematic and replicable role in accounting for individual differences in the language learning outcomes.

While we acknowledge that there are multiple methods of analyzing, describing, or documenting second language learning outcomes over time, in this volume we restrict our focus to methods of quantitative longitudinal data analysis. Our goal in this collection of studies is to provide samples of how longitudinal data can be analyzed using a variety of quantitative methods useful for providing generalizable inferences about factors affecting learning outcomes. To this end, we build on the existing literature pertaining to second language learning phenomena using some of the methods utilized in the chapters to follow.

The collection of studies in this volume features methods of analysis that build on conventional comparative group analyses of repeated measures of language learning, such as those used by Derwing and Munro (2013), in which group means are compared on the same measures spaced over time during which second language acquisition takes place. Methods of analysis that involve regression analyses to investigate influences on individual differences in outcomes (Daller and Phelan, 2013), or regression over time comparing factors affecting growth and change across cohorts in a language program in the form of path analyses (Noels, 2001; Ross, 2003) are featured in the chapters by Zheng, Ono, and Masters. Research designs focusing on the effects of context (Kozaki and Ross, 2011) or clustering of individuals (Casillas, 2020) or involving both fixed and random effects (Crossley, Kyle and Salsbury, 2016; Nagle, 2018; Raudszus, Segers, and Verhoeven, 2021) are featured in the chapter by Isbell and Zhang. Individual difference factors, now commonly analyzed with latent growth models (Ross, 2005; Jia and Fuse, 2007; Retelsdorf, Becker, Koller, and Moller, 2012; Grimm, Solari, and Gerber, 2018), are exemplified in chapters by Nishitani and Mackey. Aggregated data analyses of group or cohort means measured repeatedly, as first exemplified by time series analyses such as those used by Mellow, Reeder, and Forster (1996), are utilized in large-scale longitudinal summaries in the chapters by Ono and by Bloomfield and Clark.

Our goal in this volume is to provide examples of how large-scale longitudinal analyses can provide a macro-level view of language learning outcomes that may otherwise remain hidden within cross-sectional research designs. We also outline how longitudinal designs can be planned and organized as a data collection project to allow for systematic database construction, and management and archiving processes that ultimately provide the input into analyses of potential utility for program evaluation and monitoring purposes. Each of the chapters in the volume features one or more longitudinal data analysis methods focused on a foreign or second language learning phenomenon. All of the data sets used were originally authentic language assessment data collected for validation, program monitoring, curricular analysis, or program evaluation. For instructional purposes, the current volume is also accompanied by an eResource companion, containing detailed statistical information undergirding primary analyses of interest.

Chapter Summaries

Chapter 1

The first chapter defines the salient characteristics of longitudinal research in language learning contexts in order to provide a contrast to cross-sectional ex-post facto correlation studies, lab studies, or short-term pre-test to post-test intervention studies commonly reported on within the fields of second language acquisition and applied linguistics. This chapter will define the optimal conditions and core assumptions for designing quantitative longitudinal research, with a focus on designs and data management. The fundamental considerations for longitudinal research are to have access to at least one stable cohort of language learners, and the possibility of repeated testing. The frequency of testing can be within a series of class meetings, as in the self-assessment of learner anxiety or motivation, or in the form of weekly assessments of learning outcomes such as accuracy in writing after corrective feedback. The essential requirement is that the measures are of the same construct, as defined by parallel or equated measures. Longitudinal studies of language learning are most commonly done with an intact and stable cohort of learners. Often, when latent variable or multi-level models are used, the required sample sizes for adequate statistical power tend to be large, at least by applied linguistics research standards. Linking contiguous cohorts within a program of instruction often suffices to build up the sample of learners into a pooled sample, as long as the programmatic processes across cohorts are maintained over the semesters of sampling. The ideal circumstance for cumulative longitudinal research appears when the institutional policy mandates that proficiency testing be conducted at least once for each cohort of learners passing through a program, or as evidence that proficiency has been sustained. More advantageous still is repeated proficiency testing. If pre-mid-post testing is mandated, archiving the repeated measures and merging them with learner-level covariates and class assignment data afford an opportunity for detailed analysis of growth and factors that affect it. A key requirement here is accurate database management. This chapter will outline R software packages useful for merging and appending archived data sets stored in spreadsheet applications for database management. The major threat to longitudinal research is non-random attrition of participants. The usual strategy is to use a data imputation algorithm to replace missing data with plausible imputations. R packages useful for imputation are exemplified in this chapter along with criteria for valid imputation.

Chapter 2

The focus of this chapter is to outline methods of longitudinal data analysis using example scripts from R packages or from freeware applications such as JASP. Longitudinal analysis methods such as *latent growth curve models* test for evidence of language learning growth, and afford the testing of possible covariates of growth in the form of growth prediction models. *Multi-level growth models* nest learners in cohorts or languages, and make possible the analysis of the effects of cohort-varying factors on growth trajectories, and on individual difference variables hypothesized to affect variation in the starting points and trajectories of growth over time. When the focus is on program processes, *recursive path models* and *cross-lagged panels with latent variables* are used to examine the influence of anterior variables on proficiency outcomes. Path analyses across languages with the same sets of anterior variables, such as aptitude, motivation, achievement, and prior learning, provide a basis for examining the commonality and uniqueness of different languages within a program. When cohorts are combined across years to provide a cumulative history of means on standardized measures, a *time series regression* can be used. In many multi-year studies, both incidental and planned interventions occur, affording researchers the opportunity to examine their influence on the post-event portion of the series while holding the prior series as the control condition. Lastly, *event history analysis* can test factors affecting both growth and decline in cohort-level measures of language proficiency over time when the outcome is defined as a specific punctual event. The assumptions, advantages, and limitations of each longitudinal data analysis method are discussed.

Chapter 3

US government organizations often have a large-scale investment in foreign language development programs for their employees. Developing foreign language proficiency is a costly investment in terms of both time and money, and the maintenance of proficiency requires additional expenditures over the career of a foreign language professional. Programs that have as their goal the promotion of foreign language skills across a workforce provide funds that can be used to provide foreign language training or other supportive services to employees. In this chapter, Amber N. Bloomfield and Martyn K. Clark use an interrupted time series analysis to investigate the impact of in-service foreign language training activities and proficiency test score outcomes over approximately a ten-year period for large samples of foreign language professionals employed across three different government organizations. As with any other program, the question arises as to whether the program costs are justified by the impact of the program in terms of one or more outcomes. In their analysis of archived longitudinal data, Bloomfield and Clark examine the impact of a foreign language training funding program designed to sustain and enhance the foreign language skills of employees across the three US government organizations.

Chapter 4

In this chapter, Beth Mackey examines the predictive validity of a language aptitude measure over a multi-year sample of language professionals in the US Government. Language aptitude tests are widely used in the US Government to select and place students into immersive training programs ranging from 26 to 64 weeks at the Defense Language Institute Foreign Language Center (DLIFLC). Graduates of these language training programs often go on to serve multi-year terms as language professionals in the military. Each linguist is required to retest in the foreign language yearly to provide evidence of sustained or improved proficiency Mackey uses merged training and proficiency records to examine growth trajectories of DLIFLC graduates over the course of their careers as linguists. Of particular interest to the prediction of long-term growth in proficiency is the role of aptitude for language learning. In this chapter, Mackey explores the predictive validity of the Defense Language Aptitude Battery (DLAB) in a latent growth prediction model.

Chapter 5

In this chapter Megan C. Masters examines a subset of languages taught at DLIFLC with the goal of examining factors that predict variation in end-of-training proficiency outcomes. For this, Masters first uses logic modeling, which describes the anticipated relationships among program inputs, activities, and outcomes in the program design. Logic modeling then sets up a presumed left-to-right temporal flow of influence from earlier- to latter-measured variables, which then can be tested empirically with path analysis, a procedure that provides a simultaneous estimation of the hypothesized causal relationships among measured variables in their temporally ordered flow. Masters further examines how individual difference factors contributed to variation in the development of foreign language achievement and proficiency over time for three languages grouped within the same difficulty category.

Chapter 6

In this chapter, Leslie N. Ono and Steven J. Ross use an elaborated logic model to describe the temporal flow from achievement assessment quality checks to dimensionality confirmation, then to expected carry-over and cross-over relations in recursive path analyses before elaborating on how proficiency growth on standardized measures of proficiency can be predicted with measures of achievement. Ono and Ross use cross-cohort comparisons of four cohorts to test how variation in the inter-relations among achievement indicators can be used to account for cross-cohort differences in proficiency gains over a four-semester, 320-hour program of foreign language instruction. Ono and Ross use path analyses within each semester to estimate a metric of *coherence*, or inter-relatedness of achievements, before testing how different analyses of coherence can be used to account for cross-cohort differences in proficiency gains. They finally test whether an aggregated measure of achievement can differentiate between high- and low-gaining cohorts in a growth prediction model.

Chapter 7

In one of the longest and largest institutional studies of foreign language learning on record, Leslie N. Ono examines the 20-year history of a foreign language program originally designed to prepare undergraduates for English-medium instruction. The data set Ono uses is a multi-cohort design appended into a cumulative time series array in which each cohort in the instructional program took a pre-instruction proficiency test (Institutional Test of English as a Foreign Language (TOEFL)), a retest using a parallel form after the first year of instruction, and then a third post-instruction proficiency test at the end of the two years of instruction. In her time series analysis of cohort means, Ono examines critical events, both factors external to the institution and those intentionally planned within the institution, that changed the series. Ono demonstrates evidence of instruction impact for each cohort while noting variation in initial proficiency levels over time, as well as the magnitude of interruptions to the series of proficiency means.

Chapter 8

Atsuko Nishitani's chapter examines the adoption of a novel division of labor within a model of foreign language curricular design – one featuring direct method aural/oral courses taught by native speakers and reading/grammar/vocabulary instruction provided by instructors using the learners' native language in cognitive code or translation-based instruction. In the two-year program Nishitani examines the hypothesis that gains in repeated measures of a standardized measure of English proficiency will be differentially predicted by within-domain (within the same skill) achievement records compared to cross-domain (across different skills) achievements. In a large sample analysis, Nishitani examines variation in growth in reading/grammar and listening comprehension using parallel latent growth models that compare within- and between-domain achievement indicators on growth trajectories.

Chapter 9

Qi Zheng examines the validity of a self-assessed self-efficacy measure in a pre–post design involving a standardized measure of foreign language proficiency.

The one-year study was at an in-service language training for employees ultimately tasked with overseas assignments in which they were to engage in a foreign language-medium technology transfer project. Study participants were pre-tested for proficiency and self-efficacy on a set of can-do foreign language tasks before the program of instruction, then post-tested with the same task-based self-efficacy instrument and a parallel form of the proficiency measure. Noting parallel changes in both self-efficacy and proficiency after the program of instruction, Zheng then uses a cross-lagged panel design in order to test the validity of changes in self-efficacy as a predictor of changes in proficiency.

Chapter 10

Daniel R. Isbell and Xiaowan Zhang examine foreign language proficiency measures collected over a three-year period of study. Noting the increased use of proficiency measures for program monitoring of learner progress and outcomes, Isbell and Zhang examine variation in three skill domains collected over a three-year period on five foreign languages taught to undergraduates at three public universities in the US. Using growth curve models in mixed-effects regression analyses, Isbell and Zhang examine how variation across target languages, learner background variables, study abroad, and majors influence both the starting point and the end-of-instruction proficiency-level attainment of the foreign language learners.

References

Barkaoui, K. (2014) Quantitative approaches for analyzing longitudinal data in second language research. *Annual Review of Applied Linguistics*, 34, 65–101.

Casillas, J.V. (2020) The longitudinal development of fine phonetic detail: Stop production in a domestic immersion program. *Language Learning,* 70(3), 768–806.

Crossley, S., Kyle, K. and Salsbury, T. (2016) A usage-based investigation of L2 lexical acquisition: The role of input and output. *The Modern Language Journal*, 100(3), 702–715.

Daller, M. H. and Phelan, D. (2013) Predicting international student study success. *Applied Linguistics Review*, 4(1), 173–193.

Derwing, T. and Munro, M. J. (2013) The development of L2 oral language skills in two L1 groups: A 7-year study. *Language Learning*, 63(2), 163–185.

Grimm, R. P., Solari, E. J. and Gerber, M. M. (2018) Longitudinal investigation of reading development from kindergarten to grade eight in a Spanish-speaking bilingual population. *Reading and Writing*, 31(3), 559–581.

Jia, G. and Fuse, A. (2007) Acquisition of English grammatical morphology by native Mandarin-speaking children and adolescents: Age-related differences. *Journal of Speech, Language, and Hearing Research*, 50(5), 1280–1299.

Kozaki, Y. and Ross, S. J. (2011) Contextual dynamics in foreign language learning motivation. *Language Learning*, 61(4), 1328–1354.

Mellow, D., Reeder, K. and Forster, E. (1996) Using time series designs to investigate the effects of second language instruction. *Studies in Second Language Acquisition*, 18, 325–350.

Nagle, C. (2018) Motivation, comprehensibility, and accentedness in L2 Spanish: Investigating motivation as a time-varying predictor of pronunciation development. *The Modern Language Journal*, 102(1), 199–217.

Noels, K. A. (2001) Learning Spanish as a second language: Learners' orientations and perceptions of their teachers' communication style. *Language Learning*, 51(1), 107–144.

Ortega, L. and Iberri-Shea, G. (2005) Longitudinal research in second language acquisition: Recent trends and future directions. *Annual Review of Applied Linguistics*, 25, 26–45.

Raudszus, H., Segers, E. and Verhoeven, L. (2021) Patterns and predictors of reading comprehension growth in first and second language readers. *Journal of Research in Reading*, 44, 400–417.

Retelsdorf, J., Becker, M., Koller, O. and Moller, J. (2012) Reading development in a tracked school system: A longitudinal study over 3 years using propensity score matching. *British Journal of Educational Psychology*, 82(4), 647–671.

Ross, S. J. (2003) A diachronic coherence model for language program evaluation. *Language Learning*, 53(1), 1–33.

Ross, S. J. (2005) The impact of assessment methods on foreign language proficiency growth. *Applied Linguistics*, 26(3), 317.

1

INTRODUCTION

Longitudinal Research Designs

Steven J. Ross and Megan C. Masters

Introduction

This chapter will outline the characteristics of longitudinal research in language learning contexts in order to provide a contrast to cross-sectional ex-post facto correlation studies, lab studies, and short-term pre-test to post-test intervention studies commonly reported on within the field of second language acquisition (SLA). This chapter will define the optimal conditions and assumptions for quantitative longitudinal research, with a focus on designs and data management. The fundamental considerations for longitudinal research are to have access to at least one stable cohort of language learners, and the possibility of repeated testing. The frequency of testing can be within a series of class meetings, as in the self-assessment of learner anxiety or motivation, or in the form of weekly assessments of learning outcomes such as accuracy in writing after corrective feedback. The essential requirement is that the *measures are of the same construct*, as defined by parallel or equated measures. Longitudinal studies of language learning are most commonly done with an intact and stable cohort of learners. Often, when latent variable or multi-level models are used, the required sample sizes for adequate statistical power tend to be large, at least by applied linguistics research standards. Linking contiguous cohorts within a program of instruction often suffices to build up the sample of learners into a pooled sample, as long as the programmatic processes across cohorts are maintained over the semesters of sampling. The ideal circumstance for cumulative longitudinal research appears when the institutional policy mandates that proficiency testing be conducted at least once for each cohort of learners passing through a program, or as evidence that proficiency has been sustained. More advantageous still is repeated proficiency testing. If pre-, mid-, and post-testing are mandated, archiving the repeated measures and merging

DOI: 10.4324/9781003087939-2

them with learner-level covariates and class assignment data afford an opportunity for detailed analysis of growth and factors that affect it. A key requirement here is accurate *database management*. Skilled use of a relational database is a key advantage for archiving and merging data within and between cohorts. This chapter will outline the merge function in R as an example of database management. The chapter will conclude with an overview of one of the biggest threats posed to longitudinal research in any discipline: non-random attrition of participants. The usual strategy to address this phenomenon is to use a *data imputation algorithm* to replace missing data with plausible imputations of missing values. Criteria for valid imputation will be included in this chapter.

Defining Longitudinal Research Designs

It has for some time been recognized that longitudinal studies have remained relatively rare in the second language and foreign language learning research literature. The need for longitudinal studies is widely recognized and is an often-stated desideratum among SLA and applied linguistics researchers. The logistics of conducting longitudinal research, both quantitative and qualitative, or using mixed methods, has always presented a daunting challenge for researchers planning to undertake it. As much applied research is conducted within graduate programs, where there are constraints on the timelines for semester-long project completion, or for junior faculty aiming to build a dossier of research output within a five-year window, the tendency has been to favor short-term experiments or brief intervention studies over longer study designs. The time frame for conducting language learning research under such circumstances can be very truncated, with, for instance, laboratory studies of exposure to pseudo languages or to manipulated word lists, presented through a pre-programmed laptop interface designed to measure priming effects or attentional focus variables, which can often be conducted in an hour or two. The questionable generalizability and ecological validity of ultra-short-term studies can be raised when we consider that instructed SLA and foreign language learning in its natural environment take hundreds of contact hours before stable measures of functional proficiency emerge. Naturalistic or untutored SLA also develops after hundreds of hours of repeated exposure to a language, especially if language learning is assessed with functional tasks resembling simulations of authentic goal-driven interactions.

As has been noted by many researchers, there is no clear definition of just how long a study must be before it can be accurately deemed 'longitudinal'. A tendency has been to refer to studies with repeated measures of the outcome of interest as longitudinal, based primarily on the fact that repeated tests of the outcome were used. Repeated measures, unfortunately, do not have any standard or fixed duration, resulting in some repeated measures separated by minutes, hours, days, and others by a few weeks or months. Menard (2002) has noted the ambiguity in classifying studies as *longitudinal*, opting to define them as studies that measure change in a variable over time – studies with at least two repeated measures. This definition provides a simple contrast with cross-sectional designs with no repeated observations of outcomes, or inclusion of a time-varying measure. With measurement over time as the criterion for defining longitudinal research, there remains the possibility of some relatively short 'longitudinal' designs possible, as long as there are repeated measures of outcomes. Some examples of repeated measures in a series are phenomena such as physiological measures of anxiety, with and without tasks hypothesized to increase or diminish state anxiety, or retrospective research that requires language learners to recall previous affective states. Here, recollections of motivational states may be assessed through self-report and plotted in a series to indicate individual and group-level variation in perceived motivation over time. We will argue that short-term repeated measures designs such as these still fall short of a distinct definition of longitudinal designs for programmatic language learning research designs – although some of the analytic methods covered in the chapters to follow are often used in such short-duration repeated measures designs.

There are various design strategies useful for conducting longitudinal research. The most straightforward approach is a panel design. Panels are cohorts of individuals who are tracked over time at different stages of development. Biographical data, surveys, and proficiency assessments are collected periodically to create a cumulative record of individual difference data. When large data sets are available, and if there are multiple waves of time-marked assessments contained in them, a developmental analysis of change over time can be constructed. Even panel designs vary in design. Some collect different assessments at varying time points, but do not include repeated measures of the same variable. Other panel designs may collect individual difference data at the outset, then repeat the measures of the criterion outcome on multiple occasions across the language learning history of the panel members. If the database contains indicators of time, such as length of residence, hours of instruction, grade levels, or even language test outcomes, a quasi-longitudinal data set can be constructed by sampling the time or proficiency measures in cross-sectional slices along a continuum (Skiba, Dittmar, and Bressem, 2008). Longitudinal panel studies, while ideal in some ways because they track the same individuals, are particularly susceptive to attrition, which happens when participants who started within a given panel drop out and no longer continue with the research program requirements. Longitudinal developmental designs require a large coherent data set from which cross-sectional samples can be taken, and these are rare in second and foreign language learning research.

A common factor in the chapters featured in this volume is the duration of the language learning programs studied. Using a semester-long term of 10–12 weeks of instruction or immersion as the minimum duration, we will argue that the studies featured in this volume are longitudinal by virtue of two definitional criteria: either they involve multiple measures of the language learning outcome of interest, separated by at least 10–12 weeks of programmatic instruction between the repeated measures, or they involve the collection of individual difference measures prior to immersive instruction lasting for 10–64 weeks, with interim developmental achievement testing prior to a final end-of-instruction measurement of proficiency.

It is imperative that the logistics of testing large enough samples of individuals are considered at the outset in terms of the likelihood of attrition and continued access to study participants. Longitudinal researchers take on a degree of risk if they assume that members of an original cohort will remain willing to participate in the study, especially if there is insufficient incentive to do so, or a high degree of mobility. The feasibility of designing and conducting longitudinal research is largely contingent on continuous access to at least a single cohort of language learners in an established and stable program. Ideally, researchers will have continued access to multiple cohorts over a period of years. Many of the studies featured in this volume are based on the merger of multiple cohorts of learners entering, progressing through, and graduating from an instructional program with a stable curriculum.

If language learning program administrators have a policy of archiving outcome measures, there is also a potential for merging historical outcomes with current cohorts' outcomes. The advantage presented in that circumstance is the volume of data and a basis for a comparison of different languages over time. A frequently met shortcoming in accessing and reorganizing archived institutional data is that measurement or outcome files are often stored in administrative cycles. Further, biographical data on the language learners pertinent to analyses of individual differences affecting long-term language learning success may be stored in unlinked files, and perhaps even archived at a different institution managed by a different bureaucracy. An issue in retroactive analysis of language learning outcomes is not only access to historical records, but the facility of merging records across waves of data collection to create a cumulative and sufficiently comprehensive longitudinal record at the individual language learner level.

Once suitable archives are located, and if the planned analyses are to focus on group or cohort means, as in conventional repeated measures analysis of variance, the serial array of measures starts with the earliest measures before the repeated measures are added later to their right. The design of the left-to-right orientation of the data file can aid other researchers who at some later date might receive the data set. For instance, if planned covariates are tested early in the data collection process, they should be positioned in a column that designates the order of data collection. Such a design provides a basis for recognizing which individual difference variables precede the outcomes, and which ones have co-evolved with language learning. If regression analyses are planned, knowing which measures are antecedent, co-evolving, or consequential by virtue of their position in the data array can avoid ambiguities that arise when co-evolving phenomena are treated as 'predictors' of the language learning outcomes. Retroactive construction of data sets without time stamps indicating when tests and possible covariates were collected can muddle any cause-and-effect argumentation that would be formulated post hoc.

When researchers plan a longitudinal study ab initio, the framework for data collection and management is relatively uncomplicated. Unless very large numbers of languages and learners are to be involved, data can be collected in waves and manually integrated over time into a central data file. The structure of the data file will need to be considered from the outset, as the planned analyses of the longitudinal outcomes will require data formatting amenable to different kinds of analyses. We will consider two common formats – a horizontal (wide) array, with persons on rows, and time-ordered variables in columns, and two variants of vertical (long) or 'stacked' arrays of data, with persons and the serial order of the measures in rows, and individual or contextual factors stored in columns.

Horizontal Data Array

In the horizontal data array, person identifiers (IDs) are uniquely in rows, and all variables describing the persons are contained in the columns. Group membership indicators denote individuals sharing common features such as cohort membership, gender, administrative categories, and the like. Repeated measures are merged into the cumulative person file with serialized subscripts such as numbers or letters denoting the sequencing of the measures. Longitudinal data involve repeated measures, with the first test of record appearing to the left, followed by the same test, often an alternate or equated form, stored in columns to the right of the pre-test. The re-testing schedule is often constructed after a period of instruction or immersion has occurred. In attrition research, the re-test data might be collected years after the original measurement. The end result of the systematic data collection is a horizontal array of repeated measures of each cohort or group of language learners. Horizontal arrays of repeated measures provide a straightforward and intuitive method of storing data at the person level. This approach can also be used to link different cohorts of language learners vertically as program administrators append the more recent cohort to the cumulative archive of learners who have already progressed through a program.

A person array of repeated measures has utility for a limited set of longitudinal analyses and has a few assumptions that must be considered. For instance, the periodicity of the repeated measures is assumed to be equal for each person such that the time difference between the serial measures is assumed to be approximately equivalent across persons. When different cohorts of learners across years are appended, this assumption must still be satisfied, and presumes that the duration and intensity of instruction have remained constant from cohort to cohort. In addition to the main research focus in person array designs, i.e., whether there has been gain or change in proficiency over time, there are some analyses that can include person-level covariates. If these are continuous measures, they can be used to test the influence of individual difference covariates such as aptitude on the repeated measures. Person-level covariates can be used to generate marginal means if proficiency changes across cohorts are the foci of the analysis. From the outset, designers of longitudinal research need to plan ahead to consider the best strategy to archive and manage repeated measures within and between cohorts, with specific analytical goals in mind. An example of the horizontal data design is in online appendix A1.1.

Cohort-Level Vertical Array

Less common than person-level repeated measures are research questions pertaining to variation across multiple cohorts of learners entering and exiting a systematic program of instruction. In large-scale university foreign language learning programs, an evaluative focus may be on cohort averages on standardized measures given across time at approximately equal intervals. For instance, the person-level horizontal array discussed above could be summarized as a cohort mean on each of the repeated measures of interest. Instead of repeated measures in the rows occupied by persons, the entire cohort of learners' average scores on the repeated measures might be the object of interest and, for a pre-mid-post-test design, compressed into three rows. The average outcomes for the whole cohort of learners would be archived and merged over time such that the measurement averages of each cohort made of a few hundred learners would be summarized in three rows, each of which is associated with a specific and constant test periodicity.

In contrast with the person-level horizontal array design, the cohort-level array is arranged vertically such that each cohort occupies three rows of data. In this kind of array, aggregate group means are used instead of individual learners' test outcomes. The serial order of the test means is coded in a test occasion variable, denoting the vertical integration of a number of cohorts into one cumulative data set. The test occasion indicator is serial and begins when the first cohort in a program is tested and ends when the last cohort's data are added. As long as the measurement scale remains constant – that is to say, the same measurement instrument, often a standardized test, is repeatedly used to measure language learning outcomes – the average outcomes per cohort on each of the repeated measures can be computed and stored in the archive. The within-cohort order of testing is contained in codes indicating the test occasion. Within each cohort, the grand mean of the group is stored in a cell. Multiple columns can be used for different test outcomes, such as listening, reading, or speaking. A binary code for the serial order of the test is needed to designate each cohort mean as a pre-test, mid-test, or post-test. In this manner, differences in cohort starting averages, as well as their trajectories of gain or change, are directly and visually comparable. Figure A1.2 in the online appendix provides an example of this kind of data array.

Another advantage of the multi-cohort vertical array allows for a cyclical analysis of proficiency changes across as many cohorts as have been updated into the data archive. The first cohort of learners' average outcomes would occupy the first three rows, while the second cohort, usually entering the instructional program a year later, begin their series occupying the fourth through sixth rows of the data. Once a sufficient number of cohort means have been tallied, a series will emerge indicating variation in the intercepts or starting proficiency levels in each skill, as well as different rates of growth from cohort to cohort. The time series designs are also useful for testing the effects of both planned interventions such as curriculum changes and the influences of other events that coincidentally affect changes to the series.

Person-Level Vertical Array

When an analysis of individual differences affecting variation in growth and change is the object of interest, the person-level vertical array of data provides the most utility. As noted by Singer and Willett (2003), the vertical arrangement of persons can contain all of their repeated measures, as well as other variables in each row denoting the time stamp of the measurement and other static measures such as bio-data and codes for continuous or binary covariates. The person-level vertical array is not only useful for analyses of gain or change, but can be integrated into growth prediction models or sequence-of-change models (Duncan, Duncan and Strycker, 2011).

Similar to the cohort-level array, the person-level vertical array has a column denoting the order of the measurement. This feature allows for individuals to have different numbers of repeated measures, providing more flexibility in analysis options and less attrition owing to case-wise deletion of subjects with missing measures. A time stamp, such as the date of testing, provides a basis for controlling the intervals between measures to ensure that assumptions important for repeated measures and growth or change modeling are met. Further, other person-level covariates can be added when updated with a key field such as the person ID.

It is noteworthy that the person-level vertical array is not only useful for longitudinal analyses of language learning gains. Indeed, a vertical array of persons allows for repeated trials to be integrated with a task or item code for the trials, as well as covariates. This approach has, in the last decade, become particularly widespread in psycholinguistics research (Baayen, 2008; Jaeger, 2008), chiefly because it allows for the inclusion of both person-level random and fixed effects, as well as fixed and random effects for items or tasks. In longitudinal language learning research, the repeated measures are test outcomes and are often the first level of a multi-level regression model, in which individual difference covariates at the second level are predictors of variation in the repeated measures, and contextual variables are at the highest level of the nested structure.

Database Archive Management

A fundamental necessity in longitudinal research involves the collection, storing, and merging of different waves of data into a comprehensive data set. Even for studies starting with a straightforward repeated measures design, the subsequent waves of data will need to be integrated into the main data archive. As noted above, the data may be stored in a horizontal format with persons in rows and variables in the columns, or in a vertical format with persons occupying as many rows as there are repeated test events. In just about all formats, at some point data will need to be merged and reformatted for the intended longitudinal analysis.

When the number of test takers is large, or when test results are first scanned with technology such as optical scanners or automated scoring devices, manipulating updates rapidly becomes tedious and impractical. Longitudinal researchers will find that the investment in learning a structured query language or a relational database will facilitate the merging and storing of data and will save many hours of labor. At a minimum, learning the merger function of a spreadsheet such as Excel will often suffice. A key feature of any database management system will be the merger function in which data from one file can be extracted from a data set and inserted into a combined file.

Queries and Data Mergers

A key requirement for the use of queries and data mergers is that there is a fixed ID for each person. This ID remains constant across all of the test administrations, and is used to ingest updated data about individuals into the archive. From the outset, the person ID needs to be an alpha-numeric string associated with a unique person. In many research settings, Institutional Review Boards require that the original names of study participants be converted into a non-identifying subject code. This can present an immediate problem for the retroactive construction of historical archives, as there is a need to convert each original study participant name to a unique ID that remains constant across the data collection waves. If this can be accomplished, the derived person ID can serve as the key field used for sorting and merging test records across time. The logistics of anonymizing archived data to meet Institutional Review Board standards needs to be considered as an early step in planning longitudinal research.

As an example of data mergers, a series of language learning achievement records of a single cohort of language learners in a language program will be merged using the merge function in the R base package (R Core Team, 2013). In this example, the learners in a foreign language program attend four different skills classes each week, and at the end of each semester a grade in each course summarizes each learner's achievement. The essential fields are person ID, and the course label with serial number to denote the semester (Figure 1.1).

ID	EC1R	EC1L	EC1W	EC1S
7001	78.08	62.92	70.50	72.67
7002	83.53	64.20	81.59	83.64
7003	80.76	86.35	78.05	82.13
7004	81.21	66.77	80.70	79.83
7005	77.97	76.40	86.28	83.63
7006	87.66	82.82	86.15	84.45
7008	88.60	84.74	92.70	84.02
7009	86.66	78.65	83.65	77.08
7010	86.39	84.10	80.35	81.93
7012	87.48	88.60	82.55	85.45
7013	91.64	80.25	90.80	92.02
7014	82.62	82.18	81.07	77.69
7015	92.13	66.13	84.45	75.60
7016	88.55	71.90	83.35	85.90
7017	82.15	80.25	75.43	28.04
7019	88.04	82.82	80.85	82.30
7020	75.74	80.89	77.38	72.33
7021	81.37	72.87	74.62	78.25
7022	88.09	67.41	85.60	72.89
7023	92.25	87.31	85.70	84.08
7024	89.10	87.74	83.78	80.75
7025	76.61	80.25	85.58	83.55

FIGURE 1.1 English Communication Program (ECP) semester 1 grades.

In this example, the English as a foreign language learners take four more skills courses in the second semester, after which a grade is given based on pre-set criteria such as attendance, participation, homework, and in-class assessments. At the end of each of the four semesters, the individual course grades are collated into a spreadsheet for checking and administrative reporting. In order to get a cumulative picture of each learner's achievement, the separate databases need to be merged into a spreadsheet that will contain all 16 course achievement records as well as repeated measures of proficiency as measured by a standardized test. The ultimate goal of the cumulative accumulation of individual records for each cohort will be to provide evidence of the learners' achievements and how these achievements relate to changes in proficiency over time. The second and subsequent achievement records must be merged into a cumulative record of outcomes. The data merger goal then is to collect the separate measures of achievement and proficiency for each cohort in the program into a single comprehensive archive.

To this end, a new Excel spreadsheet is used for each semester. Into it, a program administrator collects grades for each instructor in each of the four skill domains and checks input grades for accuracy. As assignment to class sections changes each semester, individual records are associated with the assigned fixed person ID and are retained throughout the duration of the program. At the end of the first of four semesters, each learner in the program will have achievement records associated with the four skills courses. By the end of the second term, each learner will have eight achievements, as well as the pre-instructional measure of proficiency in three domains, and a mid-program measure of proficiency given after two semesters of instruction. By the end of the first year of instruction in the program there will be four separate spreadsheets of data that need to be merged before longitudinal analyses can be undertaken. After each wave of data collection, the spreadsheets containing the person-sorted achievements and test scores should be deposited in a single well-labeled folder with a serialization of the test waves, such as EC1L, EC1R, etc., to denote the course content and semester. Sorting on the ID number of the cohort members is needed for all tables in which learners appear.

Merging different spreadsheets can be efficiently accomplished with the use of the R base package (R Core Team, 2013). Prior to performing the merger, the individual spreadsheets containing the separate archived achievement or proficiency records need to be sorted on the learner ID and then saved into a comma-separated file with the .csv extension.

```
ecrd1<-read.table("e:\\RM Longitudinal\\EC1GRD.csv",header=T,sep=",")
names(ecgrd1)
ecgrd2<-read.table("e:\\RM Longtiudinal\\EC2GRD.csv",header=T,sep=",")
names(ecgrd2)
combo=merge(ecgrd1,ecgrd2,by="ID",all.data=TRUE)
names(combo)
write.csv(combo,"ecgrd12.csv")
```

In the first line of the R script above, the set of four first-semester grades is defined as 'ecgrd1' and read into R from an Excel spreadsheet labeled EC1GRD, saved as a comma-separated file (.csv). The content of the file is listed for confirmation. The same is then done for the second-semester grades (ecgrd2). The R package data. table is called from the library before the merge operation begins. The merged file is temporarily named 'combo' before the merged contents are checked with the names function. Finally, the combined files are written back to a comma-separated variable (csv) spreadsheet for archiving, as shown in Figure 1.2.

The merged files should be saved with a serial number denoting how many waves of longitudinal data are thus far contained within it. In the present example, we would name the merged file ECGRD12.xls to denote that the current file contains two waves of data. The R script can be modified when more achievements or proficiency measures are available. An example of this would be the merger of the achievement records with proficiency tests archived in a separate spreadsheet. The merger script in R needs only a few modifications

ID	EC1R	EC1L	EC1W	EC1S	EC2L	EC2R	EC2W	EC2S
1	7001	78.08	62.92	70.50	72.67	76.99	71.68	65.74	81.00
2	7002	83.53	64.20	81.59	83.64	65.82	70.54	55.10	69.58
3	7003	80.76	86.35	78.05	82.13	71.99	70.30	75.40	96.60
4	7004	81.21	66.77	80.70	79.83	67.11	82.90	58.40	59.25
5	7005	77.97	76.40	86.28	83.63	67.74	69.48	77.80	87.50
6	7006	87.66	82.82	86.15	84.45	90.40	80.35	85.50	72.60
7	7008	88.60	84.74	92.70	84.02	75.99	77.85	76.90	68.50
8	7009	86.66	78.65	83.65	77.08	72.49	71.98	83.00	85.00
9	7010	86.39	84.10	80.35	81.93	73.41	76.15	87.00	89.00
10	7012	87.48	88.60	82.55	85.45	85.48	82.80	78.46	85.38
11	7013	91.64	80.25	90.80	92.02	91.23	83.537	81.8	92.1
12	7014	82.62	82.18	81.07	77.69	71.91	69.40	92.10	86.00
13	7015	92.13	66.13	84.45	75.60	77.03	76.60	83.28	83.20
14	7016	88.55	71.90	83.35	85.90	84.52	75.48	68.94	80.05
15	7017	82.15	80.25	75.43	28.04	79.07	71.65	85.80	70.25
16	7019	88.04	82.82	80.85	82.30	90.11	84.88	79.00	88.00
17	7020	75.74	80.89	77.38	72.33	69.49	65.83	93.40	61.50
18	7021	81.37	72.87	74.62	78.25	66.57	70.03	65.00	69.90
19	7022	88.09	67.41	85.60	72.89	79.62	85.13	73.70	72.60
20	7023	92.25	87.31	85.70	84.08	81.40	66.58	72.66	61.75
21	7024	89.10	87.74	83.78	80.75	89.48	80.28	82.90	81.35
22	7025	76.61	80.25	85.58	83.55	72.16	71.13	75.00	81.50

FIGURE 1.2 Merged ECGRD1 and ECGRD2 records.

before it can be reused to update the product of the previous merger of two achievements with an archive of standardized test results for members of the same cohort.

```
ecgrd12<-read.teable("e\\RM Longitudinal\\ecgrd12.csv",header=T,sep=",")
names (ecgrd12)
ec7itp<-read.table("e:\\RM Longitudinal\\ec7itp.csv",header=T,sep=",")
names(ec7itp)
combo=merge(ecgrd12,ec7itp,by="ID",all.data=TRUE)
names(combo)
write.csv(combo, "ec7achpro12.csv")
```

The modified R script imports the merged achievement data (ecgrd12) and then imports the separate spreadsheet containing the pre-test and mid-test proficiency test outcomes for the same cohort of learners (ec7ipt). The merger of the two data tables keyed on the ID of the cohort members produces the interim 'combo' file, which is then written back to an Excel readable comma-separated file (ec7achpro12.csv). The merged data set is then ready for an interim pre–post comparison or can be archived until the third- and fourth-semester achievements and the final end-of-program proficiency data are ready for merger into a comprehensive longitudinal data set for the cohort (Figure 1.3).

Once mergers are completed, unneeded fields in the data set can be easily deleted from the Excel spreadsheet. If multiple cohorts are to be compared, standardized alignment of the spreadsheet columns is advisable before sequential

ID	X	EC1R	EC1L	EC1W	EC1S	EC2L	EC2R	EC2W	EC2S	STREAM	LC1	LC2	RC1	RC2
7001	1	78.08	62.92	70.50	72.67	76.99	71.58	65.74	81.00	0	34	41	39	37
7002	2	83.53	64.20	81.59	83.64	65.82	70.54	55.10	69.58	0	45	46	50	43
7003	3	80.76	86.33	78.05	82.13	71.99	70.30	75.40	96.60	0	41	43	48	47
7004	4	81.21	66.77	80.70	79.83	67.11	82.90	58.40	39.25	0	45	47	48	46
7005	5	77.97	76.40	86.28	83.63	67.74	69.68	77.80	87.50	0	40	39	42	39
7006	6	87.66	82.82	86.15	84.45	90.40	80.35	85.50	72.60	0	48	67	43	52
7008	7	88.60	84.74	92.70	84.07	75.99	77.85	76.90	68.50	0	44	47	44	39
7009	8	86.66	78.65	83.65	77.08	72.40	71.98	83.00	95.00	0	44	46	46	40
7010	9	86.39	84.10	80.35	81.93	73.41	76.15	87.00	89.00	0	43	48	48	47
7012	10	87.48	88.60	82.55	85.45	65.48	82.80	78.46	85.38	0	52	55	46	48
7013	11	91.64	80.25	90.80	92.02	91.23	83.537	81.8	92.1	0	45	47	50	51
7014	12	83.62	82.18	81.07	77.69	71.91	68.40	92.10	86.00	0	44	47	35	46
7015	13	92.13	66.13	84.45	75.60	77.03	76.60	83.28	83.20	0	48	51	48	47
7016	14	88.55	71.90	83.35	85.90	84.52	75.48	68.94	80.05	0	45	45	45	37
7017	15	82.15	80.25	75.43	28.04	79.07	71.65	85.90	70.25	0	43	45	47	47
7019	16	88.04	82.82	80.85	82.90	90.11	84.88	79.00	86.00	0	48	57	43	51
7020	17	75.74	80.89	77.38	72.33	69.49	65.83	93.40	61.50	0	52	52	37	50
7021	18	81.37	72.87	74.62	78.25	66.57	70.03	65.00	69.90	0	40	41	38	34
7022	19	88.09	67.41	85.60	72.89	79.62	85.13	73.70	72.60	0	46	47	54	49
7023	20	92.25	87.31	85.70	84.08	81.40	66.58	72.66	63.75	0	54	53	44	50
7024	21	89.10	87.74	83.78	80.75	69.48	80.28	82.90	81.35	0	48	48	44	50
7025	22	79.61	80.25	85.58	83.55	72.16	71.13	75.00	81.90	0	43	43	42	49

FIGURE 1.3 Merger of achievement with proficiency.

cohorts of learners from the same program are stacked into a vertical array of data for cross-cohort comparisons.

Missing Data and Imputation

In addition to ensuring the systematicity and accuracy of database entry and maintenance, another key component of conducting longitudinal research is identifying appropriate methods for addressing missing data. Missing data occurs when data values are not stored for observed variables within a given data set, subsequently reducing the representativeness of the sample and potentially distorting inferences made about the larger population of interest. When conducting longitudinal analyses, typically taking place over months, years, or even decades, data points for individuals across all variables within a data set are often missing. The data imputation process replaces missing data with substituted values, allowing researchers to avoid having to use case-wise deletion of missing data, which has been found to result in the overestimation of statistical outcomes and often significantly reduces the *n*-size of a given data set (Tabachnick and Fidell, 2007). The substituted values become *estimated values* calculated from other available information within the data set.

Prior to engaging in the data imputation process, it is imperative to examine the missingness of one's data since the parameters associated with the imputation procedures are influenced by how the missing data within a data set are characterized. For a detailed explanation of the basic types of missing data: (1) missing completely and random (MCAR); (2) missing at random (MAR); and (3) missing not at random (MNAR), see Rubin (1987), Little and Rubin (2002), and Enders (2010). To explore the patterning of missing data, descriptive statistics are used to determine the number of missing cases associated with a given data set. When analyzing missing data, it is often prudent to review data in both tabular and visualized forms, since the visualization of missing data can often show patterns of missingness that may otherwise go unnoticed. Table 1.1 shows an example of missing data from a longitudinal data set containing pre- and post-Test of English as a Foreign Language (TOEFL) scores (in bold) and 16 achievement-related grades from which learners' grade point average (GPA) were computed. Learners' progression through their language learning coursework took place over four semesters of instruction.

As shown in Table 1.1, at program onset, all 285 learners enrolled in the program took the TOEFL listening comprehension, reading comprehension, and speaking proficiency tests. When working with missing data, it is important to differentiate between a 'real' score of 0 and the use of 0 to indicate a missing value. The use of 0 in Table 1.1 denotes the number of missing cases associated with a given measurement instrument. Sixteen learners did not complete the second iteration of

TABLE 1.1 Test of English as a Foreign Language (TOEFL) longitudinal data set

	Missing	Not missing
LC 1	0	285
ST 1	0	285
RC 1	0	285
L1	0	285
S1	0	285
R1	0	285
W1	0	285
L2	0	285
P2	0	285
S2	0	285
W2	0	285
LC2	16	269
ST2	16	269
RC2	16	269
L3	0	285
P3	0	285
S3	0	285
W3	0	285
X4	0	285
Z4	1	284
S4	0	285
W4	1	285
LC3	104	181
ST3	105	180
RC3	105	180

proficiency testing for all three skills, and over 104 learners did not complete the final suite of proficiency testing upon program completion.

Longitudinal researchers have a number of different options to employ when faced with the challenge of missing data. One straightforward solution is to simply delete the missing cases from the analysis for those learners with incomplete records. A drawback to this approach, as mentioned above, is that this strategy often significantly reduces the research study's sample size and hence, statistical power. An alternative to this solution is the use of data imputation. Common methods include 'hot deck' imputation, where the averages of different, but comparable cases, are used to replace missing values. Alternatively, mean imputation, which replaces missing data with the average score of a given variable from the same data set, can be used. A third approach is to use regression imputation, in which linear regression is used to estimate values for the missing variables (Little and Rubin, 2002). The challenge associated with these traditional methods is that they do not take into account the uncertainty or variability of data within the imputation model. To address this issue, Rubin (1987) argues that repeated or multiple imputations greatly improve the quality of estimates generated for missing data. As described by van Buuren (2017), multiple imputation involves three main steps. The first step entails imputing (or filling) missing entries of incomplete data sets multiple times, resulting in imputed values drawn from a distribution which can be different for each missing case. This process results in the generation of m complete datasets, depending on the number specified by the researcher (typically about ten). The second step involves analyzing the data specified within the given analytical framework using the m unique imputed data sets. The final step involves integrating the results of the m analyses into the final set of statistical outcomes. The outcomes of this final, pooled set of data result from each of the m analyses conducted on the separate m imputed data sets.

An Example

Working with a TOEFL data set for a single cohort of language learners, we will explore potential differences in statistical outcomes between complete versus imputed data sets. As noted above, imputation is most accurate if there are ample observed data about each case in the data set. In longitudinal data sets, the ideal data management system includes all prior proficiency test scores, and each individual grade or achievement indicator in a cumulative file. As data attrition usually is most frequent in the most recent, or right-most columns of a cumulative data set, all of the prior information about individual learners can be used for the imputation of the missing data.

To illustrate this, we use the MICE (Multiple Imputation with Chained Equations) package in R (van Buuren and Groothuis-Oudshoorn, 2011). The goal is to use the available data accumulated for learners in a data set (Cohort4) to impute missing Institutional TOEFL subtest scores on the mid-program, and post-program administrations of those tests. The R code in MICE and two other associated R packages, 'nainar' (Tierney, Cook, McBain, Fay, Ohara-Wild, Hester, and Smith, 2020) and 'miceadds' (Robitzch, Grund, and Henke, 2021), is used here to generate five imputed data sets.

The R script first invokes the three R packages from the library and installs them.

```
library(mice) # for imputation
library(naniar) # for recoding missing to NA, the missing code used in R
library(miceadds) # for saving the imputed files
```

The source data set (Cohort4) is read in after it is converted from its original storage in SPSS, Excel, etc. into a csv-type file. The source data set (cohort4miss. csv) is read into R and renamed cohort4.

```
cohort4<-read.table("f:\\RM Longitudinal\\cohort4miss.csv",header=T,sep=",")
names(cohort4)
```

The R package naniar (Tierney, Cook, McBain, Fay. Ohara-Wild, Hester, and Smith, 2020) is then used to recode the missing code from the original data storage file (zeros) into the R system code for missing (NA). This is done for all test outcomes with a missing code.

```
cohort4$LC2[cohort4$LC2 == 0] <- NA
cohort4$ST2[cohort4$ST2 == 0] <- NA
cohort4$RC2[cohort4$RC2 == 0] <- NA
cohort4$LC3[cohort4$LC3 == 0] <- NA
cohort4$ST3[cohort4$ST3 == 0] <- NA
cohort4$RC3[cohort4$RC3 == 0] <- NA
```

After the recoding of the missing zeros to 'NA', the R package MICE is started and imputes five data sets ($m = 5$), each of which will replace the missing TOEFL data in cohort4 with plausible replacements. Because MICE uses a Monte Carlo estimation for each imputation run, the actual imputed values for each imputed data set will differ slightly.

```
co4im <- mice::mice(cohort4, m=5, maxit=10)
write.mice.imputation(mi.res=co4im, name="mice_cohort4")
```

After the desired number of imputed data sets is generated, each one is available for a replication analysis for comparison with the original data set with missing cases deleted. The multiple analyses with the imputed data sets permit a comparison with the original analysis so that the influence of the original missing data can be compared with the replications with replaced data. Inferences about the longitudinal changes in the data set can then be formulated considering the influence of the missing data, and a confidence interval around the magnitude of changes can be derived from multiple imputations. In some data, the influence of missingness after imputation is marginal, and inferences about growth or change in the original data set containing missing cases will not substantially differ from the analyses on the imputed versions of the data with no missing data. In other data, the imputed data will lead to a substantive modification of the original inferences about the magnitude of change over time. Whether the effects of attrition affect the conclusions drawn about growth and change over time will depend on the extent of non-random loss of repeated measures data and the accuracy of the imputations.

References

Baayen, R. H. (2008) *Analyzing Linguistic Data*. Cambridge: Cambridge University Press.

Duncan, T. E., Duncan, S. C., and Strycker, L. A. (2011) *An Introduction to Latent Variable Growth Curve Modeling* (2nd ed.). New York: Lawrence Erlbaum.

Enders, C. (2010) *Applied Missing Data Analysis (Methodology in the Social Sciences)*. New York, NY: Guilford Press.

Jaeger, F. T. (2008) Categorical data analysis: Away from ANOVAs (transformation or not) and towards logit mixed models. *Journal of Memory and Language*, *59*, 434–446.

Little, R. J. A., and Rubin, D. (2002) *Statistical Analysis with Missing Data*. New York, NY: John Wiley.

Menard, S. (2002) *Longitudinal Research. Quantitative Applications in the Social Sciences 76*. Thousand Oaks, CA: Sage.

R Core Team (2013) R: A Language and Environment for Statistical Computing. Vienna, Austria: R Foundation for Statistical Computing. www.R-project.org/

Robitzch, A., Grund, S., and Henke, T. (2021) R package miceadds. https://CRAN.R-proj ect.org/package=miceadds" https://CRAN.R-project.org/package=miceadds.

Rubin, D. B. (1987) *Multiple Imputation for Nonresponse in Surveys*. New York, NY: John Wiley.

Skiba, R., Dittmar, N., and Bressem, J. (2008) Planning, collecting, exploring, and archiving longitudinal L2 data: Experiences from the P-Moll project. In L. Ortega and H. Byrnes (Eds.) *The Longitudinal Study of Advanced L2 Capabilities*. New York, NY: Routledge.

Singer, J., and Willett, J. (2003) *Applied Longitudinal Data Analysis: Modelling Change and Event Occurrence*. Oxford: Oxford University Press.

Tabachnick, B. G., and Fidell, L. S. (2007) *Using Multivariate Statistics* (5th ed.). Boston, MA: Allyn & Bacon.

Tierney, N., Cook, D., McBain, M., Fay, C., Ohara-Wild, M., Hester, J., and Smith, L. (2020) R Package naniar. https://CRAN.R-project.org/package=naniar.

van Buuren, S. (2017) Multiple Imputation. www.stefvanbuuren.nl/mi/MI.html

van Buuren, S., and Groothuis-Oudshoorn, K. (2011) MICE: Multivariate Imputation by Chained Equations in R. *Journal of Statistical Software*, 45(3), 1–67.

2

APPROACHES TO LONGITUDINAL DATA ANALYSES

Steven J. Ross and Megan C. Masters

Often, the focus of longitudinal language learning research turns to the issue of attrition over time. For such research issues, time serves as the key independent variable, with other covariates tested for their influence on the rate of attrition. *Event history analysis* can test the immediate and long-term impacts of planned and unplanned disruptions to a repeated measures series, and thus can be used to design interventions and identify incidental factors, if the focus is on group-level effects.

In some longitudinal designs, the repeated measures are of individual language learners, and the learners are clustered into schools, classes, or other stable groupings. In such designs, the issue of growth across different contexts becomes the key variable of interest. *Multi-level growth models* nest learners in clusters such as cohorts or even languages and make possible the analysis of the effects of cohort-varying factors on growth trajectories, and on individual difference variables hypothesized to affect variation in the starting points and trajectories of growth over time. Longitudinal analysis methods, such as *latent growth curve models,* measure individual learner variation as latent factors. These models are among the most flexible, as they can test for evidence of language learning growth, and concurrently afford the testing of possible covariates of growth in the form of growth prediction models. In contrast with the group focus of repeated measures analysis of variance (ANOVA), the latent variable approach incorporates person-level variation in the change process. The growth factor can serve as the focus of analysis, or can itself be a predictor of other outcomes, and in some designs, may be tested for covariance with a parallel growth process. The advantages and limitations of each longitudinal data analysis method, along with short examples, will be outlined in this chapter.

DOI: 10.4324/9781003087939-3

Repeated Measures ANOVA

A very commonly used approach for longitudinal data analysis in applied linguistics research is the repeated measures ANOVA. Repeated measures ANOVA are often referred to as a mixed ANOVA because they can include within-person measures, the repeated measures, and between-group factors, such as experimental conditions or non-experimental cross-cohort comparisons. The key requirement is for the dependent variable to be measured more than once, and for repeated measures to be approximately in the same time interval for all persons. The repeated measures are assumed to be the same measurement instrument – an actual repeated use of a single instrument, or more commonly, a parallel or equated standardized test or assessment procedure. The between-groups factor can in some designs be optional. If the research focus is on testing the degree of change over time, the repeated measures can be tested in a within-persons design using a single group or cohort. More commonly, researchers will randomly assign persons to groups and test the effects of one or more interventions relative to a control group. In such designs there are main effects of interest, the within-persons change, and between-groups difference in that change. Interactions between the within and between factors assess the parallelism of the change across groups.

Repeated measures analysis of variance has several important assumptions. One is that the repeated measurements have equal variances across time and constant correlations among the residual error terms. Most applications feature a diagnostic test of this sphericity assumption, and options to correct for minor violations of sphericity.

Figure 2.1 shows a design common in longitudinal applied linguistics research. The repeated measures are arrayed in a pre-mid-post format with equal time periods between the administration of each measure. The between-group factor

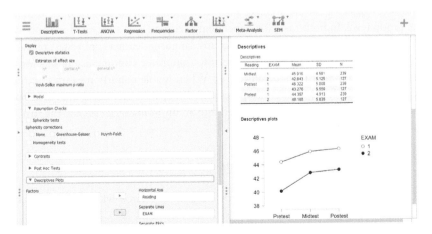

FIGURE 2.1 Repeated measures analysis of variance (JASP).

is a non-experimental one, a code denoting whether the group members entered college through one or another admissions processes. The repeated measures factor shows nearly parallel and significant change because of instruction, but large significant differences in the starting point. As the design was not experimental, the results are essentially descriptive.

A useful feature of most repeated measures applications is that they can incorporate covariates measured at the person level. For quasi-experimental designs without random assignment, the covariates allow for hypothesis testing while controlling for initial group differences, as might be the case in quasi-experimental designs. In repeated measures analysis of covariance, complex interactions between change, groups, and covariates can be modeled.

Time Series Regression

Time series regression tests whether there have been systematic changes over time for a repeated measure. Unlike shorter-duration repeated measures ANOVA designs with two to four time points, time series designs have many measures of the dependent variable using the same metric for measurement each time over approximately equally spaced intervals. For large-scale program evaluation projects, where standardized testing is done in equally spaced intervals for each cohort entering and exiting a program of instruction, multi-cohort time series can test linear and non-linear trends, as well as planned and unplanned events that change the series over time.

While time series are usually modeled with specialized software, especially in economics and price-forecasting research, language learning outcomes compiled in cumulative program archives are relatively less complex, and generally can be modeled with linear regression techniques (Huitema, 2011) available in common statistical packages. Although person-level data can be collected in longitudinal case study designs, cohort averages provide a more general tally of outcomes at the group level. In both cases the dependent variable (Y) is a repeated measure of the outcome of interest. In many programs, language learners are tested repeatedly for program monitoring purposes, or for employee continuance of incentive programs, such as merit pay qualifications. When whole cohorts' measures on the dependent variable are of interest, aggregated data spaced over equal time intervals can first be averaged before being placed into an on-going series such as the structure outlined in Figure 2.2.

$$\underline{Y_1 Y_2 Y_3 Y_4 Y_5 Y_6 Y_7 Y_8 Y_9} \ldots \ldots \ldots \underline{Y_n},$$

FIGURE 2.2 A figure showing a dependent variable of interest with aggregated data spaced over equal time intervals.

In this figure the cohort averages (*Y* bars) are archived over equal time periods in serial time (*T*) order 1 through *n*. The series can then be tested for a trend to diagnose if the series is constant, declining, increasing, or varying. Prior to this step, a visualization of the series can provide a starting point for model diagnostics and building.

The time series plot for the Structure subtest (Figure 2.3) shows that for each of the ten cohorts, each of which is measured three times over a two-year, four-semester sequence of instruction, there is a general pattern of gain from the pre-instruction measure to the mid-test after one year of instruction, and then considerable between-cohort variation in the gains from mid- to post-instruction measures. There is also a clear downward trend for the whole series, with a pre-cipitous drop visible between time points 21 and 22, beginning with the eighth cohort. The time series regression analysis first tests for an overall trend using serial time (*T*) as the only factor in the model (Figure 2.4).

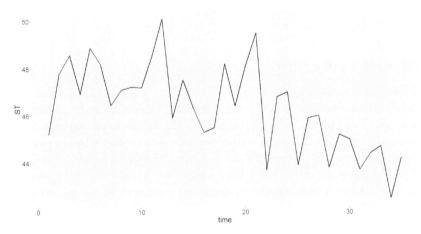

FIGURE 2.3 Time series of institutional Test of English as a Foreign Language (TOEFL) Structure subtest.

$$Y_{ij}=B_0+B(T)+e_{ij}$$

FIGURE 2.4 Basic regression equation.

Periodicity

Variation in the value of *Y*, or average *Y*, over time is initially tested for the overall trend, and then for periodicity, which are typically defined as cycles of variation in *Y* recurring in regular patterns. When multiple cohorts of learners progressing through a stable program are aggregated, natural periodicity tends to occur, beginning with the pre-test starting level for each cohort, and for the gains each cohort subsequently achieves on the series of retests. The time series graphic in Figure 2.2 suggests a cycle recurring every third time period, which coincides with a new cohort of learners into the program of instruction. When a cyclical pattern is apparent, a second independent variable needs to be put into the linear regression model. A dummy code that indicates the peak of each season will usually capture the periodic change in the series.

```
Time   12345678910111213141516171819202122232425262728293031323334 3536
Cycle  12312312312312312312312312312312312312312312312312312312312 3123
```

The regression model is expanded to include cycles 2 (C2) and 3 (C3) for each cohort, leaving the pre-test out of the model to denote a new starting level for each cohort (Figure 2.5).

$$Y_{ij}=B_0+B(T)+B(C2)+B(C3)+e_{ij,}$$

FIGURE 2.5 Expanded regression model with cycles C2 and C3.

Interruption to the Series

In many time series analyses, the focus of hypothesis testing is on an event that is tested as an *interruption* to the foregoing series. The event can be planned as an experimental intervention or a change in the instructional curriculum, or can be an event that is tested post hoc for its influence on the series change. For a test of a discrete event, a third independent variable is used. For time periods prior to the event, those time periods are identified as the counterfactual condition, which reflects the trend and periodicity before the event of interest took place.

```
Time    12345678910111213141516171819202122232425262728293031323334 4353
Cycle   12312312312312312312312312312312312312312312312312312312312 312
Event   00000000000000000000000000000000000000011111111111111111111 11111111
```

Times at and to the right of the start of the event (*E*) hypothesized to interrupt the series are coded 1 (Figure 2.6). If the event changes the series upwards, the unstandardized regression coefficient (*B*) will be positive. If the impact shifts the series downwards, the coefficient will be negative. The statistical tests (*t*-ratio) will be significant at the level chosen by the researcher.

$$Y_{ij}=B_0+B(T)+B(C2)+B(C3)+B(E)+e_{ij,}$$

FIGURE 2.6 Expanded regression model to include the event (*E*).

Post-Event Change to the Series

In many research situations, the interruption attributable to an event may be short-lived, permanent, or display a gradual return to the prior pattern (Mohr, 1995). In order to test the pattern of changes on Y after the start of the intervention or event, a fourth term can be added to the regression model. This term is analogous to a time by event interaction:

Time   123456789101112131415161718192021222324252627282930313233343536
Cycle 123123123123123123123123123123123123123123123123123123123123123
Event 000000000000000000000000000000000000111111111111111111111111111111
TxE   0000000000000000000000000000000000001234567891011121314151617 18

The time by event interaction effectively starts a secondary trend, which can indicate the duration of the post-event trend and its direction (Figure 2.7).

$$Y_{ij}=B_0+B(T)+B(C2)+B(C3)+B(E)+B(TxE)+e_{ij},$$

FIGURE 2.7 Time by event interaction regression equation.

As with hierarchical regression models in general, the main effects and interactions are tested and removed if they are not significant. Note that in time series regression, the absolute impact of each variable, its unstandardized coefficient, B (time, cycle, event, or TxE), is the focus of interest.

The baseline test is whether time is at all correlated with the outcome, and thus first establishes if there is any non-random change in the series. In time series regression, each Y or mean of Y is predicted serially, resulting in a series of residuals (e_{ij}) associated with each time period in the series. The residuals are assumed to be uncorrelated with each other.

$$Y_{t2} = B_0 + B_{(T1)} + e_{t1}$$
$$Y_{t3} = B_0 + B_{(T1)} + B_{(T2)} + e_{t12}$$
$$Y_{t4} = B_0 + B_{(T1)} + B_{(T2)} + B_{(T3)} + e_{t123}$$
$$Y_{t5} = B_0 + B_{(T1)} + B_{(T2)} + B_{(T3)} + B_{(T4)} + e_{t1234}$$

The significance tests for the time factor will be inaccurate if there are serially correlated residuals (McDowell, McCleary, Meidinger, and Hay, 1980), so a diagnostic such as the Durbin–Watson (DW) statistic is commonly used (Figure 2.8).

$$d = \frac{\sum_{t=2}^{T}(e_t - e_{t-1})^2}{\sum_{t=1}^{T} e_t^2},$$

FIGURE 2.8 Durbin–Watson test statistic.

The d statistic falls within a range in a DW table. If the observed d is *below the lower bound* of the DW for degrees of freedom (number of predictors in the current model), the inference is that there is autocorrelation among the residuals. Field (2009) offers a rule of thumb for the DW test: d statistics below 1 and above 3 suggest autocorrelation among the residuals. In that event, the regression model would need to be transformed and adjusted for correct re-estimation of main effects (t-ratios), with a follow-up adjustment such as Cochrane–Orcutt, or Prais–Winsten, which are included as R packages that can be called for the linear regression module in R, as well as in the AREG module of SPSS. Alternative methods (Huitema, 2011) are also available, and are particularly useful for short series. In the event there is serial correlation of the residuals, corrective adjustments are needed.

A number of language learning phenomena can be collected and archived in time series format. A program level archiving system might, for instance, include all standardized test scores across multiple cohorts of learners entering and graduating from a program. The conjoined cohorts in aggregate would provide a picture of growth and change over time, and be expanded each year of the program to yield a comprehensive historical account of learning outcomes. One such example is outlined here and elaborated by Ono in Chapter 7. A series of Institutional Test of English as a Foreign Language (TOEFL) Structure subtest scores archived over ten cohorts of language learners in a college foreign language program is plotted, modeled, diagnosed for autocorrelation of the residuals, and if need be, corrected before final interpretation. For this, purpose, the R packages *car* (Fox and Weisberg, 2019), *ggplot2* (Wickham, 2016), *orcutt* (Spada, Quartagno, Tamburini, and Robinson, 2018), and *lmtest* (Zeileis and Hothorn, 2002) were used:

```
library("car")
library("ggplot2")
library("orcutt")
library(lmtest))

itpseries<-read.table("e:\\RM Longitudinal\\itpseries.csv",header=T,sep=",")
names(itpseries)
```

The data are read from the comma-separated file 'itpseries.csv', and named itpseries in the subsequent analyses. Initially a visual of the series is useful, and for this, the ggplot2 package in R is used (Wickham, 2016).

```
stseries <- ggplot(data = itpseries, aes(x = TIME, y = ST,))
stseries+geom_line()
```

The series is modeled using a linear regression, with the use of a series of models starting with the trend, followed by the cyclical factor, and then the event and post-event trend added sequentially.

```
sttime<-lm(ST~TIME+ITP2+ITP3+EVENT+EVENTTIME,data=itpseries)
summary(sttime)
```

The resulting linear regression is assessed with a focus on the unstandardized coefficients, which reflect the absolute impact of the variables on the value of the dependent variable. The intercept, trend, and effects of the cyclical factors, which reveal the influence of within-cohort instruction on language learning gains, are expected to be statistically significant. The events added as specific hypotheses about causes for a change in the series may in some research be the focal interest.

```
durbinWatsonTest(lm(ST ~ TIME+ITP2+ITP3+EVENT+EVENTTIME,data=itpseries))
rcorc=cochrane.orcutt(rctime)
summary(rcorc)
```

Time series have the assumption of uncorrelated residuals, so a DW diagnostic test of that assumption is standard. If the DW test indicates autocorrelation of the residuals, a corrective adjustment such as the Cochrane–Orcutt transformation can be invoked with the use of the *orcutt* package in R (Spada et al., 2018).

In this volume, Ono (Chapter 7) uses interrupted time series analyses to examine macro-level educational policy changes in Japan, and institutional level admissions policy changes on 20 years of Institutional TOEFL data. Bloomfield and Clark (Chapter 3) also use interrupted time series to examine evidence of a planned intervention's impact on the foreign language proficiency sustainment in three US government agencies.

Regression over Time

Path Analysis

When variables are gathered over time or have a hypothesized evolutionary order, time can be combined into a regression model to create a path analysis, or a more complex mediation analysis with direct and indirect influences on the latter-measured outcomes. Path analysis is a method to examine possible causal influences among variables arrayed over time. If the variables are measured over time to form an antecedent to consequent order, and if the latter-measured variables did not pre-exist the earlier-measured variables, a flow of influence can be tested (Asher, 1990; Winship and Morgan, 2007). When designing a path or mediation analysis, the collection of data needs to be planned in a manner to ensure that the time order is maintained. The first wave of data collection should measure the individual difference variables that pre-exist those that will follow. Both static variables, measured only once in the first waves of the data collection, and repeated measures, measured in the first wave of data collection and again later in time, can be integrated into the analysis. The number of waves will depend on the duration of the study, and as long as the antecedent to consequent order is maintained, a flow of influence hypothesis can be tested for direct and indirect effect on one or more outcome variables measured in the last, or rightmost wave of data collection.

As an example of a path analysis with tests of mediation, consider whether prior academic success and individual differences in metalinguistic knowledge have direct and indirect effects on language proficiency developed after two semesters of instruction. The Achievement in High School (ACD) measure and a test of metalinguistic knowledge (MET) are considered exogenous (also referred to as independent) variables because they are antecedents and are not predicted by other measures. Exogenous variables are represented as rectangles to show that they are measured variables with errors associated with them. To their right are later two measures, also represented as rectangles, taken during college foreign language instruction. These occupy the middle of Figure 2.9, and indicate achievements (grade point averages in foreign language courses) in the first (EC1) and second semesters (EC2). Rightmost is the outcome of interest, a standardized foreign language proficiency test given after the first year of instruction (TF2).

The strategy for testing direct and indirect effects on post-instruction proficiency can use recursive linear regression, where latter-measured variables first serve as interim dependent variables and later serve as independent predictor variables as relationships are tested further downstream within the model. More commonly and conveniently, simultaneous equations are used. JASP offers a

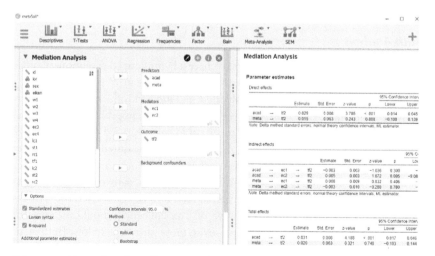

FIGURE 2.9 Example of mediation module in JASP estimating direct and indirect effects.

mediation module useful for estimating direct and indirect effects in the structural equation module, as shown in Figure 2.9 (JASP Team, 2022).

As shown in Figure 2.10, the effects of the MET (metalinguistic knowledge) variable show no systematic influence on achievements or on proficiency. ACD, representing overall academic performance in high school, shows both direct effects on foreign language proficiency and an indirect effect through the second-semester grade point average. Figure 2.10 also indicates the standardized path coefficients for all variables in the model, including the covariation between the exogenous variables and the achievement outcomes. The left-to-right flow of effects show direct, indirect, and total effects for the variables in the path model.

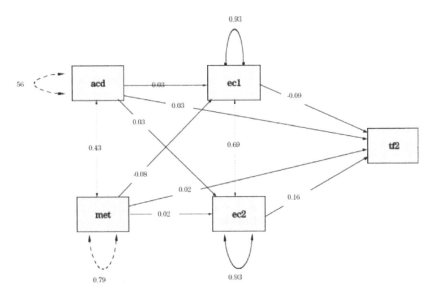

FIGURE 2.10 Direct and indirect influences on post-tested proficiency.

Path analysis is a useful tool for testing the flow of influences from early measures on variables that evolve or are measured later in time, and then from the intermediate states to the outcomes of interest. This approach to longitudinal analysis can identify sustained long-range influences and differentiate them from more ephemeral influences and show how some individual difference variables exert direct and indirect influences on language learning outcomes. In Chapter 5, Megan C. Masters uses a recursive path analysis to test how the same factors differ in predicting individual differences in proficiency outcomes across three languages taught within a US Government language training program. Qi Zheng in Chapter 9 uses a latent cross-lagged panel design to test the validity of self-assessed task-based abilities as predictors of measures of proficiency in a year-long single-cohort study.

Event History/Survival Analysis

When discrete events occur to individuals in different times over a longitudinal period, binary logistic regression can be used with time as the primary independent variable. In language learning research, such events might be leaving a program, graduating, failing a course, deciding on participation in a study-abroad program, or reaching a particular level of proficiency. Other covariates or independent variables can be added to test their effect on the probability of an event of interest happening or not happening. A fundamental issue is the unit of time used, with the assumption that the same time metric must be used for all cases. Individual cases are tracked over time until a discrete event of interest occurs. If it does not occur, the case 'survives' and remains in the census or population until the end of the data collection period. The actual event to be modeled can be any phenomenon of interest, as long as it is a discrete or binary outcome that is occurring at the case level. For instance, at the case level, if the research interest is language attrition, the event is the time at which a repeated measure of proficiency results in a lower level of proficiency of a predetermined magnitude for any given individual relative to that individual's prior level of proficiency. The metric of time would be a standard measure, such as days or months, that lapse between the first testing event, and the last test of record for each individual in the data set. The number of days or months varies across cases and is calculated from the date stamp for each test event and the outcome of the test taken at that date for any particular individual. The event is a binary code for the case experiencing attrition or not.

Event History Analysis in R Module 'Survival'

R offers different types of event history analyses in the 'survival' package. Once 'survival' and a graphics module 'ggfortify' are installed, an R script like the one below can be written. In the scripts below, the measure of time is lag, which is the difference in months between the first test on record and the last. The event of interest is the binary code denoting whether the last listening comprehension test for each case was lower than the first, and thus considered a loss of proficiency, in this example a loss of listening proficiency.

```
library("survival")
library("ggfortify")
listenloss<-read.table("e:\\RM Longitudinal\\listenEHA.csv",header=T,sep=",")
fitKM<-survfit(Surv(lag,loss)~lang, data=listenloss)
autoplot(fitKM)
fitCX<-coxph(Surv(lag,loss)~lang+sus, data=listenloss)
summary(fitCX)
```

The 'fitKM' command line models the time and event (lag and loss), with a single binary covariate, 'lang'. Here the object of interest would be whether there is a difference in attrition between two different foreign languages. The autoplot line provides a survival graph for the loss event by lang, which gets a default label 'strata' representing the two languages (Figure 2.11).

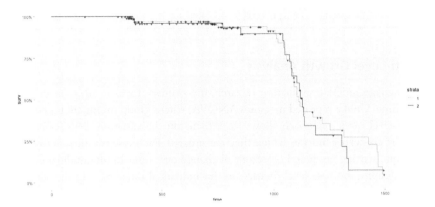

FIGURE 2.11 Language attrition event by language.

The survival graph suggests that listening attrition increases the longer the time lag between the first and last test events. For the two contrasted languages, attrition starts after about 1200 days between testing events. The graphical display indicates that the two languages attrite at about the same rate over time. A conventional statistical test is also provided to support the inference that the two languages in question do not differ in the rate of attrition.

Attrition researchers are likely to have individual difference variables they wish to test as factors that affect the probability of language attrition, or whatever the event of interest may be. For this, a Cox regression model is fit:

```
fitCX<-coxph(Surv(lag,loss)~lang+sus, data=listenloss)
summary(fitCX)
```

The object fixCX is defined with a model with time (*lag*) and the event (*loss*) as a function of languages contrasted (*lang*), plus another independent variable, in this case, *sus*, which here is a binary code denoting whether the individual had participated in an in-service refresher course to maintain his or her proficiency between the first and last testing events. The two covariates *lang* and *sus* are tested for their effect on the odds of attrition, and reported in the summary of the analysis object fitCX.

The results are shown as the coefficient, and an odd ratio, exp(coef), and a test of significance (Table 2.1). In this example, the two languages do not differ in their rate of attrition over time, and the in-service program (*sus*) does not have an effect on delaying attrition for learners experiencing it.

TABLE 2.1 Language and sustainment training are tested for their effect on the odds of attrition

	Coef	Exp(coef)	Se(coef)	Z	Pr (> |z|)
Lang	1.553e – 02	1.016e + 00	2.823e – 01	0.055	0.956
Sus	−1.708e+01	3.811e – 08	3.388e + 03	−0.005	0.996

Multi-Level Growth Analysis

In language program evaluation research, the primary focus is often on growth over time. Unlike repeated measures ANOVA, where group means are tested, the multi-level model approach allows for a focus on the variation *across individuals* and the clustering units in which they are situated. Each case is modeled to have a unique starting point and trajectory of change over time. In longitudinal multi-level designs, the base level focuses on the individual differences in the starting points (intercepts) and the variation in growth or change over time (slopes) at the case or individual person level. Language learners in programs are usually clustered in larger organizational units such as languages studied, class sections, or institutions. For growth analysis in the multi-level approach, longitudinal data need to be transposed so that they are 'stacked' with the cases in rows and a time (repeated measure) variable denoting each test event. The multi-level approach accommodates missing data so that individual person level repeated measures can still be included without imputation to replace the missing cells with estimates of the outcomes.

Multi-Level Growth in R Module LME4

In longitudinal language learning research, learners are usually clustered into intact classes that are taught by an individual instructor or team of instructors over a semester or longer. In contrast to the repeated measures ANOVA approach, which focuses on group means, the multi-level growth analysis can also focus on individual learner growth trajectories as well as variation across the clusters or class sections. The multi-level modeling of growth can also include a separate level that includes individual difference measures describing possible sources of variation among the learners, in addition to the growth trajectories of learners. The person-level covariates can then be tested for their influence on variation in individual growth trajectories. A third level is also frequently used in multi-level analysis – variables that describe how the clustering units, most commonly class sections, or even schools, differ. These can be indicators describing the class units in terms of average class abilities, aptitude, motivation, aspiration (Kozaki and Ross, 2011; Sasaki, Kozaki, and Ross, 2017), or variables that describe characteristics of the individual instructors of the class sections. An advantage of the multi-level approach to growth over time is that it can test hypotheses about contextual factors that go beyond the exclusive focus on individual differences, essentially integrating cognitive person-level phenomena with context-varying phenomena hypothesized to interact with individual difference variables.

The R package LME4 (Bates, Maechler, Bolker, and Walker, 2015) provides a dynamic set of analysis procedures for repeated measures, repeated trials, and clustered data. When included with a graphics module such as ggplot2 (Wickham, 2016), multi-level growth phenomena can be modeled and graphically represented. As an illustrative example, repeated measures of foreign language proficiency are tested over a two-semester period for 1373 members of a university foreign language cohort. Class sections (60) are constant over the year of instruction in a pre-mid-post-test design using a standardized proficiency measure with reading and listening subtests.

```
library("lme4")
library("ggplot2")
tbgains<-read.table("e:\\RM Longitudinal\\TBunivST.csv",header=T,sep=",")
names(tbgains)
lcbase<-lmer(LC~TIME+(1|ID)+(1|SECT),data=tbgains)
summary(lcbase)
```

The baseline model tests whether there has been change in the listening comprehension subtest over the year of instruction. Time (pre-mid-post) is treated as a fixed effect, while the individual learners' starting proficiency levels, and the sections into which they were placed, are treated as random effects. The pre-instruction measure is used for placement into sections, so the expectation is that learners and sections will not have a common starting point.

The individuals (ID) and classes into which they were placed (Sect) are variable at their intercepts or starting points, as anticipated (Table 2.2). The size of the variation across persons and classes provides corroborating evidence of heterogeneity that exists in the starting levels of proficiency. Had individuals been randomly assigned to sections, the expectation would be that the section variance would be much smaller.

TABLE 2.2 Random effects

Groups	Name	Variance	Standard deviation
ID	Intercept	7.69	2.773
Sect	Intercept	35.30	5.942
Residual		25.50	5.050

Number of observations: 4119, groups: ID, 1373; SECT, 60.

The fixed effect for the repeated measures (Time) shows a 3.15-point increase in proficiency for each year of instruction (Table 2.3). This would be the starting point for further exploration of other factors, individual difference covariates at the person level, or class or instructor covariates at the section level. A common research question in language program evaluation is whether the classes are homogeneous in proficiency growth over time. The variation in growth trajectories can be graphed to provide a picture of variation across the streamed class sections.

```
lcplot <- ggplot(data = tbgains, aes(x = TIME, y = LC, group = SECT))
lcplot+geom_smooth()
```

TABLE 2.3 Fixed effects

	Estimate	Standard error	t-value
Intercept	50.29546	0.79978	62.89
Time	3.15076	0.09637	32.70

The overall growth is positive as made evident with the test of time as a fixed effect. There is still, however, considerable variation across the class sections in the growth patterns (Figure 2.12). To explore factors that could explain the variation in listening over time, learner level variables can be tested for their fixed effects. If class sections are the focus, variables that are features of the class sections can be modeled. For instance, the years of experience of an instructor assigned to any class section could be such a focus. To test the effect of instructor experience, the baseline model is expanded to include a measure of each listening course teacher's years of experience (CEXP).

```
lcTexp<-lmer(LC~TIME+CEXP+(1|ID)+(1|SECT),data=tbgains)
summary(lcTexp)
```

The inclusion of instructor experience into the model in addition to the growth in listening suggests a small but non-random benefit provided by more experienced instructors (Table 2.4).

TABLE 2.4 Fixed effects

	Estimate	Standard error	t-value
(Intercept)	46.44295	1.79205	25.916
Time	3.15076	0.09637	32.695
CEXP	0.37424	0.15715	2.381

The multi-level modeling of growth permits detailed tests of interactions and conditional outcomes. For instance, growth in listening might be presumed to

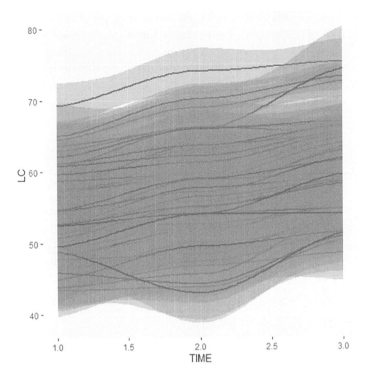

FIGURE 2.12 Listening growth by class section.

have a fixed effect across sections such that all class sections grow in listening proficiency in a parallel way. Alternatively, growth in listening can be tested as varying across class sections, with some classes growing, others declining, and some not growing in proficiency over the year of instruction.

```
lcTSECT<-lmer(LC~TIME+(1|ID)+(TIME|SECT),data=tbgains)
summary(lcTSECT)
```

Rather than modeling growth as fixed, it can be tested as depending on the class section by replacing the (1 | SECT) term with (TIME | SECT) (Table 2.5). This allows each section to have its own growth trajectory in the form of a random-slopes model.

TABLE 2.5 Random effects

Groups	Name	Variance	Standard deviation	Corr
ID	(Intercept)	7.69886	2.7747	
SECT	(Intercept)	34.38484	5.8639	
TIME		0.02846	0.1687	0.20

The small amount of variance across sections over time suggests that a random-slopes model does not fit the data better than a simpler model with random intercepts for class sections. The random-slopes model can be tested contrastively with the random-intercepts-only model with the use of a model comparison function (ANOVA).

```
lcbase<-lmer(LC~TIME+(1|ID)+(1|SECT),data=tbgains)
summary(lcbase)
lcTSECT<-lmer(LC~TIME+(1|ID)+(TIME|SECT),data=tbgains)
summary(lcTSECT)
anova(lcbase,lcTSECT)
```

Models can be tested to confirm that a parsimonious model fits the data better than a more elaborate alternative model. Here the baseline model with growth over time as a general fixed effect allowing for different starting points for individuals and class sections is explicitly compared with the random-slopes alternative (Table 2.6).

```
Models:
lcbase:    LC ~ TIME + (1 | ID) + (1 | SECT)
lcTSECT: LC ~ TIME + (1 | ID) + (TIME | SECT)
```

TABLE 2.6 Baseline model

	Df	AIC	BIC	$logLik$	$Deviance$	$Chisq$	$ChiDf$	$Pr>Chisq$
lcbase	5	26154	26186	−13072	26144			
lcTSECT	7	26158	26202	−13072	26144	0.2117	2	0.8995

In contrast, here, the random-slopes version of the model (TIME | SECT) is compared with the random-intercepts model for learners (ID) and class sections (SECT). The Chi-square difference between the models indicates that the more complex random-slopes (lcTSECT) model does not, in fact, fit any better than the baseline model. A similar test can be performed with class-level covariates such as CEXP to confirm that their addition to the model improves it to the data.

Latent Growth Curve Modeling

A clear advantage for analyzing growth as a latent variable comes from the fact that the individual differences in the latent growth factor can serve as dependent variables when predictors of the variation in growth are included. The latent growth factors can also be used as predictors of other measured or latent variables and can be combined into more complex models of parallel change or growth processes. Rather than focus on group means as in the repeated measures ANOVA approach, a latent growth model can use the same data and include individual differences in the starting proficiency level, as well as individual differences in the growth trajectories. As an example, the research focus might be on evidence of cohort-level growth in reading proficiency over time. A foreign language reading test given in evenly spaced test periods over two years of instruction would provide three waves of repeated measures, RC1–RC3.

Unlike confirmatory or structural equation models (SEMs), all of the path loadings to the latent intercept and slopes are fixed to a constant '1' for the intercept to establish a starting point for all cases, while the slope loadings are hypothesized to have a particular trajectory. The latent factor SLOPE RC1 is set to 0, the SLOPE RC2 is set to 1, and the SLOPE RC3 is set to 2 if the hypothesis is a linear incremental growth in reading skill over time. When a non-linear growth pattern is hypothesized, or when the actual trajectory is unknown, the SLOPE RC3 can be estimated as a free parameter.

The R package *lavaan* (an abbreviation of 'latent variable analysis'; Rosseel, 2012) can be used directly in R or invoked through the JASP SEM interface. The basic model for a latent growth model such as Figure 2.13 would be:

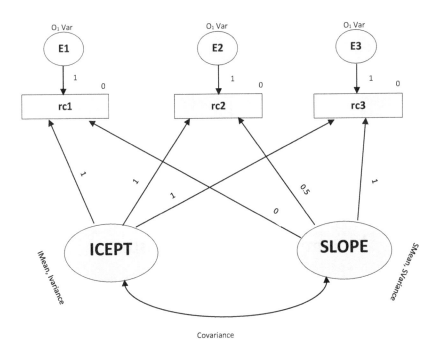

FIGURE 2.13 Basic latent growth model.

```
library("lavaan")
rcgrow<-read.table("e:\\RM Longitudinal\\cohort7shrt.csv",header=T,sep=",")
names(rcgrow)
rclgm <- ' ir =~ 1*RC1 + 1*RC2 + 1*RC3
          sr =~ 0*RC1 +1 *RC2 + 2*RC3 '
  fit <- growth(rclgm, data=rcgrow)
  summary(fit)
```

The basic growth model would fit the trajectory of growth and summarize the overall increase from the first to the last repeated measures. Because the latent intercept (*i*) and latent slope (*s*) are factors, individual learners have their own trajectories of change. The variation in change is then a typical focus of analysis when the basic growth model is elaborated. For instance, program evaluators would be interested in confirming that individual differences in achievement, as measured by a grade point average computed over all of the language courses taken during the two years of instruction (ecgpa), are correlated with the individual differences in growth on the standardized measure of proficiency in the foreign language.

For a growth prediction model, individual differences in reading growth trajectories (slope in Figure 2.14) are predicted by prior achievement (ecgpa).

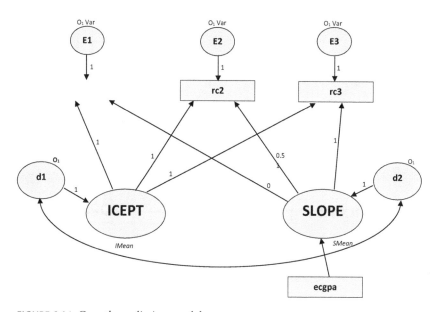

FIGURE 2.14 Growth prediction model.

TABLE 2.7 Model with addition of term s ~ ecgpa

	Estimate	Standard error	z-value	P(> |z|)
s~ecpga	0.037	0.015	2.533	0.011

```
library("lavaan")
rcgrow<-read.table("e:\\RM Longitudinal\\cohort7shrt.csv",header=T,sep=",")
names(rcgrow)
rclgm <- ' ir =~ 1*RC1 + 1*RC2 + 1*RC3
           sr =~ 0*RC1 + 1*RC2 + 2*RC3
           sr ~ ecgpa '
   fit <- growth(rclgm, data=rcgrow)
   summary(fit)
```

The addition of the term s ~ ECGPA in the *lavaan* code will test the hypothesis of interest, producing evidence of a small but non-random path between achievement and proficiency growth (Table 2.7).

Other predictors or covariates of growth can be added to the model in the same way. The model specifications in *lavaan* interface with the JASP SEM. Moving from R *lavaan* over to JASP will also provide an expanded menu of the fit statistics needed to provide evidence that the growth models actually fit the observed data. There are also options to convert the coefficients to standardized coefficients for comparative analysis variables in the model. JASP also provides a graphical presentation of the growth models with latent variables.

Summary

Once data sets have been constructed and prepared for analysis, the transition from data management to data analysis should require a few steps. Longitudinal researchers nevertheless need to plan their studies well in advance in order to identify the key variables of interest and gain sustained access to continued data collection through maintaining contact with the study participants, or through integration of existing archives of data. In short, longitudinal data collection and analysis require considerable logistical planning and sustained effort to collect and archive data, as well as strategies to deal with the contingencies that inevitably arise. In some research, archival data may be available. It is not uncommon, for instance, for institutional data to be collected systematically and archived. When such data are made available, there are often opportunities to create multi-cohort data sets which can be used to diagnose changes in outcomes over time. Such analyses can be invaluable for program evaluation and for establishing benchmarks for future outcomes analyses.

Software Applications

Several software packages have modules that are useful for longitudinal data analysis. Standard statistics packages such as SPSS (AMOS) or SYSTAT can be used for repeated measures ANOVA, linear regression models, and event history analysis. More flexible applications like M*plus* (Muthen and Muthen, 2007) can model multilevel and latent variable models, and like the R package *lavaan*, it uses a syntax-driven interface. Latent growth models with graphics interfaces are useful for drawing models before testing them against data. EQS (Bentler (2006) and Wu) and AMOS (X and Hamagami) are long-standing applications that are useful for these kinds of models. More recently, JASP has come on the scene, with a growing collection of modules useful for longitudinal data analysis. The *lavaan* packages in R interface with JASP SEM, providing a wide array of fit statistics and some model visualization.

References

Asher, H. B. (1990) *Causal Modelling. QASS Series 3*. Thousand Oaks, CA: Sage Publications.

Bates, D., Maechler, M., Bolker, B., and Walker, S. (2015) *lme4: Linear mixed effects using Eigen and S4. R package version 1.1-8*. https://CRAN.R-project.org/package=lme4.

Bentler, P. (2006) EQS 6 *Structural Equations Program Manual*. Encino, CA: Multivariate Software.

Field, A. (2009) *Discovering Statistics Using SPSS (3rd ed.)*. New York, NY: Sage.

Fox, J., and Weisberg, S. (2019) *An {R} Companion to Applied Regression (3rd ed.)*. Thousand Oaks, CA: Sage. https://socialsciences.mcmaster.ca/jfox/Books/Companion/

Huitema, B. E. (2011) *Analysis of Covariance and Alternatives (2nd ed.)*. New York, NY: Wiley.

JASP Team (2022) JASP (Version 0.16.3) (computer software).

Kozaki, Y., and Ross, S. J. (2011) Contextual dynamics in foreign language learning motivation. *Language Learning, 61(4)*, 1328–1354.

McDowell, R., McCleary, R., Meidinger, E., and Hay, R. (1980) *Interrupted Time Series. QASS Series 21*. Thousand Oaks, CA: Sage Publications.

Mohr, L. B. (1995) *Impact Analysis for Program Evaluation*. Newbury Park, CA: Sage Publications.

Muthen, L. K., and Muthen, B. O. (2007) *Mplus User's Guide (6th ed.)*. Los Angeles, CA: Muthen & Muthen.

Rosseel, Y. (2012) lavaan: An R package for structural equation modeling. *Journal of Statistical Software, 48(2)*, 1–36.

Sasaki, M., Kozaki, Y., and Ross, S. J. (2017) The impact of normative environments on learner motivation and L2 reading ability growth. *The Modern Language Journal, 101(1)*, 163–178.

Spada, S., Quartagno, M., Tamburini, M., and Robinson, D. (2018) *orcutt: Estimate Procedure in Case of First Order Autocorrelation*. https://CRAN.R-project.org/package=orcutt.

Wickham, H. (2016) *ggplot2: Elegant Graphics for Data Analysis*. New York, NY: Springer Verlag. https://ggplot2.tivverse.org.

Winship, C., and Morgan, S. L. (2007) *Counterfactuals and Causal Inference. Methods and Principles for Social Research*. New York, NY: Cambridge University Press.

Zeileis, A., and Hothorn, T. (2002) lmetest: Diagnostic checking in regression relationships. *R News*, 2(3), 7–10. https://CRAN.R-project.org/doc/Rnews/

3

USING EXTANT DATA TO ASSESS THE IMPACT OF IN-SERVICE FOREIGN LANGUAGE PROFICIENCY SUSTAINMENT PROGRAMS AT THREE US GOVERNMENT ORGANIZATIONS

Amber N. Bloomfield and Martyn K. Clark

Introduction

We first describe in general the impact analysis approach we will apply in investigating how the foreign language training (FLT) program affected foreign language skills at each of the organizations receiving FLT funding. The approach we describe in this report can be situated within the general tradition of impact analysis (Mohr, 1995). Before investigating the FLT program in detail, it is useful to consider the relationship between goals, activities, and impacts at a conceptual level to provide a framework for program assessment. Programs are funded to solve some kind of problem, though the ultimate problem may be implicitly rather than explicitly understood. Program activities are often undertaken as part of the larger overall effort, with the particular activity in question intended to support some aspect of the larger goal. As such, an individual activity may be effective, even though the larger problem it was intended to address may remain to some degree. Thus, the efficacy of an activity must be measured against the goals and objectives of that specific activity.

The FLT program had the goal of increasing employees' foreign language skills. Each type of funded expenditure supported this overall goal of nurturing foreign language skills, albeit from different angles. In other words, to investigate the overall impact of the FLT program, we must first lay out the separate activities for which these foreign language enhancement training funds were used and the goals associated with each of these activities. The logic of the FLT funding program is as follows. At each organization studied, there are incumbents whose job duties require some level of foreign language proficiency. However, maintaining or developing foreign language proficiency can require additional training opportunities outside of daily work activities; in fact, a language professional's current

DOI: 10.4324/9781003087939-4

role may not involve foreign language skills on a regular basis. The FLT program provides funding that can be used to offset costs associated with providing such opportunities, either through the direct costs associated with instruction (e.g., training events) or through the provision of interim foreign language professionals (*offset hires*) who can take over the incumbents' job duties while they are attending a training event. After participating in a training event, the incumbents return to their posts, ideally with an increased level of foreign language proficiency.

The assessment of success for individual activities conducted as part of a program can occur at a variety of levels. The work of Kirkpatrick (1998) has been influential in explicating these different levels as they apply to the evaluation of training programs. In Kirkpatrick's system, there are four levels of evaluation:

- Level 1: The reaction to the training in terms of participant satisfaction
- Level 2: The increase in participants' learning or knowledge due to training
- Level 3: Changes in participants' behavior due to training
- Level 4: The impact of the participants' attending the training in terms of improved job performance

In-service training programs can be evaluated by collecting data at each of these levels. This conceptualization rests on the assumption that each level is causally related to the one above – one would not expect a poorly received training event to show a positive effect on job performance, for example.

Phillips and Phillips (2009) expand on Kirkpatrick's idea of level of impact in their conceptualization of return on investment (ROI). ROI is the evaluation of the overall benefit of a program activity, given its financial cost, and is of primary concern to executive decision makers. The ROI model mirrors the Kirkpatrick model with one additional, higher level (Level 5, below):

- Level 1: Reaction and planned action
- Level 2: Learning
- Level 3: Application and implementation
- Level 4: Business impact
- Level 5: ROI

As with the Kirkpatrick model, Phillips and Phillips (2009) argue that relevant information can and should be collected to evaluate each of these levels. For each level, the appropriate outcome measure must be identified and analyzed. In some cases, level-appropriate measures may be collected as a matter of course (e.g., a participant satisfaction survey for a training event), whereas other situations may require significant planning and data-gathering efforts to select the best measure or proxy. This is especially true when it comes to evaluating the higher levels. For this reason, organizations may choose to have different evaluation targets for the various levels across a portfolio of initiatives such that, for example, 100% of programs are evaluated at Level 1, 60% of programs are evaluated at Level 2, 30% at Level 3, and so on (Phillips and Phillips, 2009).

Ideally, the evaluative component is incorporated into new programs from the outset: targeted levels are identified before implementation and relevant outcome data are continuously captured. If not, as was the case with the FLT funding initiative, it is necessary to rely on extant data that capture outcomes at one or more levels to glean project impact. The goal of an impact analysis is to investigate the link between a program activity and the outcome of that activity. A key element of impact analysis is the notion of the counterfactual – that is, the assumed state of the world had the program in question not been implemented (Mohr, 1995; Morgan and Winship, 2007). Simply put, the impact of a program can be defined as the difference between the observed results of a given program and what the results would have been had that intervention not been implemented. The greater the difference between program results and the counterfactual, the greater impact the program can be said to have. Note that this difference can be expressed from either a positive or negative direction, depending on whether the desirable state of the world is seen as an increase in something positive (e.g., an increase in the number of people receiving language training) or a decrease in something negative (e.g., a decrease in the number of people without sufficient language ability). Thus, the interpretation of program impact depends on program context and how the intended outcome of the program has been conceptualized.

Background

To properly assess the impact of FLT program spending, we need to first identify the types of activities that were made possible through the program and consider what outcomes those activities were intended to or could reasonably be expected to produce. Those program activities with quantifiable outcomes can provide data needed to assess the impact of the program. Although there are a variety of program activities for which funds are used across the organizations that receive them, most activities can be divided into two broad categories: (1) human resources expenditures; and (2) training costs:

1. Human resource expenditures: Spending in this category involves costs directly associated with personnel, such as paying for offset hires for employees participating in training or covering the salaries of language instructors.
2. Training costs: Spending in this category includes a variety of costs associated with language training activities, such as developing new courses or paying tuition for training activities offered outside the organization.

As we will discuss below, the outcome measures likely to detect the impact of the FLT program will differ depending on the type of expenditure. For instance, hiring foreign language instructors should, in most cases, impact language proficiency for the employees who take courses from those instructors; hiring a language program manager is unlikely to affect language proficiency in such a straightforward manner, though there may be a more general, diffuse, or long-term impact on language proficiency within the organization. To the extent that there is diversity in how funds are used, there will be diversity in the outcome measures most appropriate for exploring how expenditures influenced foreign language skills. In our case, the available sources of information were organization proficiency testing and training records. As it was not always possible to tie specific training events directly to the FLT program funding initiative, we were obliged to first consider changes in workforce, rather than individual, proficiency levels.

The Impact of FLT Program Funding on Language Proficiency

To investigate how FLT program allocations affect foreign language proficiency at the participating organizations, we first examine how workforce proficiency at each organization has changed since the advent of FLT funding. For this, a time series regression approach is used (Ostrom, 1990; Mohr, 1995; Ono, Chapter 7 in this volume). Time series analyses are used for a wide range of economic, legal, political, biomedical, and social policy research questions. The input to time series analyses are historical records on the same scale that stretch back in time prior to an intervention or event hypothesized to have affected the series of measures arrayed from the earliest recorded measure through to the most recent.

The test of record for all three organizations was the Defense Language Proficiency Test, or DLPT, a multiple-choice test that requires examinees to read/listen to a passage in the target language and respond to a set of questions based on the information presented (DLIFLC, n.d.). As with most foreign language testing in the US Government, proficiency is reported on the Interagency Language Roundtable (ILR) scale, an 11-step functional continuum ranging from 0 (no proficiency) to 5 (proficiency equivalent to a well-educated native speaker), with plus levels (1+, 2+, etc.) between each base level. Each step in the continuum has a corresponding skill level description which characterizes the functional language ability expected of a person at that level for a given skill (Clark and Clifford, 1988; ILR, n.d.). To analyze DLPT scores, we follow the common practice of treating the ILR levels as integers, with plus levels as fractional values (e.g., ILR 2 = 2, ILR 2+ = 2.6).

Organization A

A visual examination approach to time series analyses starts with a longitudinal view of the series over time. The graphical representation of the series shows variation in the series on a wide-focus lens reflecting the ILR measurement scale used by stakeholders. For the present study, repeated test records for Organization A were available for about ten years of data. Based on these test record data,

Organization A's language professionals' average proficiency level was calculated for each 50-day interval from the earliest test date in the data to the most recent. The wide-lens view of Organization A series in Figure 3.1 depicts a change wherein scores shift from a more erratic, slightly downward pattern in the beginning of the series to a pattern of consistent improvement. Note that to reduce figure size and improve readability, the space between each x-axis tick mark in the figure represents three 50-day intervals rather than individual intervals. October 1, 2009 corresponds to when the intervention program for in-service FLT funding began for Organization A, roughly indicated by the vertical line. Two foreign language skills are tested – listening and reading – and both are reported on the ILR scale to convert all foreign languages to a common proficiency metric. Reading test scores tend to be higher than listening test scores across all time intervals.

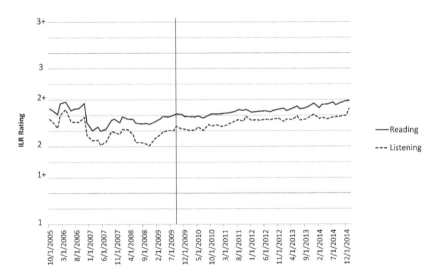

FIGURE 3.1 Average reading and listening test scores at Organization A over time. ILR = Interagency Language Roundtable.

Organization B

Testing and training records were available for Organization B employees for roughly nine years of data. Based on the testing records provided by Organization B, we calculated the average reading and listening proficiency test score for each 50-day interval from the earliest date in the dataset through the end of the dataset.[1] The average workforce proficiency levels at each time point are displayed in e-Figure 3.1 in the e-resources. A vertical line corresponds to the point at which FLT funds were first allocated to Organization B (the beginning of fiscal year (FY) 12). The view of the series indicates that there has been stability over the time series for reading and listening test scores. The time series for Organization B appears more jagged in general than that for Organization A; this is due to the smaller number of Organization B employees contributing to the average proficiency score at each time point. There seems to be a disturbance to the series around the point at which FLT funding began, wherein the series shifts from a pattern of stability to a pattern of decreasing scores over time. We will explore this disturbance and potential reasons for it below. Similar to the pattern for Organization A, average Organization B reading test scores tend to be higher than average listening test scores across all time intervals. As with Organization A, the multiple-choice DLPT was the test of record.

Organization C

Testing and training records were available from Organization C from FY2007 through FY2015. The available test information listed FYs rather than specific calendar dates associated with each score. As a result, the time series for Organization C is at the level of FYs and thus considerably coarser-grained than the Organization B and Organization A time series, which gives the Organization C time series a much smoother appearance (see e-Figure 3.2 in the e-resources). There appears to be a slight disturbance in the time series around FY2010, when the in-service FLT program funds became available. Yet the visible change to the time series for reading and listening is very slight for this organization, likely due to the smaller number of measurement points in the series. Like the time series for Organization A, the time series for Organization C shows an upward trajectory, with reading test scores consistently higher than listening test scores.

We next conducted time series regression analyses to investigate the potential impact of FLT program allocations on the patterns of test scores over time for Organization A, Organization B, and Organization C employees. For all of the time series analyses, statistical modeling is needed to detect impacts that are not obvious in the visual inspection of the graphical representation of the series. Although disturbances to all three of the time series are suggested by the figures above, it is unclear whether these changes to the series are statistically stable or what factors may motivate them. In addition to investigating these issues, the analyses can test each series for violations of the assumption of independent error terms at each time period in the series. Correlated error terms are common in time series data and indicate that the relationship between values in a time series is dependent on the lag between them (typically, that values from closer time points are more related to each other than to others that are more distant in the series). The graphical representation does not reflect possible correlated errors, and thus regression models provide both the diagnostics needed for accurate inferences about the hypothesized impacts of the FLT program as well as tests of overall trends and changes to the trends.

The approach to time series regression models follows a hierarchical sequence of models. The first model noted in Figure 3.2 tests whether there is a trend in the series, and whether there is any evidence of correlated errors across time.

$$Y_t = \beta_0 + \beta(T_t) + e_t$$

FIGURE 3.2 Basic statistical regression model.

The baseline time series analysis tests if the effect (β) for time (T) is positive, negative, or random. Positive coefficients denote upward trends for the dependent variable (Y, here, DPLT averages in each time period), or negative downtrends, suggesting a gradual decline. The series do not show any evidence of periodicity or cyclical variation. Once the trend is estimated, an event, either planned or identified as a historical event (e.g., the onset of FLT program funding, which is the independent variable (X) in these analyses), is added to the model to test if it has an impact on the series average immediately after it is introduced (Figure 3.3).

$$Y_t = \beta_0 + \beta(T_t) + \beta(X_t) + e_t$$

FIGURE 3.3 Statistical regression model with the addition of the independent variable, X, representing foreign language training program funding.

The impact of the intervention (X) may be hypothesized to be immediately interrupting the series by moving the averages upward or downward, or to be manifesting a slower effect over the series after the intervention has started. In the present case, the program should impact the average proficiency of the workforce positively.

The last model in the hierarchical time series approach tests whether the introduction of the intervention changes the series with a post-intervention trend. The second trend tests how the intervention reverses or continues the trend observed prior to the onset of the interruption (Figure 3.4).

$$Y_t = \beta_0 + \beta(T_t) + \beta(X_t) + \beta(T_t X_t) + e_t$$

FIGURE 3.4 Statistical regression model examining the impact of the intervention on average proficiency trends.

As noted earlier, the models are continuously tested with regression diagnostics for the key assumption of independent residuals (errors).[2] If needed, appropriate transformations are invoked to correct for any non-independent residuals.[3] The corrected coefficients provide the basis for more accurate inferences about the impact and changes to the series thereafter. For each organization receiving FLT funding, the time at which these funds became available can be estimated as the first day of the FY in which they were allocated. The event was estimated as occurring on October 1, 2009 for Organization A, December 1, 2011 for

Organization B, and in FY2010 (October 1, 2009–September 30, 2010) for Organization C. Figure 3.5 displays the time series with the introduction of the FLT program event, schematically represented as Period 10.

$$\bar{Y}_1\bar{Y}_2\bar{Y}_3\bar{Y}_4\bar{Y}_5\bar{Y}_6\bar{Y}_7\bar{Y}_8\bar{Y}_9\boxed{F\bar{Y}_{10}}F\bar{Y}_{11}\ F\bar{Y}_{12}\ F\bar{Y}_{13}\ F\bar{Y}_{14}\ F\bar{Y}_{15}.....\ F\bar{Y}_n$$

FIGURE 3.5 Single series with antecedent averages as the counterfactual condition.

The time series analysis facilitates estimation of the trend of change and any cyclical patterns (possibly a result of periodic influxes of new employees entering service) prior to the onset of the FLT initiative. At the point in time that FLT program funds became available, the series is tested for changes in the trend lines or cyclical patterns established prior to the start of the FLT program funding. The effect of the FLT program can be assessed as immediate, or as a gradual change to the trend established before the FLT program. Both of these potential effects of the FLT program are tested in the time series analyses below.

We fit a series of regression models to the average proficiency test scores for reading and listening test scores at Organization A separately. The average reading test scores at Organization A over time are shown in Figure 3.6, this time scaled to ILR2–ILR3 to better display the variation in test scores seen over time. The vertical line represents the point at which FLT program funds became available, and could potentially have impacted the series. There does not appear to be an immediate shift in the time series at this point, though the average test scores seem to stabilize into a steady upward trend after the FLT program funds were first allocated.

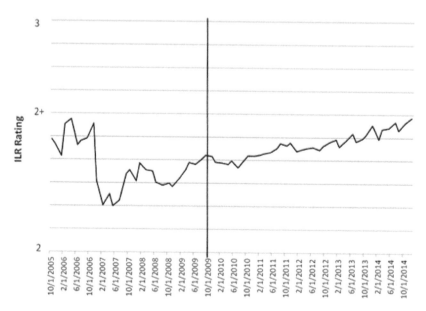

FIGURE 3.6 Average reading test scores at Organization A. ILR = Interagency Language Roundtable.

To investigate the impact of the FLT program statistically, we first fit a regression model to the reading test scores with time as the only covariate.[4] This model examines the extent to which average reading test scores change over time at Organization A. The results of the analysis indicate that there was a marginally significant positive relationship between average reading test scores and the time interval, implying that reading scores tended to improve over time, at a rate of about 2.3% of an ILR rating per 50-day time interval (Table 3.1).

TABLE 3.1 Results of the time series analyses for reading test scores at Organization A

Included in model	Predictor	B	p value	Implication
Time	Trend in scores over time	0.023	$p < 0.06$	There was an overall positive trend in average reading test scores over time
Time + FLT program	Immediate impact of FLT program	0.037	ns	There was no significant impact of the onset of the FLT program on the mean for the reading time series
Time + FLT program + FLT program × time	Impact of FLT program on trend	0.097	$p < 0.01$	The onset of the FLT program positively impacted the trend in reading test scores over time
Time (pre-FLT program scores only)	Pre-FLT program trend	−0.041	ns	Prior to the FLT program, there was stability in reading test scores
Time (post-FLT program scores only)	Post-FLT program trend	0.048	$p < 0.001$	Following the onset of the FLT program, there was a positive trend in reading test scores over time

FLT = foreign language training.

In the next step in the analyses, we included the FLT program "event" to explore whether the introduction of FLT program funds resulted in a shift in the trend for reading test scores. The results of this analysis indicate that the FLT program did not have an immediate impact on the positive trend. As one would anticipate a lag between the initial availability of funds and the completion of training events and subsequent testing, this lack of immediate impact is not unexpected.

The final step in these analyses investigated whether the introduction of FLT program funding altered the trend of the time series significantly. The results indicate that FLT program funding had a positive impact on the trend, suggesting the reading test scores improved to a greater extent over time once FLT program funds became available. Compared to the increase of 2.3% of an ILR rating per time interval prior to FLT program funding, scores increased about 9.7% of an ILR rating per time interval following the onset of FLT program funding. This result echoes what can be seen by examining Figure 3.6: reading test scores show a steeper and more consistently positive trend after Interval 31 than earlier in the series.

To confirm the above results, we conducted separate analyses on the "pre-FLT program" and "post-FLT program" reading test scores. While there was not a significant trend in the average reading scores prior to the start of FLT program funding, there was a significant positive trend in the time following the start of FLT program funding.

The same sets of analyses were conducted with Organization A listening test scores (shown in e-Figure 3.3 in the e-resources) and yielded similar results.[5] As displayed in Table 3.2, there was a marginally significant positive trend for listening test scores over time, indicating about 2.8% of an ILR rating increase with every 50-day time interval. FLT program funding did not have an immediate impact on the average listening test score but did influence the trend of listening test scores over time, such that scores showed a steeper pattern of improvement over time (about 12.3% of ILR rating per time interval) following the start of FLT program funding. In support of this last result, listening test scores prior to FLT program funding showed stability over time and those following FLT program funding showed a significant positive trend.

TABLE 3.2 Results of the time series analyses for listening test scores at Organization A

Included in model	Predictor	B	p value	Implication
Time	Trend in scores over time	0.028	$p < 0.07$	There was an overall positive trend in average listening test scores over time
Time + FLT program	Immediate impact of FLT program	−0.091	ns	There was no significant impact of the onset of the FLT program on the mean for the listening time series
Time + FLT program + FLT program × time	Impact of FLT program on trend	0.123	$p < 0.01$	The onset of the FLT program positively impacted the trend in listening test scores over time
Time (pre-FLT program scores only)	Pre-FLT program trend	−0.063	ns	Prior to the FLT program, there was stability in listening test scores
Time (post-FLT program scores only)	Post-FLT program trend	0.051	$p < 0.001$	Following the onset of the FLT program, there was a positive trend in listening test scores over time

FLT = foreign language training.

Changes in Workforce Language Proficiency for Organization B

As with Organization A data, the Organization B time series analyses to follow were based on proficiency test scores sampled at 50-day intervals. The date ranges in the Organization B data were from January 1, 2006 through January 29, 2015,[6] slightly narrower than that for Organization A. Further, Organization B did not receive its first allocation of FLT program funds until FY12, so the onset of FLT program funding for this organization was estimated to be December 1, 2011. E-Figure 3.4 in the e-resources shows the average reading test scores at Organization B over time with a narrower range of proficiency (ILR2–ILR3) to illustrate the variability in scores over time. The vertical line shows the approximate time point at which FLT program funds were available to Organization B. In contrast to Organization A reading test scores, scores at Organization B appear to show a stable, though jagged, pattern over time up until the advent of FLT program funding, after which time there is the appearance of a downturn.

The visual representation of the whole series (e-Figure 3.4 in the e-resources) suggests a gradual decrease in average proficiency over time. The stability and direction of the trend are initially tested with time as the only predictor of the reading proficiency test scores (Table 3.3). This analysis indicates that there is indeed a significant negative relationship between time and reading test scores that is very small but consistent (about 0.3% of an ILR rating for each time interval).

TABLE 3.3 Results of the time series analyses for reading test scores at Organization B

Included in model	Predictor	B	p value	Implication
Time	Trend in scores over time	−0.003	$p < 0.001$	There was an overall negative trend in average reading test scores over time
Time + FLT program	Immediate impact of FLT program	−0.104	$p < 0.05$	There was a negative impact of the onset of the FLT program on the mean for the reading time series
Time + FLT program + FLT program × Time	Impact of FLT program on trend	0.002	ns	The onset of the FLT program did not affect the trend in reading test scores over time

FLT = foreign language training.

The next model fit to the data included the immediate impact of FLT program funds. This analysis revealed that there was a significant immediate negative impact of the onset of FLT program funding on reading test scores. A model including a change in trend following the onset of FLT program funding did not find a significant change in the trend of reading test scores, however. In sum, the results for the time series analyses involving reading test scores at Organization B indicate that reading scores had an overall negative trajectory over time, and the availability of FLT program funds had a negative immediate impact on the average reading test score. Both of these findings are unexpected. We will discuss possible reasons for the results below.

E-Figure 3.5 in the e-resources displays the average listening test score at each time interval for Organization B. The ILR rating range shown here is 1+ to 3, as some of the averages were below ILR 2. The pattern of scores over time is very similar to reading test scores: there is a long period of general stability in scores and a period of apparent decline in scores for roughly the last third of the time series, coinciding with the timing of initial FLT program funding allocation.

The model including only the impact of time on listening test scores found a significant negative relationship, suggesting that the average listening test score at Organization B decreased over time at a slight but consistent rate (0.3% of an ILR rating per time interval; Table 3.4). Adding the immediate impact of FLT program allocations to the model revealed no significant impact of FLT program on listening test scores, but the model including a change in trend following FLT program allocations did reveal a significant negative relationship. This result indicates that the availability of FLT program funds coincided with an increase in the downward trajectory for listening test scores at Organization B to a rate of about 1% of an ILR rating decrease per time interval, contrary to what would be expected. To confirm these results, we fit the model including time as a predictor of listening test scores to the test data prior to the onset of FLT program and scores after the onset of FLT program separately. Time had a non-significant relationship to listening test scores for the pre-FLT program series, indicating that scores were relatively stable prior to the time FLT program funds became available at Organization B. There is a marginally significant negative trend for scores following the onset of the FLT program. We discuss this result further below.

Summary of Changes in Organization B Workforce Language Proficiency

For reading test scores at Organization B, the introduction of FLT program funding had an immediate negative impact on scores, but did not change the trend of test scores over time. Further, reading scores showed a significant pattern of decline over all time intervals. Listening test scores showed the same pattern, but for these

TABLE 3.4 Results of the time series analyses for listening test scores at Organization B

Included in model	Predictor	B	p value	Implication
Time	Trend in scores over time	−0.003	$p < 0.001$	There was an overall negative trend in average listening test scores over time
Time + FLT program	Immediate impact of FLT program	−0.116	$p < 0.05$	There was a negative impact of the onset of the FLT program on the mean for the listening time series
Time + FLT program + FLT program × time	Impact of FLT program on trend	−0.012	$p < 0.05$	The onset of the FLT program negatively impacted the trend in listening test scores over time
Time (pre-FLT program scores only)	Pre-FLT program trend	0.000	ns	Prior to the FLT program, there was stability in listening test scores
Time (post-FLT program scores only)	Post-FLT program trend	−0.013	$p < 0.08$	Following the onset of the FLT program, there was a negative trend in listening test scores over time

FLT = foreign language training.

scores, the onset of FLT program funding significantly changed the trend to be more negative over time. Negative impacts are rare for training FLT programs intended to increase the mean outcome relative to the status quo ante. However, the relationship between the onset of FLT program funding and test scores could be due to the way Organization B used the FLT program funds. Depending on mission needs, language professionals may need to develop skills in additional languages not originally trained in. Broadly speaking, ILR2 is considered minimal working proficiency. Placing a focus on language acquisition courses (ILR0–ILR2 range) devised to increase the number of employees who have minimal proficiency in languages for which there is current need would introduce more lower-proficiency individuals into the pool of employees testing at Organization B. In support of this explanation, Organization B training records indicate that nearly 50% of the courses directly supported by FLT program funding, and 38% of all courses offered in the time since FLT program funds became available to Organization B, were acquisition courses. Comparatively, only 19% of all courses offered prior to the start of FLT program funding were acquisition courses. Acquisition courses are designed to take learners from no and very low language skill levels to levels at or below ILR2; sustainment courses, comparatively, have the goal of maintaining skill levels, typically at ILR3 or higher. More acquisition courses are likely to result in a greater proportion of lower-level language professionals taking the DLPT. While this is a possible explanation for the results of the time series analyses, it is not possible to show definitively that it was the availability of FLT program funds that led to the greater proportion of language acquisition training at Organization B, nor is it possible to know that this is the root cause of the downward trend in test scores.

The results for Organization B reading and listening test scores illustrate some of the complexities of a time series approach with regard to investigating the impact of the FLT program initiative. While the use of new funds for new language training activities might be expected to increase the average listening and reading proficiency at an organization, this perspective assumes a closed system in which the employees testing prior to the new funding are the same employees who are testing after the new funding, or the same employees testing in the same languages. This is not necessarily the case. While a conclusion that could be drawn from the Organization B results is that the FLT program funding had no positive impact on the average language proficiency level, an increase in the number of analysts with proficiency in languages that were hitherto without sufficient numbers of linguists is a valuable outcome. Further, if foreign language professionals are moved to a third or fourth language for ab initio training, the means at each interval can be expected to include retested L2 professionals as well as those starting from near-zero proficiency. Ideally, disaggregation of data would tease out gains that are obscured in aggregated data.

Another reason why the negative trend in listening and reading test scores at Organization B is unexpected is that the results of previous analyses of Organization B employee test and training data found generally positive trajectories for test scores over time (reported in Ross et al., 2011 and Bloomfield et al., 2012). These results were generated with latent growth analysis, which estimates the change in individual employees' proficiency test scores over time; this analysis then calculates an average slope representing the typical pattern of change across all employees (see Mackey, Chapter 4 in this volume). In contrast, the time series analyses reported above analyze proficiency test scores at the aggregate level of the language professional workforce (i.e., averaged across all employees). To confirm that the individual pattern of change in scores over time is still positive, we fit a latent growth model to the current sets of Organization B listening and reading data. The model fit for listening scores found a positive average slope across employees, indicating that individual employees tended to show increasing listening test scores over repeated test events. For reading, the slope trended toward positive, though it was not significant. These findings provide additional evidence that variation in the pool of employees contributing to the average proficiency test score at different time points may have led to the workforce-level results found in the Organization B time series analyses, rather than a decline in test scores over time for individual employees per se.

Changes in Workforce Language Proficiency for Organization C

As noted above, the time series for Organization C had to be at the level of FYs due to the test records available. E-Figure 3.6 in the e-resources shows the average reading test scores at Organization C over time on a narrower scale from ILR 2 to ILR 3 to better show the detail of change in average score over time. The vertical line at FY2010 shows the time point at which FLT program funds were available and thus the starting point from which these funds could have begun to affect proficiency test scores. Compared to the Organization A and Organization B time series described above, the Organization C time series shows a more constant upward trajectory, both pre- and post-FLT program funding.

The stability and direction of the upward trend are first tested with time as the sole predictor of the reading proficiency test scores (Table 3.5). This analysis indicates that there is a significant positive relationship between time and reading test scores (about 5% of an ILR rating for each time interval). The next analysis, including the immediate impact of the FLT program, found a significant positive impact of the onset of FLT program funding on reading test scores. The final model including the change in trend at the time FLT program funds were introduced did not reveal a significant change in the trend of reading test scores. The results for the time series analyses involving reading test scores at Organization C indicate that the availability of FLT program funds positively affected the average test score, but did not increase the rate at which test scores improved over time.

TABLE 3.5 Results of the time series analyses for reading test scores at Organization C

Included in model	Predictor	B	p value	Implication
Time	Trend in scores over time	0.053	$p < 0.001$	There was an overall positive trend in average reading test scores over time
Time + FLT program	Immediate impact of FLT program	0.100	$p < 0.05$	There was a positive impact of the onset of the FLT program on the mean for the reading time series
Time + FLT program + FLT program × time	Impact of FLT program on trend	0.003	ns	The onset of the FLT program did not affect the trend in reading test scores over time

FLT = foreign language training.

E-Figure 3.7 in the e-resources shows the average listening test score for Organization C employees across FY2007–2015. Again, the vertical line at FY2010 indicates the onset of FLT program funds for this organization. Like reading test scores, the average listening test scores over time show a positive trajectory both before and after FLT program funds became available.

The first model including only the impact of time on average listening test score revealed a significant positive relationship between time and scores: listening test scores improved over time (Table 3.6). When the immediate impact of the FLT program was added to the model, this predictor had a marginally significant positive relationship to listening test scores, indicating the average score for the series increased following the availability of FLT program funds. As with the reading test score series, however, the onset of the FLT program did not affect how much listening test scores improved over time.

TABLE 3.6 Results of the time series analyses for listening test scores at Organization C

Included in model	Predictor	B	p value	Implication
Time	Trend in scores over time	0.057	$p < 0.001$	There was an overall positive trend in average listening test scores over time
Time + FLT program	Immediate impact of FLT program	0.041	$p < 0.07$	There was a positive impact of the onset of the FLT program on the mean for the listening time series
Time + FLT program + FLT program × time	Impact of FLT program on trend	−0.013	ns	The onset of the FLT program did not affect the trend in listening test scores over time

FLT = foreign language training.

Summary of Changes in Organization C Workforce Language Proficiency

Compared to the Organization A and Organization B time series, the Organization C time series was much coarser-grained: instead of capturing the average workforce proficiency in reading and listening every 50 days, we were only able to calculate the average for each FY, due to the available test records. As a result, the series had a much smoother and more apparent consistent upward trend than did the Organization B or Organization A series. Also unlike Organization A and Organization B series, the Organization C series showed a significant immediate impact of the introduction of FLT program funding, but the overall trend, the upward trajectory of listening and reading test scores, was not significantly affected by the FLT program. That is, scores were trending upwards prior to the intervention. The lack of an interaction between FLT program funding and the improvement in listening and reading test scores over time could be due to the smaller number of time points in the Organization C series (FYs instead of 50-day intervals). Nonetheless, the results of the time series analyses for this organization indicate that workforce language proficiency significantly improved after the allocation of FLT funds.

The Impact of FLT Program-Funded Training on Employees' Language Proficiency

Ideally, it would be possible to examine how FLT program expenditures translated into change in foreign language proficiency for individual employees at each organization receiving funding. However, this approach proved difficult for many of the organizations. For Organization A, the specific employees who participated in language training as a result of FLT program funds were not identified in extant data sources. Data received from the other organizations did identify the employees who participated in FLT program-funded activities. Yet in many cases, these employees did not have proficiency test scores both before and after the training activity, so change in their language proficiency could not be investigated. In addition, it was often the case that the number of employees participating in program-funded training at a given organization was either too few to conduct statistical comparisons between these individuals and other employees who did not, or the test scores for the other employees were unavailable.

Impact of FLT Program-Funded Training for Organization B Employees

For the Organization B data, a field in the training dataset indicated whether a training event was supported with FLT program funds. This information and the fact that activities funded with FLT program funds at Organization B affected specific employees rather than increasing the number of language training generally available (e.g., through hiring language instructors) made the identification of employees directly affected by FLT program funding straightforward. Fifty-three Organization B employees were indicated as having participated in FLT program-funded training. However, only 11 of these 53 employees had reading test scores both before and after FLT program-funded training events, and only 13 had listening test scores before and after FLT program-funded training events. The distribution of pre- and post-training test scores is shown in e-Figure 3.8 in the e-resources. Due to the small number of employees, we did not conduct statistical tests on the impact of the FLT program-funded training. Examining e-Figure 3.8 reveals that there was a shift to the right (i.e., higher proficiency levels) for test scores following the FLT program-funded training. Specifically, seven of the 11 employees showed an improvement in reading test scores and six of the 13 showed an improvement in listening test scores.

Impact of FLT Program-Funded Training for Organization C Employees

Organization C provided extensive data that included a number of different groups of employees who had participated in training, along with their pre- and post-training test scores for these employees. Two of the groups, 167 employees in total, were identified as having participated in FLT program-funded training. We compared the pre- and post-training proficiency test scores for these individuals. Paired-sample t-tests revealed that post-training test scores were significantly higher for both reading and listening ($t = -8.83$ and -6.77, respectively, both $p < 0.001$). The distribution of pre- and post-training test scores is shown in e-Figure 3.9 in the e-resources.

Conclusions

The analyses reported here indicate that the introduction of FLT program funds had a positive impact on foreign language proficiency at participating organizations, although observing the positive effects was not always simple. At the workforce level, the positive change in proficiency levels following the onset of FLT program funding was clearly evident for Organization A, both when looking across all tested languages and when comparing the languages to which FLT program funding was applied and the languages not targeted with FLT program funding. This relationship was also straightforward for Organization C: following the availability of FLT in service training resources, average reading and listening proficiency improved significantly. For Organization B, on the other hand, the onset of the FLT program seemed to correspond with an overall decrease in reading and listening proficiency at the workforce level. A closer look at the training and test data revealed that this was likely due to FLT program funding being used primarily for initial language acquisition training, which would result in a larger number of employees from the overall workforce with lower language proficiency being tested, bringing down the workforce average score.

At the individual employee level, FLT program-funded training had a largely positive impact on proficiency. Organization B employees who received FLT program-funded training tended to improve their reading and listening test scores, and the difference between pre- and post-test scores was statistically significant for Organization C employees who participated in FLT program-funded training.

Each organization received funds and used those funds to support activities with a direct relationship to employees' foreign language proficiency (e.g., hiring language instructors, developing new language courses, supplying a back-fill employee for employees attending training); each organization showed an increase in their employees' language proficiency as a result. However, focusing on proficiency test scores as an outcome can only partially portray the impact of the FLT program. For impact assessments of this type, ideally outcomes will be identified before the start of the program so that measures of each can be established before any change occurs, allowing a baseline to be measured.

Notes

1 The last 50-day interval in the Organization B dataset included scores for only eight employees; the average for this interval was excluded from the time series analyses.
2 Auto-correlation among residuals (e_t) is tested with the Durban–Watson statistic.
3 In the event the Durban–Watson statistic detects significant serial correlation, the series is transformed with the Prais–Winsten method, available in the AREG function in SPSS.

   The series is transformed iteratively until the Durban–Watson statistic is larger than the upper bound of the range for the indicators (variables and time periods), and the auto-correlated residuals become independent (Ostrom, 1990).
4 The Durbin–Watson statistic generated by the initial regression indicated substantial auto-correlation in the time series; we corrected for this using an auto-regression procedure for all Organization A reading score time series analyses.
5 Again, the Durbin–Watson statistic generated by the model fit including time indicated substantial auto-correlation in the time series; we corrected for this using an auto-regression procedure for all Organization A listening score time series analyses.
6 As noted above, the last 50-day interval for Organization B data included only eight test scores, so the average for this interval was excluded from the time series analyses.

References

ADNI/Human Capital: Foreign Language FLT Program Office (2011). Intelligence Community Foreign Language Training Initiative for Fiscal Year 2011. Arlington, VA: ADNI/Human Capital: Foreign Language FLT Program Office.

Bloomfield, A. N., Gynther, K., Masters, M. C., O'Connell, S. P., & Ross, S. J. (2012). *Foreign Language Proficiency Change Over Time. Preliminary Explorations of Training, Test Version Changes, and Initial Proficiency Levels.* College Park, MD: University of Maryland, Center for Advanced Study of Language.

Bloomfield, A. N., Masters, M. C., Clark, M. K., & Ross, S. J. (2015). *FLT Program Initiative Full Time Equivalent (FTE) Allocation Use among Organizations: Categories of Funding Use, Available Data, and Planned Analyses.* College Park, MD: University of Maryland, Center for Advanced Study of Language.

Clark, J. L. D., & Clifford, R. T. (1988). The FSI/ILR/ACTFL proficiency scales and testing techniques: Development, current status, and needed research. *Studies in Second Language Acquisition*, 10(2), 121–147.

Clark, M. K., Masters, M. C., & Bloomfield, A. N. (2015). *Interim Report: An Overview of FLT Program-Related Data Received and Planned Analyses.* College Park, MD: University of Maryland, Center for Advanced Study of Language.

DLIFLC (Defense Language Institute Foreign Language Center) (n.d.). DLPT Relevant Information and Guides. Retrieved October 8, 2020 from: www.dliflc.edu/resources/dlpt-guides/.

ILR (Interagency Language Roundtable) (n.d.). Descriptions of proficiency levels. Retrieved October 8, 2020 from: www.govtilr.org/.

Kirkpatrick, D. (1998). *Evaluating Training Programs: The Four Levels.* San Francisco, CA: Berett-Koehler.

Mohr, L. (1995). *Impact Analysis for Program Evaluation.* Thousand Oaks, CA: Sage.

Morgan, S., & Winship, C. (2007). *Counterfactuals and Causal Inference: Methods and Principles for Social Research.* New York, NY: Cambridge University Press.

Ostrom, C. W. (1990). *Time Series Analysis: Regression Techniques* (Vol. 9). Newbury Park, CA: Sage.

Phillips, P. P., & Phillips, J. J. (2009). Return on investment. In: *Handbook of Improving Performance in the Workplace: Volumes 1–3,* 823–846. Wiley Online Library. https://doi.org/10.1002/9780470592663.ch53

Ross, S. J., Bloomfield, A. N., Masters, M. C., Nielson, K. B., Kramasz, D. M., O'Connell, S. P., & Gynther, K. (2011). *How Does Foreign Language Proficiency Change Over Time? Results of Preliminary Data Mining.* College Park, MD: University of Maryland, Center for Advanced Study of Language.

4
INVESTIGATING LANGUAGE APTITUDE AND ATTRITION

Beth Mackey

Introduction

Language aptitude tests are widely used in the U.S. Government to select and place students into long-term language training programs. Within the Department of Defense (DoD), the Defense Language Aptitude Battery (DLAB) has been administered to select potential language professionals for future military service since the 1970s. Service members who are accepted into positions as linguists receive their language training at the Defense Language Institute Foreign Language Center (DLIFLC) in Monterey, California. This training is intensive and lasts 36–64 weeks, depending on the language, and service members are expected to reach Interagency Language Roundtable (ILR) Skill Level 2 upon graduation. The length of language training is dependent upon the language difficulty, which is defined in terms of distance from English. DLI uses a four-category system, with languages considered easier to learn (e.g., French, Spanish) as Category I, and the most difficult languages to learn (e.g., Arabic, Chinese) as Category IV.

Research on the predictive validity of the DLAB, though it spans 40 years, has been focused on its ability to predict these outcomes at DLIFLC. Because graduates of language programs go on to serve multi-year terms as language professionals in the military, their language performance across time is of interest to the DoD. A longitudinal design is critical to investigating change in behavior over time (Duncan & Duncan, 2004). This study explores how cognitive ability and language aptitude predict language proficiency growth. It also provides a benchmark of the current status.

This study used latent growth modeling (LGM) to analyze language proficiency test scores. LGM allows the researcher to model initial proficiency level and growth trajectories. Growth in reading and listening language proficiencies was

DOI: 10.4324/9781003087939-5

analyzed using test scores and other information from a sample of military language professionals. Cognitive ability and language-specific aptitude were entered into the model as predictor variables to assess their impact on language learning outcomes over an eight-year period. It was hypothesized that both cognitive ability and language aptitude would be significant predictors of not only initial proficiency outcomes (per the original test purpose), but also of growth.

Background

The traditional entry point into the language profession in the U.S. military services is through successful performance on the Armed Services Vocational Aptitude Battery (ASVAB). The ASVAB is a multiple-abilities test used for selection and classification by the DoD.[1] Successful performance on the ASVAB, in turn, leads to an offer to take the DLAB. Recruits with high scores on the DLAB are then encouraged to accept positions that require foreign language proficiency in the Armed Services. To be qualified to serve as language professionals in the military, recruits must graduate from language training. Over the past 40 years, studies (Lett et al., 2003; Petersen & Ali-Haik, 1976; Silva & White, 1993) have confirmed that DLAB predicts success in foreign language learning at the DLIFLC.

Throughout the U.S. DoD, language proficiency in reading and listening is measured by the Defense Language Proficiency Testing (DLPT) system. Tests are now in their fifth generation, although some older-generation tests are still in use in some languages. Military linguists are required to test annually. DLPT scores are reported against the ILR Skill Level Descriptions (Interagency Language Roundtable, 1985). The ILR[2] descriptors date back to the 1950s when the Civil Service was charged with cataloging U.S. Government language professionals. Following decades of research and use of a proficiency scale led by the Foreign Service Institute, what became known as the "ILR Scale" was broadly adopted in 1985 to describe language proficiency across 11 levels (six base levels and five "plus" levels) in listening, reading, speaking, and writing (Herzog, n.d.). The ILR served as the basis for the American Council on the Teaching of Foreign Languages (ACTFL) scales (Clifford & Cox, 2013).

At the time of this study, though graduates of the DLIFLC programs were expected to reach ILR Level 2 in listening, Level 2 in reading and Level 1+ in speaking, the work these graduates go on to do demands a much higher level of language proficiency (Department of Defense, 2005). Graduates from the DLIFLC serve as language professionals across the DoD, and they are expected not only to maintain, but to improve their language proficiency. Foreign language and regional expertise are considered "critical competencies essential to the DoD mission" (Department of Defense, 2005a). One of the four goals of the Defense Language Transformation Roadmap (Department of Defense, 2005b), which grew out of congressionally mandated follow-on actions after September 11, 2001, is to "establish a cadre of language specialists possessing a level 3/3/3 ability (listening/

reading/speaking ability)" (p. 10). ILR Level 3 is considered to be the professional level. Language training is mandated for those in language-enabled positions, so in addition to using their language skills on the job, graduates from DLIFLC continue to receive classroom and on-the-job training in their languages with the goal of as many as possible attaining professional level proficiency. They are also encouraged to continuously refresh their language skills through self-study.

Published research on the ASVAB and DLAB as predictors of language learning is limited. In a seminal study, Silva and White (1993) found that DLAB did contribute significant incremental validity in the prediction of DLPT scores over and above both general ability (*g*) and ASVAB subscores. DLAB multiple correlation increments were significant, though small, ranging from 0.02 to 0.04 for listening and reading and 0.02 to 0.13 for speaking (p. 87). Similar results were found for the prediction of academic attrition, with DLAB consistently adding to the correlations by a range from 0.01 to 0.12 (p. 89). Silva and White (1993) concluded that their results supported a theory of differential aptitude (Ree & Earles, 1990; Wagener, 2016) and that ASVAB and DLAB should be used to predict outcomes at DLIFLC. Given the numbers of students and the cost associated with language training, even small improvements in prediction were seen to be of value to the U.S. Government.

In more recent studies, language testing researchers have taken up the challenge to explore patterns in language growth. Surface et al. (2004) studied second language (L2) proficiency change in an analysis of U.S. Special Operations language professionals, analyzing DLPT reading and listening scores over five test occasions. Individual differences were found in initial scores and rates of development (both linear and curvilinear). The average change in proficiency for both listening and reading followed an overall positive linear pattern but listening exhibited a downward curvature (p. 5). Their analysis found that language difficulty negatively impacted initial proficiency and constrained growth. Education level and cognitive ability were found to only predict initial proficiency level, and not growth. They suggested that these latter findings were perhaps attributable to limitations such as range restriction and unknown factors, such as training, that would have influenced growth over time.

Differing patterns of language proficiency growth in reading and listening were also found in a study by Bloomfield et al. (2012). Their analysis of language professionals at the Defense Intelligence Agency found that listening and reading proficiency scores improved over time. Unlike the Surface et al. (2004) study, their modeling took into account factors such as training, which was predicted to influence growth over time, but their analysis did not include aptitude measures as predictors. They found that for listening and reading modalities, training had a significant negative relationship with starting proficiency and a significant positive relationship with growth. This was interpreted to mean that those who were at lower ILR levels were likely to receive training, and that the training was more likely to improve their level of proficiency as compared to those who were not trained.

In summary, previous research shows that language aptitude is predictive of static proficiency outcomes over and above general intelligence, and that language proficiency among military language professionals improves over time. However, there are only limited studies using a longitudinal design to investigate the relationship between aptitude and growth beyond initial acquisition.

Research Questions

The ASVAB and DLAB have shown their value as predictors of success at the DLIFLC. While the graduation outcome from DLIFLC is critical to the language training program, it is also important to the broader DoD that language professionals continue to grow in their language proficiency after graduation from the Institute. Understanding how aptitude influences this language proficiency growth is of interest to the DoD, given its long-term investment in language professionals over the course of their careers. This study built upon the research described above in the following ways:

- It used a longitudinal design, rather than static, as in Silva and White (1993).
- It included additional predictor variables (language training, work in the language), as suggested by Surface et al. (2004) and Bloomfield et al. (2012).
- It employed LGM techniques, rather than correlational studies or multiple regression, as in Petersen and Ali-Haik (1976), or Silva and White (1993).

Aptitude was measured with a general cognitive measure (specifically the Armed Forces Qualifying Test (AFQT) composite score from ASVAB) and a language-specific instrument (DLAB). Outcomes in foreign language proficiency were measured with the DoD standard proficiency test, the DLPT.

The study was designed to investigate the following questions:

RQ1: To what extent do general cognitive ability and language aptitude predict learning outcomes following training at DLIFLC?

RQ2: To what extent do general cognitive ability and language aptitude predict growth in language proficiency?

RQ3: To what extent do other variables (language difficulty, language training, language use) impact the relationships between language aptitude and language proficiency?

Methodology

Extant data were provided by two organizations, the Defense Manpower Data Center (DMDC) and a DoD agency that employs DLIFLC graduates. Data included AFQT scores, DLAB scores, language studied, DLPT listening and reading results, and dates tested, a dichotomous variable indicating attendance in post-DLI language training, and a dichotomous variable indicating whether an individual ever worked in the language.

The subject pool comprised DLIFLC graduates between January 1, 2004 and January 1, 2008 who served in assignments in a cryptologic branch of one of the military services (Army, Navy, Air Force, and Marines) between 2004 and 2013. The final sample included listening test scores for 5678 individuals and scores for 5673 individuals for reading.

LGM takes into account group level information (as expressed by factor means) as well as individual differences (the variances). The analysis can be used to describe growth at the group and individual level, as well as to see which variables influence growth. According to Duncan and Duncan (2004), the strengths of LGM include: "an ability to test the adequacy of the hypothesized growth form … to correct for measurement error in observed indicators … and to develop from the data a common developmental trajectory, thus ruling out cohort effects" (p. 8).

LGM allows for change to be linear or curvilinear. As Surface et al. (2004) and Bloomfield et al. (2012) found in their studies, changes in proficiency growth do not always follow a linear path. LGM allows the researcher to test for linear and non-linear patterns of growth to select the best model. Another advantage of LGM is that explanatory variables can also be entered into the model.

Languages taught at DLIFLC are categorized by their difficulty for an English learner. In the current dataset, there are 23 languages, with the majority (60%) in the most difficult languages, Category IV, and only 10% in the easiest, Category I. Because there were only seven cases of Category II languages, they were combined with Category III languages (30%) for the subsequent analyses.

The mean AFQT score for individuals in this dataset was 89.35 (SD 8.47), and the mean DLAB score was 112.94 (SD 12.09) with scores on both aptitude tests reflecting a negative skew and a ceiling effect (see Figures 4.1e through 4.4e in the e-companion of this book). To minimize the effect of range restriction in the latent growth analysis, scores were standardized (*ASVABZ* and *DLABZ*, below).

Other variables of interest included whether an individual reported working in the language (58%), took training in the language (59%), or experienced a change in DLPT test version (43%). Just over half of the individuals worked in the language, and a similar percentage received further training beyond DLI in the language tested. Just under half of the individuals experienced a version change at some point in their test-taking history. The percentages of personnel who worked in the language, received training, and experienced a version change for both the reading and listening skills are detailed in Table 4.1e in the e-companion of this book.

Because LGM assumes that the periodicity of testing is constant, following Bloomfield et al. (2012), new variables were created to represent test scores at five 400-day intervals, starting with the DLI graduation score as the initial score (400 days). Scores in reading and listening both show a drop in score in the first 800 days, followed by a very slight increase in scores. All scores remain in the Level 2 range, with the average reading test scores higher than listening scores. The number of available test scores in both listening and reading dropped when the scores were transformed to 400-day intervals (Figure 4.1), with 3786 individuals with scores at the 400-day mark and 2411 at the 2000-day mark.

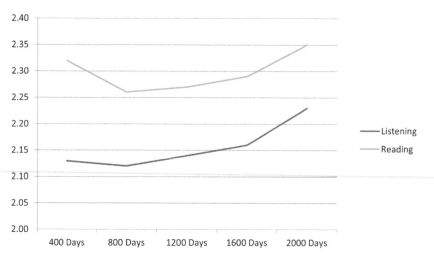

FIGURE 4.1 400-day interval test scores.

Latent growth models provide estimates that describe both inter-individual differences and intra-individual growth trajectories. The initial status, or intercept, is the estimate of the average proficiency score upon graduation from DLIFLC across individuals, and the slope is the average growth pattern across individuals. The variance of the intercept describes the extent of variability across individuals at the initial time point, and the variance of the slope represents the variability in rates of change across individuals. Finally, the covariance of growth parameters shows the relationship between the initial status and the rates of change (Surface et al., 2004). The model included measures representing whether or not a version change was noted in the data (DLPT IV to DLPT 5, *VerDiff*), the language difficulty category (*LangDiff*), the standardized ASVAB and DLAB scores (*ASVABZ, DLABZ*), whether or not the individual ever worked in the language (*Work*) and whether or not the individual attended any post-DLI training (*Train*).

Listening

Two growth models, linear and non-linear, were compared: the linear model, Model 1A, assumed a pattern of change over time with fixed values for the slope parameters (400 days at 0, 800 days at 1, 1200 days at 2, 1600 days at 3, and 2000 days at 4); the non-linear model, Model 2A, fixed a slope parameter of 0 for the first occasion and set the last parameter at 1. This allowed the rest of the factor loadings to be freely estimated from the data. Fixing the initial slope parameter at 0 (in both models) allows for the intercept factor to be interpreted as the initial status at the initial score, the 400-day mark. As anticipated based upon earlier research, the non-linear Model 2A indicated a slightly better model fit (chi-squared difference $\Delta\chi^2 = 3.26$). Therefore, Model 2A, the non-linear growth model, was accepted as the base model. All fit statistics met assumptions for adequate model fit (comparative fit index (CFI) > 0.95 and root mean square error of approximation (RMSEA) < 0.06, Duncan & Duncan, 2004).

Variables of interest were then added to the non-linear base model sequentially in the following order: difference in test version (*VerDiff*), language difficulty category (*LangDiff*), standardized ASVAB scores (*ASVABZ*), standardized DLAB scores (*DLABZ*), whether or not the individual ever worked in the language (*Work*), and whether or not the individual ever attended a subsequent training event in the language (*Train*). With each additional variable, model fit was checked again. Version difference and language difficulty categories were added first due to their demonstrated impact on growth (Bloomfield et al., 2012). The aptitude variables were added in the order that they are given to the military (ASVAB prior to DLAB). Whether or not an individual is assigned to the language (*Work*) was added before the training variable (*Train*) based on an assumption that this order represents the chronology of events in the work environment.

As each variable was added to the model, fit statistics continued to indicate an adequate fit (Table 4.1). The final model, Model 2G, includes all of the predictor variables of interest, and model fit remained adequate ($\chi^2 = 146.6$, df = 30, CFI = 0.986 and RMSEA = 0.026). Significant correlations in the model were allowed to covary to improve model fit.

TABLE 4.1 Model fit statistics

	Model variables	χ^2	df	p^3	CFI	RMSEA
2A	Base	79.9	7	0.000	0.985	0.043
2B	2A + *VerDiff*	114.8	10	0.000	0.979	0.043
2C	2B + *LangDiff*	121.2	14	0.000	0.979	0.037
2D	2C + *ASVABZ*	124.0	18	0.000	0.981	0.032
2E	2D + *DLABZ*	126.5	21	0.000	0.985	0.030
2F	2E + *EWM*	131.7	25	0.000	0.986	0.027
2G	2F + *ETR*	146.6	30	0.000	0.986	0.026

CFI = comparative fit index; RMSEA = root mean square error of approximation.

The mean intercept in the final listening model was 2.31, slightly higher than ILR Level 2, with a variance of 0.21. These numbers represent the mean of the true intercept (initial level in the dataset, i.e., DLI graduation) and the true variation of initial test score that were explained by the latent growth model. The estimated mean is quite close to the actual mean in the dataset.

The mean slope in the model was 0.055, indicating some growth in listening proficiency. As anticipated by the flat trajectory of scores, the slope mean was not significant, however ($p = 0.225$), indicating that there is not an overall pattern of growth. The variances were all significant, however, indicating that there were meaningful inter-individual differences in intercept, slope, and predictor variables.

The correlation between intercept and slope was negative (−0.051) and significant ($p < 0.001$), indicating that people who had a higher starting ILR level showed less growth over time.

The path coefficients for listening carry information about the shape of growth. The 400-day and 2000-day paths were fixed at 0 and 1, respectively. The 800-day, 1200-day, and 1600-day estimates were 0.305, 0.644, and 0.94, indicating that scores initially increased (somewhat evenly across the period from 400 days to 1600 days), and then leveled off between the last two occasions (1600 and 2000 days), although the increase was not statistically significant. Figure 4.2 graphically displays the final model for listening.

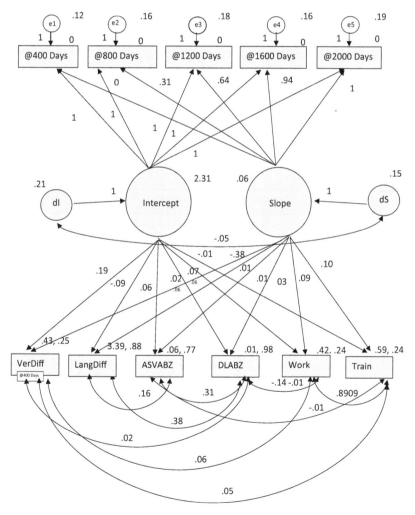

FIGURE 4.2 Listening model with parameter estimates.

We saw in Model 2G, the final model, that the mean intercept was significant, but the slope was insignificant. This was interpreted to mean that there was not an overall pattern of growth. However, the paths between the variables of interest and the intercept and slope provide information regarding between-person variation, and many of these relationships were significant. Version change had a significant positive impact on intercept (standardized beta weight = 0.20, $p < 0.01$). Version change had a negative impact on slope (standardized beta weight = -0.45, $p <$ 0.01), with those experiencing a version change over their test history showing a decline in proficiency.

Language difficulty category had a significant negative impact on intercept (standardized beta weight = -0.18, $p < 0.01$) and no significant relationship to slope. This result is somewhat surprising given that the initial training length at DLIFLC is adjusted by language category, with longer training times at DLIFLC for the more difficult languages. The fact that language difficulty does not constrain growth suggests that it is equally difficult to retain listening proficiency following graduation, regardless of language.

ASVAB had a significant positive relationship on intercept (standardized beta weight = 0.10, $p < 0.01$) and no significant relationship to slope. This suggests that individuals with higher AFQT scores tended to have a higher level of listening proficiency upon graduation from DLIFLC, but that there was not a subsequent relationship to growth. The DLAB, in contrast, was not a significant predictor of score upon graduation, but it did explain between-person variation in change for those who did show growth (standardized beta weight = 0.03, $p = 0.03$). This result is contrary to expectations and will be discussed below.

Whether or not an individual reported ever working in the language significantly predicted both intercept (standardized beta weight = 0.07, $p < 0.01$) and slope (standardized beta weight = 0.10, $p < 0.01$). The relationship between working in the language and growth is somewhat intuitive, given that working in the language offers increased exposure to the language, and those who do work in the language are required to test. It is less clear why this variable is associated with the intercept, i.e., a higher score at DLI graduation.

Individuals who attended at least one training event over the period of interest were more likely to improve their listening proficiency, as expected (standardized beta weight = 0.12, $p < 0.01$).

The covariances between residuals associated with intercept and rate of change are negative and significant, meaning that a person with lower proficiency upon DLI graduation has a greater rate of increase in proficiency score over time. This is intuitive, as there is more room to improve. Other covariances confirm relationships that have been seen in previous research. Positive covariances between DLAB and ASVAB suggest that those with higher AFQT scores have higher DLAB scores; higher DLAB and AFQT scores were also related to language difficulty, attributed to the fact that higher-aptitude students are assigned to the more difficult languages.

Reading

A similar analysis was conducted with the reading data. Model fit statistics are provided in Table 4.2.

TABLE 4.2 Model fit indices (reading)

	Model variables	χ^2	df	p^4	CFI	RMSEA
2A	Base	75.1	7	0.000	0.986	0.041
2B	2A + VerDiff	94	10	0.000	0.984	0.038
2C	2B + LangDiff	107	14	0.000	0.983	0.034
2D	2C + ASVABZ	113.5	18	0.000	0.983	0.031
2E	2D + DLABZ	119.6	21	0.000	0.987	0.029
2F	2E + EWM	110.9	25	0.000	0.989	0.025
2G	2F + ETR	116.8	30	0.000	0.99	0.023

CFI = comparative fit index; RMSEA = root mean square error of approximation.

As each variable was added to the model, fit statistics indicated a continued adequate fit. The final model, Model 2G, includes all the variables of interest, and model fit was adequate (χ^2 = 116.8, df = 30, CFI = 0.99, and RMSEA = 0.023).

The mean intercept in the final reading model was 2.62 and significant (p < 0.001), meaning that average score upon graduation was ILR Level 2+. The mean slope in the model (0.01) was not significant, indicating that, as seen in the listening data, there is no overall pattern of change in reading proficiency. The variances were all significant, however, indicating that there were meaningful inter-individual differences in intercept, slope, and predictor variables.

The correlation between intercept and slope was negative (–0.092) and significant (p < 0.001), indicating that people who had a higher starting ILR level showed less growth over time.

The standardized path coefficients for reading showed even growth that then levels off between the fourth and fifth occasions ([0.0] 0.414, 0.746, 1.01 [1.00]), although this increase was not significant.

Version change had a significant positive impact on intercept, as seen in Bloomfield et al. (2012), which means that people who had a version change in their history tended to have a higher score leaving DLI (standardized beta weight = 0.19, p < 0.01) than when tested at the agency. Version change also constrained growth (standardized beta weight = –0.336, p < 0.01). Other results also mirrored listening: the language difficulty category had a significant negative impact on intercept (standardized beta weight = –0.25, p < 0.01) and no significant relationship to slope. ASVAB scores had a significant positive relationship on intercept (standardized beta weight = 0.12, p < 0.01) and no significant relationship to slope. Unlike the listening data, however, DLAB was a significant predictor of initial level (standardized beta weight = 0.06, p = 0.002) and it had a positive significant relationship to slope (standardized beta weight = 0.08, p = 0.002). This suggests that individuals with higher DLAB scores graduated DLIFLC with higher proficiency scores and increased at a faster rate. The final model is shown in Figure 4.3.

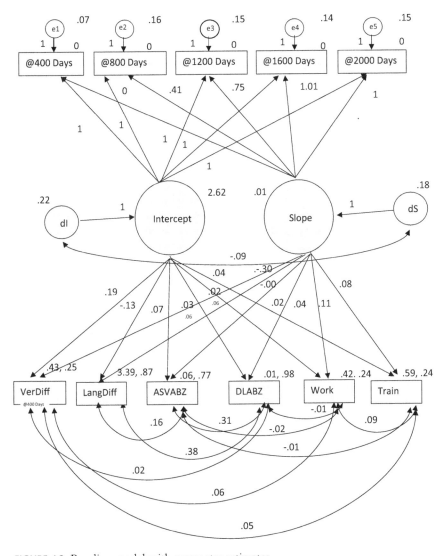

FIGURE 4.3 Reading model with parameter estimates.

Two other predictor variables also had a different pattern in reading than in listening: whether an individual ever worked in the language had no significant relationship to the 400-day score, but it was related to growth (standardized beta weight = 0.12, $p < 0.01$). Whether an individual attended a training course had a positive, significant relationship to initial level (standardized beta weight = 0.04, $p = 0.02$) as well as slope (standardized beta weight = 0.09, $p < 0.01$). This suggests that those who attended follow-on training were more likely to have a higher score at the first 400-day interval and show an increase in proficiency after leaving DLIFLC.

As seen in listening, covariances between residuals associated with intercept and rate of change in level were negative and significant, suggesting that those individuals with a lower proficiency at graduation have a greater rate of increase in level over time. Covariances between residuals associated with DLAB and ASVAB suggest that those with higher ASVAB have higher DLAB. Higher DLAB and ASVAB scores were also related to language difficulty (once again, due to language assignments).

Discussion

This study investigated the extent to which aptitude influences language proficiency growth across a 2000-day period, while controlling for other known moderating variables such as version change, language difficulty, job assignment, and ongoing training. Given that previous research on language aptitude focuses only on initial acquisition, this study contributes to the literature by describing its impact on growth over time. LGM allows for the investigation of average initial status and average growth rate, as well as providing estimates of the variation across individuals of initial status and of growth rate (Muthen & Khoo, 1998).

The above analyses provided some evidence to answer the three research questions posed above:

> RQ1: To what extent do general cognitive ability and language aptitude predict learning outcomes following training at DLIFLC?

For both the listening and reading modalities, cognitive ability, as measured by the AFQT composite score from ASVAB, was a significant predictor of the initial level of language proficiency. This relationship was positive, i.e., those with higher scores on the AFQT were more likely to have higher ILR levels upon graduation from DLI. With general cognitive ability already accounted for in the model, language aptitude was also a significant predictor of initial status in reading, but it was not a significant predictor of listening.

> RQ2: To what extent do general cognitive ability and language aptitude predict growth in language proficiency?

For both modalities, listening and reading, general cognitive ability was not found to be a significant predictor of growth. Language aptitude, however, was shown to be a significant predictor of growth in both modalities.

RQ3: To what extent do other variables (language difficulty, language training, language use) impact the relationships between language aptitude and language proficiency?

Language difficulty negatively impacted initial acquisition but was not significantly related to growth in both listening and reading. Rates of change were positively impacted for both language training and language use in both reading and listening.

The finding that general cognitive ability was a significant predictor of DLI outcomes was expected based on previous research, with higher scores on the ASVAB associated with higher ILR levels upon graduation. The findings related to how well language aptitude predicts initial status, however, were somewhat surprising, given that in previous research, DLAB was a significant predictor of both listening and reading graduation results even when cognitive ability is accounted for (e.g., Silva & White, 1993; Wagener, 2014; Wagener, 2016). In the present study, however, DLAB did not predict initial status in the listening model, while it did in the reading model.

Cognitive ability did not predict rates of change, but language aptitude did. This finding confirms the practice of giving both the ASVAB and the DLAB to military recruits, and it parallels the findings in Surface et al. (2004), wherein cognitive ability predicted the intercept only in reading and was not found to be a significant predictor of rate of change.

Possible reasons for these differences in aptitude measures may be attributed to the following. First, the longitudinal nature of this study may impact the relationships that underpin the analysis. Second, to standardize the lag between test scores, new time variables were created to represent scores at 400-day intervals. This transformation may have impacted model estimates in ways not completely investigated here. Third, the range restriction and ceiling effect in the cognitive and language aptitude measures may also impact the model estimates.

While the focus of this study is on the relationship of cognitive ability and language aptitude as predictors of ILR level upon graduation from DLI and growth over time, there are other findings that will be useful to the government.

Most notably, there was no significant pattern of growth across individuals. On average, DLI graduates do not improve their language proficiency over the course of their career. This research also confirms findings from previous studies (Bloomfield et al., 2012) indicating the important role that the test version plays in interpreting test scores. If, during this time period, a test version shifted to the DLPT 5, proficiency growth was constrained. In fact, version change exercised the most influence on the model. Therefore, we conclude that any analysis of language growth that fails to account for version change across the DLPT system may be misleading: proficiency loss may reflect this version change, rather than a true loss in language skill (Ross, 2012).

Despite attempts to provide additional time on task at DLIFLC for acquisition of more difficult languages, language difficulty still negatively impacted initial acquisition: language proficiency at the time of graduation is significantly lower in the more difficult languages. Unlike the findings in Surface et al. (2004), however, language difficulty was not significantly related to growth. This suggests that language ability is equally difficult to maintain or improve regardless of language difficulty. It also implies that the varied course lengths at DLI, with longer courses for the more difficult languages, do not ensure that ILR levels are, on average, consistent upon graduation.

Whether an individual worked in the language was a significant positive predictor of initial level in listening but not in reading; it was, however, a significant positive predictor of growth in both modalities. Thus, working in a language is more likely to improve the rate of growth. This finding is intuitive, as work experience would provide more exposure to the language. Additionally, language professionals are incentivized to reach higher levels intrinsically and extrinsically (i.e., through incentive pay).

Whether an individual received any follow-on language training accounted for significant variance in rates of change. Because this variable was summarized as a dichotomous "training" or "no training," more research is necessary to further investigate the relationship of training events with proficiency growth.

Potential Limitations

There are several known limitations to the study. As noted above, only those with high ASVAB scores are offered the opportunity to take the DLAB; only those with high DLAB scores are offered the opportunity to become military linguists. Therefore, there is reduced variation in this sample, an evident ceiling effect, and a correlation between the aptitude measures. Such range restriction is common in studies using extant data. As the military services push to increase minimum DLAB scores, the range of scores will be restricted further. However, because range restriction typically suppresses correlations, if correlations are discovered, any findings of correlation would only be strengthened if corrected. Options such as those suggested by other authors in this volume should be pursued.

A second limitation has to do with the lack of specific information on the measures in the study. Despite the high-stakes nature of the tests involved in this study, no reliability information is publicly available on either the DLAB or the DLPT. Estimated reliability statistics for the AFQT are reported as 0.94 for the paper-and-pencil version and 0.97 for the computer-adaptive version (ASVAB website).

Conclusion

The findings here suggest that aptitude measures differentially impact proficiency, with ASVAB showing a positive influence on initial DLPT level in both reading and listening, and DLAB positively impacting initial proficiency in only reading, and growth in both reading and listening, even while accounting for other important moderating variables such as version change and language difficulty. Therefore, this study confirms the warrant for continuing to use both ASVAB and DLAB as selection measures. The impact of this finding is tempered by the fact that the standardized regression weights are low, indicating that these measures explain very little of the initial level or subsequent growth, although there may still be a return on investment given the size and scope of the DoD language program.

One interesting finding in the present study is the fact that DLAB differentially influences proficiency by modality: in the listening modality, DLAB is not significantly related to initial level and is only marginally significantly related to growth ($p < 0.03$). In the reading modality, DLAB is significantly related to both intercept and slope. As reported earlier, Silva and White (1993) found that DLAB, when added to ASVAB, increased the multiple correlation with reading and listening proficiency by 0.02–0.04 (p. 87). The authors concluded that their data also supported differential aptitude theory and that DLAB contributed to improved prediction of DLI graduation results. The current findings support these conclusions.

The shape of growth seen in this study is also interesting, with a slight dip in scores followed by a very slight increase (in fact, not significant) in proficiency over a 5½-year period. Future studies could investigate these relationships further and see how they might relate to overall patterns of growth.

While there was much individual variation in the dataset, the overall pattern of growth was not significant. This is an important finding for the DoD, as it suggests that despite investments in language training post-DLIFLC, language proficiency does not substantially improve. There were significant inter-individual changes in proficiency, with increases associated with higher cognitive and language aptitude and increased exposure (job assignment and language training). However, as mentioned above, it is also clear from these findings that aptitude measures do not explain much of the variation in initial level and growth. Aptitude measures that account for other cognitive and non-cognitive measures may prove to be better predictors.

Other future analyses could take advantage of more sophisticated LGM techniques, such as multi-group analyses to test for potential differences that are masked in the current study, such as branch of service or the language itself, or a multi-level approach that accounts for language differences. Other potential avenues for research include multi-variate analyses that would allow for the modeling of reading and listening proficiency in a single model.

Nevertheless, this study establishes a benchmark that will be useful for upcoming validity studies involving the next generation of aptitude tests in the government domain (DLAB2 and the High Level Language Aptitude Battery, known as Hi-Lab). It also makes a valuable contribution to the validity argument for the current use of ASVAB and DLAB as predictors of foreign language success in the military.

Notes

1 For further information on the ASVAB, please visit www.officialasvab.com.
2 For further information on the ILR Scale, please visit www.govtilr.org.
3 Significance probably due to sample size.
4 Significance attributed to sample size.

References

ASVAB Website (n.d.) Official website of the ASVAB testing program. Retrieved from: http://officialasvab.com/validity_res.htm

Bloomfield, A., Masters, M., Ross, S., O'Connell, S. and Gynther, K. (2012) Change in foreign language skills over time. *Proceedings of the 34th Annual Conference of the Cognitive Science Society* (pp. 1350–1355). Austin, TX: Cognitive Science Society.

Clifford, R. and Cox, T. (2013) Empirical validation of reading proficiency guidelines. *Foreign Language Annals, 46(1)*, 45–61.

Defense language proficiency test frequently asked questions (n.d.). Retrieved from www.dliflc.edu/dlptfaq.html.

Defense language proficiency test availability schedule (n.d.). Retrieved from www.dliflc.edu/dlptguides.html

Defense Language Institute (2011) Annual program review 2011. Retrieved from www.scribd.com/doc/120546270/2011-APR.

Defense Language Institute (2012) Information sheet. Retrieved from www.dliflc.edu/about.html.

Defense Manpower Data Center (2012) Armed services vocational aptitude battery technical bulletin number 4 P&P-ASVAB forms 23-27. Retrieved from http://officialasvab.com/docs/asvab_techbulletin_4.pdf.

Defense Manpower Data Center (n.d.) Armed services vocational aptitude battery program. Retrieved from www.asvabprogram.com/index.cfm?fuseaction=overview.test.

Department of Defense (2005a) Defense language program: Department of Defense directive 5160.41E. Retrieved from www.dtic.mil/whs/directives/corres/pdf/516041p.pdf.

Department of Defense (2005b) Defense language transformation roadmap. Retrieved from www.defense.gov/news/mar2005/d20050330roadmap.pdf.

Duncan, T.E. and Duncan, S.C. (2004) An introduction to latent growth curve modeling. *Behavior Therapy*, 35, 333–363.

Herzog, M. (n.d.) How did the language proficiency scale get started? Retrieved from www.govtilr.org/Skills/IRL%20Scale%20History.htm

Interagency Language Roundtable (1985) Interagency Language Roundtable skill level descriptions. Retrieved from www.govtilr.org.

Lett, J., Thain, J., Keesling W. and Krol, M. (2003) New directions in foreign language aptitude testing. *Proceedings from the 45th annual conference of the International Military Testing Association*, 734–741.

Muthen, B.O. and Khoo, S. (1998) Longitudinal studies of achievement growth using latent variable modeling. *Learning and Individual Differences, 10(2)*, 73–101.

Petersen, C.R. and Ali-Haik, A.R. (1976) The development of the Defense Language Aptitude Battery (DLAB). *Educational and Psychological Measurement, 36*, 369–380.

Ree, M. and Earles, J. (1990) *Differential validity of a differential aptitude test.* Air Force Human Resources Lab Brooks AFB TX. Retrieved from https://apps.dtic.mil/sti/citatios/ADA222190.

Ross, S.J. (2012) Second language attrition: Separating authentic loss from test artifact. Paper presented at the East Coast Organization of Language Testers Conference. 2 November 2012.

Silva, J.M. and White, L.A. (1993) Relation of cognitive aptitudes to success in foreign language training. *Military Psychology, 5(2)*, 79–93.

Surface, E.A., Dierdorff, E.C. and Donnelly, J. (2004) *Modeling second language proficiency change for US Special Operations personnel.* Paper presented at the 19th annual conference of the Society for Industrial and Organizational Psychology, Chicago, IL.

Wagener, T. (2014) *Aptitude and achievement measures as predictors of growth in second language proficiency.* Unpublished manuscript, University of Maryland.

Wagener, T. (2016) *The influences of aptitude, learning context and language difficulty categorization on foreign language proficiency.* Unpublished doctoral dissertation. University of Maryland.

5

PATHWAYS TO PROFICIENCY

Megan C. Masters

Introduction

The United States Government (USG) has developed various language difficulty categorization (LDC) frameworks to predict the length of initial second language (L2) acquisition instructional time and to plan for resource allocation.[1] The main goal of these frameworks is to establish a comprehensive, policy-based system through which large numbers of Department of Defense (DoD) language analysts can matriculate as efficiently as possible (Lett & O'Mara, 1990; Clark, Ross, O'Rourke, Jackson, Bloomfield, Aghajanian-Stewart, & Kim, 2016a). The Defense Language Institute Foreign Language Center (DLIFLC), located in Monterey, California, is home to a residential foreign language training and testing program designed to train military linguists to proficiency levels approximating those of traditional four-year undergraduate foreign language majors (J. Lett, personal communication, May 2007). Managing and coordinating the training of military linguists for over 20 languages is a complex process requiring unparalleled investments of time and taxpayer resources. Recently, costs for training a single military linguist have been estimated at upwards of $250,000 (Brecht, personal communication, March 2018). In addition to being used to group languages for initial acquisition training, they are also used for a wide variety of purposes once learners meet minimum proficiency criteria, including instructor-to-student classroom training ratios, academic credit earnings, and ncentive pay (see Mackey, Chapter 4, this volume; Clark et al., 2016a, p. 15). Despite the widespread adoption of LDC frameworks across all USG agencies, few research studies have examined empirically the coherence of initial acquisition patterns of languages grouped within the same category.

Foreign language groupings within the various frameworks tend to be based largely upon the subjective expertise of L2 instructors or upon typological

DOI: 10.4324/9781003087939-6

differences between a given L2 and English. Undergirding the categorization system is the assumption that languages grouped within the same category require the same amount of instructional time to meet the minimum proficiency standards. The systematic examination of the LDC framework can either provide corroborating evidence concerning how well languages grouped within the system appear to be functioning or reveal differential patterns in proficiency development for languages otherwise assumed to function similarly. If the categorization system is wrong, it could be the case that military personnel graduate from the DLIFLC without the language skills necessary to perform their assignments, suggesting that additional training may be required. As the stakes for training, and subsequently deploying, military linguists are quite high, the need for robust empirical evidence validating the categorization and use of the LDC framework is critical.

Background

The notion of developing a systematic framework through which large numbers of military linguists could be efficiently trained received attention throughout the 1950s through 1970s as the need for government linguists with advanced levels of foreign language proficiency vastly increased. During this time, government policy makers grew keenly interested in developing training programs that efficiently produced linguists who could serve as expert transcriptionists, translators, and/or interpreters. A number of USG entities extended the conceptualization of grouping language features both *typologically*, in terms of English first language (L1) and L2 linguistic and structural differences, and *hierarchically*, in terms of anticipated difficulty, from isolated linguistic features to entire languages themselves. As described in detail by Clark et al. (2016a), this approach resulted in a number of different language difficulty hierarchies, referred to across the DoD as LDC frameworks. The authors note:

> While there are many sources that cite the LDC, only a few detail the initial, conceptual development of the framework. Furthermore, the LDC is not a uniform system within the United States Government (USG). For example, the difficulty category system at the Foreign Service Institute (FSI) is similar, but distinct from, the framework used at the Defense Language Institute Foreign Language Center (DLIFLC) and in the Department of Defense (DOD) at large. In addition, there have been some fluctuations over time in the number of categories as well as the category assignment of languages.
>
> *p. 2*

The authors also point out that USG-based approaches to grouping languages within a hierarchy of difficulty have typically been informed by subjective observations made by expert instructors or training specialists, but have not examined the extent to which empirical evidence supports or refutes hypothesized groupings.

Given the scant amount of published research detailing the grouping of languages with the LDC framework, Clark et al. conducted semi-structured interviews with subject matter experts. The interviewees relayed their recollections about how the initial frameworks were designed. After aggregating the results collected across each interview, the authors concluded that the initial LDC frameworks were first designed by the Department of State's Foreign Service Institute and later adopted by the DLIFLC in the 1950s. These frameworks were informed by post hoc, expert observations from USG course instructors about how long it had been taking students to meet established graduation criteria in their target language. The authors note that frameworks were designed using a bottom-up rather than top-down approach. That is, rather than conjecturing where a given language would fall within a hierarchy a priori, the creators of the framework worked from their observations of student learning and placed the language into a respective category within the hierarchy a posteriori. Jackson and Kaplan (2001) argue that this approach is thus based on empirical, albeit merely observational, evidence. Table 51, adapted from Clark et al. (2016a, b, c), denotes the current categorization system, number of weeks of language instruction, and associated Defense Language Aptitude Battery (DLAB) scores as of September 2016.[2]

TABLE 5.1 Current language difficulty categorization (LDC) framework at the Defense Language Institute Foreign Language Center (DLIFLC)[12]

Category I No. wks instruct. 26 Min. DLAB score: 95	*Category II* No. wks instruct. 36 Min. DLAB score: 100	*Category III* No. wks instruct. 48 Min. DLAB score: 105	*Category IV* No. wks instruct. 64 Min. DLAB score: 110
French	German	Hebrew	Modern Standard Arabic
Portuguese	Indonesian	Hindi	Arabic-Egyptian
Spanish		Persian Farsi	Arabic-Iraqi
		Russian	Arabic-Levantine
		Serbian/Croatian	Arabic-Sudanese
		Tagalog	Chinese Mandarin
		Turkish	Japanese
		Urdu	Korean
			Pashto

DLAB, Defense Language Aptitude Battery.

As shown in Table 5.1, the higher the difficulty category of a given language, the greater the predicted interference between the two languages, the longer the amount of time that instructors and students are given to teach and learn the language, and the higher minimum DLAB score required for language assignment.

A white paper written by researchers at the Human Resources Research Organization, Koch and McCloy (2015), concluded that the order in which languages were assigned to categories within the LDC were based on two main criteria: (1) difficulty and (2) distance from English. Clark et al. (2016a, b, c) define difficulty as the use of "different indices that reflect the relationship between time spent learning and [an established] proficiency [level]." Distance refers to "the degree of difference in vocabularies, phonetic inventories, grammars, etc. between…two languages" (p. 3). In their review, the authors found that difficulty was typically defined by two criteria: (1) the number of hours it takes a learner to reach Interagency Language Roundtable 3 (ILR-3) or (2) the level of speaking proficiency that students reach after 24 weeks of instruction (p. 3).[3] The researchers calculated a Spearman's rank order correlation coefficient from data previously collected by Cysouw (2013), which reported the results of the observed relationship between hours required to reach ILR-3, and data from Hart-Gonzalez and Lindemann (1993), which investigated the level of speaking proficiency attained after 24 weeks of instruction. The authors note that the results revealed a "strong relationship" between DLIFLC's categories and the two indices of difficulty: time to ILR-3 ($r = 0.95, p < 0.001$) and proficiency level after 24 weeks [of instruction] ($r = -0.88, p < 0.001$), providing initial validity evidence for DLIFLC's current categorization system.

Turning to the examination of how distance from English was measured, Clark et al.'s (2016a) research did not uncover a robust empirical foundation for grouping languages by linguistic features. Although it can be noted that all of the languages grouped in Categories III and IV differ substantially from English, in that they have different scripts than English, as noted by Lowe (1998), this does not necessarily indicate homogeneity in language features within a given category grouping. In other words, the fact that languages have been grouped within the same category does not indicate that they contain typological features that function in a similar manner.[4] To explore empirically the homogeneity of languages grouped within the same difficulty categories, Clark et al. (2016b, c) systematically mined more than 234,000 unique test records representing 108 different languages for nearly 20,000 language analysts within a large government organization who had already reached L2 proficiency criteria of ILR scores of 2/2/1+ in the listening, reading, and speaking skills, respectively. The goal of their research was to investigate statistically the extent to which similar patterns in Defense Language Proficiency Test (DLPT) outcomes would be observed for languages grouped within the same category.[5] The authors state, "if the language difficulty categories are a primary driver in explaining the success with which individuals can master a foreign language, we would expect to see a great deal of homogeneity [in observed DLPT outcome patterns] among languages in the same difficulty category" (p. 5). In other words, if the contrastive analytic approach of grouping languages based on difficulty or distance from English is valid, it would follow that languages grouped within the same category would display largely invariant patterns.

The authors subjected the data to three separate analyses in order to explore observed statistical patterns of languages grouped within the same category. Results of an event history analysis, used to predict the likelihood of a language analyst reaching an ILR-3 proficiency level on a subsequent test, while also controlling for covariates such as hours of training and test version change, found significant variation in the amount of time it took analysts to reach the ILR-3 proficiency level for languages grouped within Category IV, suggesting that it takes less time for some languages to reach this benchmark than others. The authors' second analysis subjected the data to logistic mixed-effects modeling, also designed to predict the likelihood of analysts scoring an ILR-3 on their subsequent test, controlling for previous DLPT scores, the amount of time between tests, the amount of training received between tests, and whether the examinee took a different version of a test. Results revealed a number of within-category outliers, with some languages being identified as more difficult than others. For example, Portuguese (Category I, reading), Tagalog, Russian, Urdu (all Category III, reading and listening), and Chinese Mandarin (Category IV, reading and listening), were all found to be harder languages in which to attain a rating of ILR-3 on subsequent proficiency tests than other languages grouped within the same category. Conversely, Spanish (Category I, listening), Hebrew (Category II, reading and listening), Modern Standard Arabic and Korean (both Category IV, reading) were identified as being more difficult languages in which to attain an ILR-3 on a subsequent testing event than their intra-language category counterparts.

In their final analysis, the research team then ran a second mixed-effects model, but this time collapsed all languages into a single analysis in order to estimate any observed differences between language difficulty categories. Results indicated that, while some languages varied randomly in terms of difficulty, many of the languages exhibited complete overlap in terms of estimated difficulty.[6] Figure 5.1 visually depicts these results.

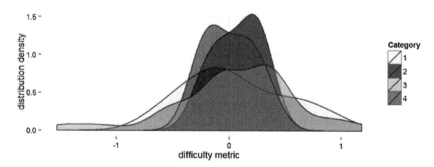

FIGURE 5.1 Distributions of empirical language difficulty by category. (Reproduced from Clark et al., 2016b.)

As shown in Figure 5.1, the overlapping distributions observed for each category suggest a lack of "significant differences between categories as a whole" (p. 7). That is, although the LDC framework rests on a variety of assumptions concerning languages' distance from English and predicted difficulty, the results depicted in Figure 5.1 show that, for the majority of languages, no meaningful distinctions between languages are observed. The authors acknowledge, however, that learners' aptitude, a variable not modeled in the results discussed above, likely plays an important role in the observed patterns, particularly given the lack of a right-hand "tail" for the more difficult language groupings. All three analyses conducted by Clark et al. (2016b, c) appear to provide converging evidence concerning heterogeneity in testing patterns observed for languages grouped within the same category. This finding indicates that the categorization system, designed to group languages during the process of initial L2 acquisition, may not adequately discriminate between language groups once minimum proficiency criteria have been attained. In other words, even though it may take learners longer to initially acquire a Category IV language, it is not necessarily the case that it takes more effort to retain their language skills thereafter.

DLIFLC Teaching and Learning Context

The overarching goal of the DLIFLC program of study is to produce foreign language-enabled enlisted personnel capable of supporting a wide variety of foreign language mission-related work across the DoD (D.K. Chapman, Commandant of DLIFLC, personal communication, May 2015). Upon completing the DLIFLC program of study, students are expected to achieve ILR proficiency ratings of 2 on the DLPT for both reading and listening skills and a 1+ on the Oral Proficiency Interview (OPI) for the speaking skill.[7] As shown in Table 5.1, the length of time students are given to achieve these program outcomes varies relative to the difficulty category to which the target language is assigned. In addition to the Armed Services Vocational Aptitude Battery (ASVAB) and DLAB described in detail by Mackey (Chapter 4, current volume), enlisted personnel within the DLIFLC are required to take a five-day Introduction to Language Studies within the Student Learning Center. This course is designed to "help increase students' levels of preparation for language studies, increase student motivation, and ultimately help reduce academic attrition rates" (DLIFLC website: www.dliflc.edu/introductiontola.html). After receiving their language assignments, and prior to engaging beginning language training coursework, students are asked to indicate an answer relative to their preference for studying their assigned language:

> I am here to study this language, which is…
> 1. Not my choice. I would prefer to do something else rather than study a foreign language.
> 2. Not my choice. I am not motivated to study the assigned language.
> 3. Not my choice, but I am still motivated to study the assigned language.

4. Based on my second or third choice.
5. Based on my first choice.

Lett, n.d.

The purpose of the activity above is to gauge learners' self-assessed preference for their assigned language prior to beginning intensive foreign language study at the DLIFLC. Previous research studies have found most correlations between self-ratings on the motivation questionnaire and DLPT/OPI outcomes to be non-significant and to vary substantially across target languages and subskills, as well as from year to year among enlisted personnel (Lett, n.d.; Lett & O'Mara, 1990).

The length of time students have to achieve the established DLIFLC program outcomes varies relative to the difficulty category to which the target language is assigned. As mentioned above, higher difficulty categories are associated with both higher minimum DLAB scores and additional weeks of target language instructional time. Once assigned to their target language of study, students enrolled at the DLIFLC attend classes five days per week for seven hours per day. Learners progress through a series of courses composed of four to five classes at the 100, 200, and 300 levels, taking place over a 26–64-week period, depending on the difficulty category to which their target language is assigned. Students typically have about two to three hours of homework per night, in addition to their regular military duties as enlisted personnel.

Research Questions

Although the data analytic techniques within the second language acquisition field have advanced significantly over the past 60 years, many of the category-based frameworks within which L2 teaching and training regimens are situated have not. Recent research has employed the use of data-mining techniques to conduct longitudinal analyses of the development of foreign language proficiency over time (see Ross et al., 2011; Bloomfield et al., 2012, 2013; Mackey, 2014; Mackey (Chapter 4 in the current volume); Wagner, 2014), but focus only on testing outcomes that have been established *after* learners' initial foreign language proficiency outcomes have been achieved. To the author's knowledge, few published research studies investigate empirically the development of within-category *initial* acquisition patterns. While languages grouped within the same category may be typologically distinct, situating languages within the same category rests on the assumption that each language will display comparable proficiency development patterns. An empirical investigation of these frameworks, modeling patterns of initial acquisition using more sophisticated, non-observational data analytic techniques, is thus warranted. Three main research questions will be examined within the current chapter:

Research Question 1 (RQ1): For languages grouped within the same category, are similar patterns of individual differences in general aptitude, language-specific aptitude, and language preference self-assessment observed in *the prediction of learners' success as they progress through coursework?*

Research Question 2 (RQ2): For languages grouped within the same category, are similar patterns of individual differences in general aptitude, language-specific aptitude, and language preference self-assessment observed in *the prediction of learners' end-of-program outcomes?*

Research Question 3 (RQ3): For languages grouped within the same category, are *homogeneous patterns of initial language acquisition observed across languages as learners progress through the DLIFLC program of study?*

Consistent with Mackey (Chapter 4 in the current volume), the cognitive aptitude variables were measured with a general cognitive measure, specifically, the Armed Forces Qualifying Test (AFQT) composite score (comprised of subsections of mathematics knowledge, arithmetic reasoning, and verbal expression scores from the ASVAB) and a language-specific aptitude measure known as the DLAB. Language preference was measured through outcomes on the language preference self-assessment questionnaire, administered prior to engaging in language training. Course-specific outcomes were measured through achievement scores given by the teachers in each of the 100-, 200-, and 300-level courses. End-of-program reading and listening skill outcomes were measured separately with the DLPT, the test of record for DoD military linguists.

Methodology

Extant data were provided by the Defense Manpower Data Center (DMDC), an identity management organization that oversees personnel records for DoD members and employees. The sampling pool was comprised of DLIFLC learner data collected between February 12, 2009 and March 22, 2010. To create longitudinal records for learners progressing through the DLIFLC program of study, data from four different systematically maintained databases were restructured, merged, and coded, resulting in the aggregation of 244 separate learner variables. Of these, six main variables are included in the current empirical model: (1) AFQT weighted scores;[8] (2) DLAB scores; (3) Language Preference Self-Assessment Scores; (4) 100-, 200-, and 300-level coursework variables; (5) DLPT reading test score outcomes; and (6) DLPT listening test score outcomes. The final sample includes listening and reading test score outcomes for 414 DLIFLC enlistees across the Arabic, Chinese, and Korean languages. eTables 5.1–5.3 in the e-resources display the raw and transformed descriptive statistics for each of the observed variables in the model separately for each language.[9]

The natural left-to-right temporal progression of learners through the DLIFLC program of study allows for the construction of a logic model. The purpose of a logic model is to make clear, via visual representation, each of the causal factors, or elements related to a program of interest and to make explicit the hypothesized connections between each component. The individual elements of a logic model include resources, activities, objectives, indicators, impacts (short-term actions) and long-term outcomes (Renger & Titcomb, 2002, p. 494). Renger and Titcomb state, "knowing what causal factors are being targeted first is essential to assessing whether an activity is appropriately targeted, identifying appropriate indicators of change, and writing sound objectives" (p. 494). Situating logic modeling within a large-scale, L2 instructional framework, programs are typically comprised of inputs (Wave 1), such as minimum entry-level indicators allowing for program admission (e.g., aptitude-related scores or prerequisite coursework), program activities (Wave 2), often including localized indicators of student achievement (e.g., class grade point average (GPA) scores) and program outcomes (Wave 3), usually represented by standardized summative assessment measures (e.g., proficiency tests) documenting end-of-program outcomes. Program outputs (Wave 4) are typically more challenging to ascertain and are not included in the current investigation. With respect to the current dataset, a potential program outcome might be a language proficiency variable, demonstrating that the DLIFLC program of study produces personnel capable of supporting a wide variety of foreign language mission-related work across the DoD well after graduation. Although the visual inspection of logic models suggests movement from left to right, when building a model, it is recommended to first start with specifying program outcomes rather than inputs (Frechtling, 2007). It is only by first establishing what a program is intending to accomplish that one can begin building a model that adequately describes the underlying goal of a given program. In most cases, foreign language programs are viewed as successful if the graduates produced by a given program are deemed to be adequately prepared to engage in a variety of foreign language-related activities. Figure 5.2 visually depicts the four major components of a logic model as they apply to the DLIFLC language learning context.

FIGURE 5.2 Main components of a logic model. AFQT = Armed Forces Qualifying Test; DLAB = Defense Language Aptitude Battery; DLPT = Defense Language Proficiency Test.

(Adapted from Frechtling, 2007, p. 22.)

When well defined, Weiss (1997) argues that if

> the predicted steps between an activity and an outcome can be confirmed in implementation, this matching of "theory" to outcomes will lend a strong argument for "causality"; if the evaluation can show a series of micro-steps that lead from input to outcomes, then causal attribution, for *all practical purposes* [original italics] seems to be within reach.
>
> *as cited in Frechtling, 2007, p. 8*

Weiss's argumentation can be extended to the empirical examination of initial L2 acquisition patterns within the LDC framework. By grouping languages within the same category, DLIFLC policy makers assume that L2 learners will acquire their assigned target languages to similar degrees of proficiency along the same required instructional timeframe. In other words, a given grouping of languages within the same category assumes that the patterns of initial acquisition proficiency development are considered invariant. It thereby logically follows that languages grouped within the same category would show similar patterns of development, thus providing validity evidence for the categorization schema. Through use of a logic model, employed to visually represent the underlying flow, or logic, of the DLIFLC language learning program, path analytic analyses can be employed in order to simultaneously estimate the hypothesized causal relationships between the measured variables of interest. If the LDC system is accurate, and languages grouped within the same category display coherence, the number and magnitude of the observed path coefficients will be comparable across languages and skills.

Results

The current investigation was run on Analysis of Moment Structures (AMOS) software associated with the SPSS statistical package. Path diagrams can be conceptualized as visual representations of the structural equations underlying each hypothesized theoretical relationship between measured variables (Hancock, 2011). As shown in Figure 5.3, there are four structural equations specified in the current model, represented by each of the four endogenous variables, expressed as a function of all elements having a direct structural effect or covariation with it. There is no modeled covariation between the error terms (also referred to as residuals) associated with each of the endogenous variables.

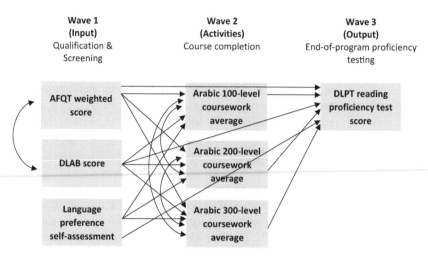

| Wave 1 (Input) Qualification & Screening | Wave 2 (Activities) Course completion | Wave 3 (Output) End-of-program proficiency testing |

FIGURE 5.3 Complete path analytic diagram.

The structural equations associated with each of the endogenous variables can be found in eTable 5.4 in the e-resources.

Reading

Wave 1 to Wave 2

Acceptable model fit was found for all languages across all skills, as visually depicted in Figures 5.4–5.9.[10] The current section discusses the results of Wave 1 to Wave 2 path analyses for all three skills, since the 100-, 200-, and 300-level average course outcomes were not broken down by skill. Path analytic outcomes for the reading skill yielded a number of notable differences between Arabic, Chinese, and Korean. As expected, DLAB scores were found to consistently predict 100-, 200-, and 300-level average course outcomes across all languages. No statistically significant differences between the established path coefficients were found across languages. The Language Preference Self-Assessment score was found to statistically predict just one causal pathway: for Arabic only, a significant and negative relationship was found between the Language Preference Self-Assessment score and 100-level average course outcomes.

Wave 2 to Wave 3

Moving from left to right within the path analytic model, an analysis of the influence of Wave 2 exogenous predictor variables to the Wave 3 endogenous DLPT reading variable yielded several statistically significant causal pathways. For Arabic, both 200- and 300-level average course outcomes predicted DLPT reading outcomes. For Chinese and Korean, 300-level average course outcomes predicted end-of-program DLPT test outcomes. The significant causal pathway from 300-level coursework to DLPT outcomes across all three languages suggests that end-of-program training likely aligns with the type of reading proficiency constructs tested on the DLPT. Multi-group invariance testing yielded no significant differences between the standardized regression weights for the 300-level average coursework outcomes to DLPT reading scores across all three languages, indicating that 300-level average course outcomes play a consistent role in predicting DLPT reading proficiency scores. This finding also provides additional evidence concerning the coherence of observed initial acquisition patterns for languages grouped within the same category.

Wave 1 to Wave 3: Full Path Analytic Model Reading

Lastly, turning to the predictive influence of Wave 1 AFQT weighted scores, DLAB scores, and learners' self-reported motivation scores on DLPT reading outcomes, just three significant causal pathways were found. Consistent with what the author hypothesized, learners' AFQT weighted scores predicted end-of-program reading proficiency test score outcomes for Chinese and Korean, but not for Arabic. Results of multi-group invariance testing yielded no statistically significant differences between the Chinese and Korean path weights. This finding suggests that the verbal expression, mathematical knowledge, and arithmetic knowledge, which comprise the AFQT weighted scores and likely require considerable reading comprehension skills, positively predict end-of-program DLPT outcomes.

In addition to the goodness-of-fit statistics, another way of exploring how well a given model explains hypothesized relationships among variables is to examine the associated squared multiple correlation indices, which are calculated for each endogenous variable within the model. These statistics denote the amount of variability accounted for by a hypothesized model as well as the amount of variability that remains to be explained. Table 5.2 reports the squared multiple correlation statistics for the Arabic, Chinese, and Korean reading models.

As shown in Table 5.2, although the squared multiple correlation indices are comparable across languages, the Korean reading model accounts for the largest amount of model variability (35.8%). Across all languages, the complete path

TABLE 5.2 Squared multiple correlation indices for the Arabic, Chinese, and Korean reading models

Language	Endogenous variable	% of variability accounted for	% of variability remaining
Arabic	100-level course outcomes	14.8%	85.2%
	200-level course outcomes	9.2%	90.8%
	300-level course outcomes	9.8%	90.2%
	DLPT Reading (Full Model)	33.9%	66.1%
Chinese	100-level course outcomes	0.9%	99.1%
	200-level course outcomes	7.5%	92.5%
	300-level course outcomes	11.4%	88.6%
	DLPT Reading (Full Model)	32.3%	67.7%
Korean	100-level course outcomes	13.0%	87.0%
	200-level course outcomes	11.2%	88.8%
	300-level course outcomes	16.5%	83.5%
	DLPT Reading (Full Model)	35.8%	64.2%

DLPT, Defense Language Proficiency Test.

analytic model for the reading skill accounts for roughly one-third of total model variability. Although this also indicates that about two-thirds of model variability remains to be explained by other unaccounted-for factors, the author argues that this finding is acceptable, particularly given that just six measured variables account for over 30% of total model variation.

Also of relevance to the full path analytic model is the number of learners for each language who met DLPT reading criterion standards. For the Arabic language, 84.6% of learners met the criterion or better; for the Chinese language, 96.9% of learners met the criterion or better, and for the Korean language, 100% of learners met the criterion or better. This finding confirms the DLIFLC "re-cycling" and "re-languaging" policies across languages, whereby only the academically strongest candidates are allowed to progress through coursework and sit for end-of-program proficiency testing. eTables 5.5–5.7 in the e-resources report the standardized regression weight, standard error, and significance level for each of the significant pathways reported in Figures 5.4–5.6.

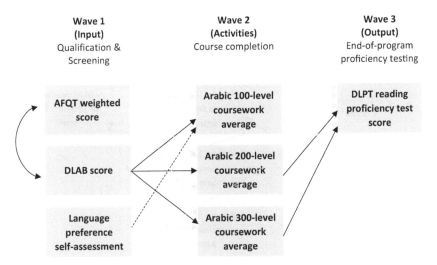

FIGURE 5.4 Full Arabic path model reading ($n = 241$, comparative fit index (CFI) = 0.999, root mean square error approximation (RMSEA) = 0.034, $\chi^2 = 2.71$, $\rho = 0.26$). AFQT = Armed Forces Qualifying Test; DLAB = Defense Language Aptitude Battery; DLPT = Defense Language Proficiency Test.

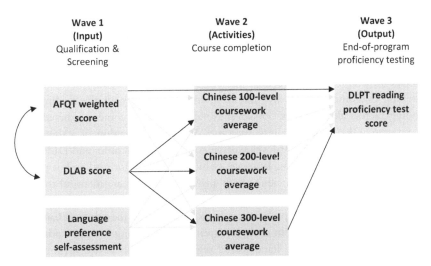

FIGURE 5.5 Full Chinese path model reading ($n = 98$, comparative fit index (CFI) = 1.000, root mean square error approximation (RMSEA) = 0.000, $\chi^2 = 0.144$, $\rho = 0.87$). AFQT = Armed Forces Qualifying Test; DLAB = Defense Language Aptitude Battery; DLPT = Defense Language Proficiency Test.

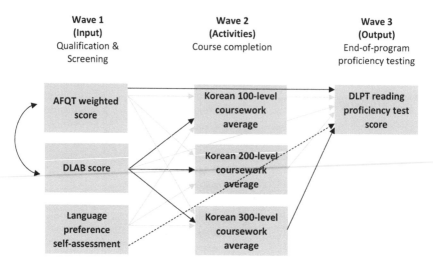

| Wave 1
(Input)
Qualification &
Screening | Wave 2
(Activities)
Course completion | Wave 3
(Output)
End-of-program
proficiency testing |

FIGURE 5.6 Full Korean path model reading (n = 75, comparative fit index (CFI) = 1.000, root mean square error approximation (RMSEA) = 0.000, χ^2 = 1.55, p = 0.46). AFQT = Armed Forces Qualifying Test; DLAB = Defense Language Aptitude Battery; DLPT = Defense Language Proficiency Test.

Listening

Wave 2 to Wave 3

For the listening skill, acceptable model fit was found for all languages. As predicted, average 100- and 200-level course outcomes did not significantly predict DLPT listening outcomes. Also as hypothesized, and consistent with the reading skill findings, across all languages, 300-level average course outcomes predicted end-of-program DLPT listening test outcomes. With the exception of a significant causal pathway between 200-level average coursework outcomes and DLPT test score outcomes for the Arabic language (which was found for reading but not for listening), the listening proficiency path analytic outcomes are identical to those found for the reading proficiency outcomes. This finding suggests a coherent pattern in foreign language proficiency development across the subset of Category IV languages. Outcomes from multi-group invariance testing found a statistically significant difference in the standardized regression weights between the Arabic and Korean language models (z = 2.077). This finding suggests that, while both causal pathways significantly predict DLPT listening outcomes, the prediction is significantly stronger for Korean than for Arabic. No significant differences were found between the Arabic and Chinese path coefficients. Table 5.3 details the outcomes of the multi-group invariance testing for the reading proficiency skill.

As shown in Table 5.3, the z-value of −2.077, established from the multi-group invariance testing between Arabic and Korean, falls outside the reference value of ± 1.96.

TABLE 5.3 Multi-group invariance testing: Wave 2 to Wave 3: listening

Path comparison	z-value (reference value ± 1.96)	Significance
Arabic and Chinese 300-level average coursework to DLPT Listening	−1.759	Not significant
Arabic and Korean 300-level average coursework to DLPT Listening	−2.077	Significant
Korean and Chinese 300-level average coursework to DLPT Listening	-0.096	Not significant

DLPT, Defense Language Proficiency Test.

Wave 1 to Wave 3: Full Path Analytic Model Listening

For listening, no significant causal pathways were found between any of the Wave 1 predictor variables and Wave 3 DLPT listening outcomes for Arabic, Chinese, and Korean. Compared to the findings associated with the reading skill, this suggests that the Wave 1 AFQT weighted score is potentially more well suited as a screening instrument for the reading skill than for the listening skill, given that the instrument itself involves the use of reading and not listening.

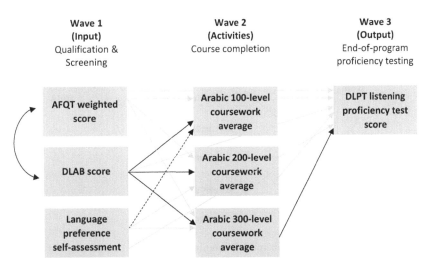

FIGURE 5.7 Full Arabic path model listening ($n = 241$, comparative fit index (CFI) = 0.999, root mean square error approximation (RMSEA) = 0.034, $\chi^2 = 2.71$, $p = 0.26$). AFQT = Armed Forces Qualifying Test; DLAB = Defense Language Aptitude Battery; DLPT = Defense Language Proficiency Test.

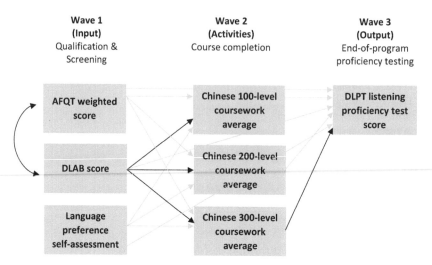

FIGURE 5.8 Full Chinese path model listening (n = 98, comparative fit index (CFI) = 1.000, root mean square error approximation (RMSEA) = 0.000, χ^2 = 0.155, p = 0.46). AFQT = Armed Forces Qualifying Test; DLAB = Defense Language Aptitude Battery; DLPT = Defense Language Proficiency Test.

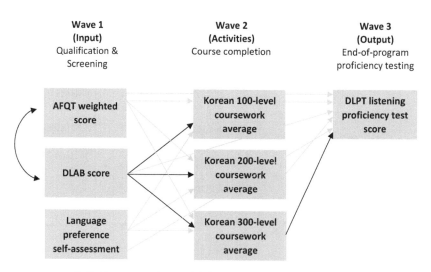

FIGURE 5.9 Full Korean path model listening (n = 75, comparative fit index (CFI) = 1.000, root mean square error approximation (RMSEA) = 0.000, χ^2 = 1.44, p = 0.87). AFQT = Armed Forces Qualifying Test; DLAB = Defense Language Aptitude Battery; DLPT = Defense Language Proficiency Test.

eTables 5.8–5.10 in the e-resources detail the standardized regression weight, standard error, and significance level of each of the significant causal pathways represented in the model.

For DLPT listening outcomes, 81.7% of Arabic learners, 90.8% of Chinese learners, and 88% of Korean learners met criterion scores or better. Across all languages, these percentages are lower than those found for the reading skill. Results of the comparison of squared multiple correlations across languages revealed substantially lower squared multiple correlation indices for Chinese than for Arabic and Korean.

As shown in Table 5.4, the Arabic and Korean listening models accounted for about 41% of total model variation, with the Chinese model accounting for just 29%. This finding is surprising, particularly given that Chinese had the highest percentage of learners to meet DLPT criterion outcomes, suggesting that other unaccounted-for programmatic variables are likely contributing to the acquisition of Chinese listening skills.

TABLE 5.4 Squared multiple correlation indices for the Arabic, Chinese, and Korean listening models

Language	Endogenous variable	% of variability accounted for	% of variability remaining
Arabic	100-level course outcomes	14.8%	85.2%
	200-level course outcomes	9.2%	90.8%
	300-level course outcomes	9.8%	90.2%
	DLPT Listening (Full Model)	40.7%	59.3%
Chinese	100-level course outcomes	0.9%	99.1%
	200-level course outcomes	7.5%	92.5%
	300-level course outcomes	11.4%	88.6%
	DLPT Listening (Full Model)	29.0%	71.0%
Korean	100-level course outcomes	13.0%	87.0%
	200-level course outcomes	11.2%	88.8%
	300-level course outcomes	16.5%	83.5%
	DLPT Listening (Full Model)	40.6%	59.4%

DLPT, Defense Language Proficiency Test.

Discussion

Although the LDC framework has been almost universally adopted across USG agencies over the past 60 years, there is very little empirical research examining the patterns of proficiency development for languages grouped within the same category. While early efforts to categorize language within a hierarchical framework were not made capriciously and were based on years of subject matter experts' insights and observations, the need for robust empirical evidence concerning how well the categorization functions is essential, particularly given the high-stakes decisions associated with its application. At its most basic level, the categorization system works under the assumption that the same amount of input (in terms of weeks of intensive language training) yields the same amount of output (in terms of minimum DLPT and OPI proficiency test score criteria) across languages. Lacking within the LDC framework is robust empirical evidence to support this assumption, despite the significant investment of resources across all levels of stakeholders, from taxpayer dollars, to the DLIFLC instructional setting, to learners, teachers, curriculum developers, and language testers. The current investigation examined individual patterns in foreign language achievement and how both cognitive (e.g., general and language-specific aptitude) and non-cognitive (e.g., language preference self-assessment scores) individual difference variables jointly influenced initial acquisition proficiency development for three Category IV languages at the DLIFLC (Arabic, Chinese, and Korean). In order to compare the coherence in patterns of proficiency development across languages, a contrastive analytic approach was employed within the framework of a logic model – a novel method applied in the L2 instructional context, within which observed outcomes between waves of proficiency development were statistically modeled.

Situating the main inputs, activities, and outcomes associated with the DLIFLC instructional paradigm within a logic model allowed for the empirical examination of the coherence and comparability of L2 initial acquisition patterns through use of a statistical path analysis. In his discussion concerning the applicability of logic modeling to L2 acquisition, Norris (2016) states:

> The potential of program logic models for advancing language education and related endeavors is tremendous, in that – if developed by educational experts, practitioners, and other insiders (i.e., versus external "logic model" experts) – they would lay bare the rationales, activities, and implicit theories that constitute language programs and thereby render them amenable to empirical confirmation (or rejection) (p. 178).

Data mining can be effective for observing longitudinal trends within a given program of interest, although it can be imperfect in its ability to account for programmatic inputs that are not systematically calculated or documented. In order to examine the coherence with which both cognitive and non-cognitive variables contribute to the development of foreign language achievement and proficiency score outcomes, a sample of course achievement and testing records, as well as other aptitude- and personality-related records, from four systematically maintained databases was used to create observed learner models. If languages grouped within the same category truly require the same amount of instructional input to meet end-of-program proficiency test score criteria, statistical examination of proficiency development patterns would be invariant across languages (Arabic, Chinese, and Korean) and skill modalities (reading and listening).

With few exceptions, a great deal of coherence was found in the development of Arabic, Chinese, and Korean foreign language proficiency skills, providing initial validity evidence for situating these languages within the same category within the current DoD classification scheme. Consistent with Masters (2016), across all languages, skills, and observed and imputed datasets, the Wave 1 DLAB variable played a robust role in predicting 100-, 200-, and 300-level average coursework outcomes. Also consistent with Masters (2016), Wave 3 300-level coursework averages consistently predicted end-of-program proficiency test score outcomes across both skills. This finding suggests a strong alignment, across all languages and skills, between 300-level instructional content and language proficiency test content.

Overall, across all languages and skills, the Wave 1 DLAB variable was found to play a robust role in predicting 100-, 200-, and 300-level coursework outcomes, thus adding to the validity evidence for use of the DLAB as a selection tool at the DLIFLC. When breaking Study 1 findings down by waves, beginning with the left-most antecedent predictor variables, although the Wave 1 qualification and screening variables were postulated to potentially predict end-of-program outcomes for all languages, only a few causal pathways approached significance. Learners' general aptitude, measured by AFQT weighted scores, was found to significantly predict DLPT reading outcomes for both Chinese and Korean. This suggests that the heavily reading-based components of this measure (e.g., paragraph comprehension and word knowledge) perform well in predicting end-of-program reading proficiency outcomes. For Korean only, Language Preference Self-Assessment scores negatively predicted DLPT reading outcomes.

The root mean square error of approximation (RMSEA) statistic for the Chinese listening model was the lowest of all models, accounting for just 29% of total model variance. Consistent with what has been recommended by Norris (2016), unexplained outcomes such as these may indicate that, for the Chinese listening skill, the logic model may not be adequately specified and that other unaccounted-for external program factors may be mediating the observed path analytic findings. Future models should account for additional contextual variables that could potentially explain Chinese listening proficiency development patterns, such as curricular content or heritage language speaking status. Lastly, across almost all languages, 300-level average course outcomes were found to significantly predict DLPT reading and listening outcomes.[11] This indicates an alignment between 300-level instructional content and end-of-training proficiency testing. It also may reflect an artifact of student placement practices at the DLIFLC. As noted previously, some learners within the DLIFLC are recommended by instructors to be "re-languaged," or reassigned to a language in a lower-difficulty category due to sub-par course grades. The significant causal pathways found between 300-level average course outcomes and end-of-program proficiency testing likely reflect this practice, as learners who complete the 300-level courses reflect the strongest learners in the cohort.

When examining the development of learners' proficiency within the same language, a great deal of model overlap is found across skills. For Arabic, almost identical causal pathways are found across the reading and listening skills (the Arabic reading skill includes an additional causal pathway from 200-level average course outcomes to DLPT proficiency test score outcomes and an unexpected negative causal pathway between Language Preference Self-Assessment scores and average 100-level coursework outcomes). For Chinese, with the exception of just two paths, identical path models are found across the reading and listening skills (a significant causal pathway was found between learners' AFQT scores and reading proficiency outcomes). Korean was found to have the most within-language variability: with the exception of the significant causal pathway found between learners' AFQT scores and DLPT reading proficiency scores and the negative causal pathway between Language Preference Self-Assessment and DLPT reading scores, identical causal pathways were found between Korean reading and listening skills.

It is hoped that the current investigation can serve as a benchmark from which evidence-based comparisons can be made. As the DLIFLC considers increasing its end-of-program graduation criteria (from 2/2/1+ to 2+/2+/2) and plans on fully operationalizing a new version of the DLAB (DLAB 2, which contains both cognitive and non-cognitive measures in its estimation of language-learning aptitude), outcomes from future research investigations, replicating (and likely improving upon) the path analytic procedure, can be compared with the findings established from the current investigation. One might expect to see increased variability in the path analytic outcomes for Arabic, Chinese, and Korean, as learners and instructors will likely implement a variety of strategies and instructional techniques to meet the updated proficiency-testing criteria. After the DLAB 2 is fully operationalized, one might expect to see even more robust significant causal pathways established between DLAB 2 and 100-, 200-, and 300-level average coursework outcomes, particularly since the DLAB 2 includes previously unaccounted-for contextual learner constructs, such as motivation and personality. While the DLAB was found to consistently predict 100-, 200-, and 300-level coursework outcomes across Arabic, Chinese, and Korean, much stronger path weights would be expected between the DLAB 2 and 100-level average coursework outcomes, since it is likely that the previously unmodeled contextual variables contained with the DLAB 2 are highly influential in the identification of learners with favorable language-learning strategies that predict initial learning success, which subsequently sustain them throughout their language studies. Lastly, future research should replicate the analyses within the current investigation with a more recent sample of DLIFLC learners and build on Masters' (2016) research to compare the development of Category IV foreign language skills with languages grouped in other categories.

The current data involved learners from a 2009 cohort of study, a time during which both program administrators and language learners alike were adjusting to an updated testing form referred to as the DLPT 5. Substantially different from its predecessor, the DLPT IV, which contained scripted, studio-based item specimens, the DLPT 5 incorporated genuine audio and written input from modern sources, such as authentic interviews, real-time conversations in public spaces (inclusive of background noise), podcasts, websites, and email correspondences. In their time series and impact analyses examining the efficacy of foreign language training programs on DLPT test score outcomes, Bloomfield et al. (2016) found a drastic decline in DLPT test scores upon introduction of the DLPT 5 in 2007, followed by an eventual recovery in test scores upon acclimation to the new test format around late 2009/early 2010, depending on the organization and skill modality. As the data used as input into the current investigation were from 2009, and the DLPT 5 was made available for operational use for Arabic, Chinese, and Korean between 2006 and 2007, observed variations in significant DLPT-related path coefficients are likely influenced by instructor and learner adjustments to the new testing formats, as well as to the potential variation in difficulty of the initial DLPT 5 test forms across languages. Lastly, it is important to note that the current analysis only investigated short-term program outputs within the logic model. Additional research, linking short-term program outputs with long-term program outcomes, would provide program administrators with the ability to model longitudinal changes in patterns of proficiency development, from the stage of initial acquisition through long-term, career-long, proficiency sustainment. Systematic, disciplined analyses such as these, which examine the coherence of acquisition patterns for languages grouped within the same category, could potentially lead to increased efficiency with acquiring a given L2, potentially yielding both short- and long-term cost savings across the DoD.

The use of logic modeling to empirically examine initial L2 acquisition patterns within large-scale instructional contexts can be a helpful framework within which to make implicit theories concerning language teaching and learning explicit. Applying the path analytic procedure to a logic model, which has been specified a priori, can be useful in establishing empirical program baselines and to examine the convergence of expected and observed patterns. Norris (2016) states,

> of course, doing so may be particularly threatening to language teachers, curriculum developers, material designers, and program administrators, as it opens up the very real possibility that they are simply not functioning with any type of program logic in mind, never mind the likelihood that expectations for how programs are functioning will not meet observable realities (p. 177).

However, it is argued that the cost of *not* taking the time to model empirically the expected and observed outcomes within a national, high-stakes L2 instructional program is dire, particularly when the cost of not succeeding or arriving at unstable proficiency levels can be devastating, in terms of taxpayer investment, resource investment, and overall foreign-language-enabled personnel readiness.

Limitations

The analyses were limited in six key ways. First, it is important to note that the sample upon which the analyses were based did not represent a full range of values that one might find in the population at large. By the time learners begin instruction at the DLIFLC, they have already been twice selected, first from their scores on the ASVAB and second from their scores on the DLAB. Further, almost all of the initial screening variables exhibited non-normal distributions. As observed by Lett and O'Mara (1990), the restricted range of the sample likely impacts the predictive power of both the cognitive and non-cognitive variables. Second, it is possible that contextual differences, rather than cognitive or non-cognitive differences alone, may have contributed to the observed differences found between the Category IV languages in each set of analyses. That is, as noted by Lett and O'Mara (1990), despite the general homogeneity of the language-learning context at the DLIFLC, it is unlikely that the programs are pedagogically equivalent either within or across Category IV initial acquisition courses. Third, the proposed analyses did not separate DLIFLC course outcome data by skill, but rather, treated each 100-, 200-, and 300-level course outcome as an overall skill-level average. As it is likely that some courses within each level specifically focused on the development of a particular modality, future analyses could separate out these courses by skill modality, rather than grouping all courses together and creating a single average. Fourth, the data used in the investigation were roughly ten years old. While ideally, more up-to-date testing and training records should be examined, these types of data are difficult to obtain, requiring a significant investment of time and effort that would likely delay the completion of the investigation by years. Since no major shifts in policy with respect to the initial acquisition training and testing processes has occurred since 2009, it is argued that the date from which the data were pulled is unlikely to substantially affect observed outcomes. Fifth, as is the case with all data-mining efforts, the current analyses were constrained by the data made available within existing datasets. All analyses assume an underlying accuracy of institutional data entry and database maintenance over time. Lastly, while the *n*-sizes associated with the current investigation met minimum criteria for structural equation modeling, it is likely that larger sample sizes, particularly for Chinese and Korean, would increase the robustness of the inferences drawn from the path analytic procedure.

Notes

1 The frameworks are designed from the perspective of adult monolinguals with English as a first language.
2 A description of the DLAB and its role within the LDC framework will be discussed in detail in the following section of the current chapter and was also described in Mackey (Chapter 4 in this volume).
3 The ILR is an unfunded federal interagency organization that sets common standards about language-related activities at the federal level. It was originally founded in 1955 by members of the Air Force, Foreign Service Institute, and Central Intelligence Agency. The ILR sets expected proficiency standards for novice- through advanced-level learners, ranging from 0 (no functional proficiency) to 5 (functional proficiency equivalent to that of a highly articulate, well-educated user of the language). For more information, see www.govtilr.org/IRL%20History.htm and www.govtilr.org/skills/ILRscale1.htm.

4   The closest approximation to a systematic categorization of language difficulty based on typological language features was research completed by Child (1987).

5   The DLPT is the foreign language proficiency test of record for the majority of DoD language analysts. The DLPT is used to test reading and listening proficiency. The Oral Proficiency Interview is used to test speaking proficiency skills.

6   Difficulty was defined by Clark et al. (2016b) as the likelihood of scoring an ILR-3 on one's next testing event (p. 6).

7   Although an integral part of linguists' training at the DLIFLC, examination of the development of the speaking proficiency skill will not be included in the current analysis.

8   The DLIFLC transforms raw ASVAB scores to AFQT weighted scores from subsections of the ASVAB battery. The equation is: (Mathematics Knowledge + Arithmetic Reasoning) + 2(Verbal Expression)). For detailed information, see www.thebalance.com/how-the-asvab-afqt-score-is-computed-3354094.

9   The AFQT, Language Preference Self-Assessment, and 100-, 200-, and 300-level values shown in eTables 5.1–5.3 show transformed values correcting for negative skew found for each across all three languages. The DLAB values shown in eTables 5.1–5.3 are transformed values correcting for positive skew found across all three languages.

10 Identical model fit was found for the full path model across all language skills for each language. With the exception of substituting end-of-program proficiency test score outcomes with DLPT reading or DLPT listening outcomes, identical models were run for each language and skill. The variability associated with each outcome measure within each language was likely not substantial enough to affect model fit across language modality.

11 Exceptions to this finding include Chinese speaking (in which 200-level average coursework outcomes predicted OPI speaking scores) and Korean speaking (in which no significant causal pathways were found between average course outcomes and OPI speaking scores).

12 Clark et al. (2016b) also note, "While the composition of the categories in the DLIFLC's system has been quite stable over the years, two languages have changed categories. In 2009, Pashto was moved from Category III to Category IV as graduation rates failed to reach the levels of other Category III languages. Similarly, Hindi was moved from Category II to Category III at some point in the 1980s."

References

Bloomfield, A. N., Gynther, K., Masters, M. C., O'Connell, S. P., & Ross, S. J. (2012). *How does foreign language proficiency change over time? Results suggest foreign language reading and listening skills are stable over time, while speaking skills are not.* College Park, MD: University of Maryland Center for Advanced Study of Language.

Bloomfield, A. N., Masters, M. C., Castle, S., Mackey, B., Ross, S. J., & Clark, M. (2013). *How language proficiency test scores change over time: Differences across language difficulty categories.* College Park, MD: University of Maryland Center for Advanced Study of Language.

Bloomfield, A. N., Ross, S. J., Masters, M. C., & Clark, M. K. (2016). Assessing the impact of new programs on language-learning outcomes. Paper presented at the Georgetown University Roundtable (GURT) at Georgetown University, Washington, DC.

Child, J. R. (1987). Language proficiency levels and the typology of texts. In Byrnes, H. & Canale, M. (Eds.), *Defining and developing proficiency: Guidelines, implementations, and concepts* (pp. 97–106). Lincoln, IL: National Textbook Company.

Clark, M., Ross, S., O'Rourke, P., Jackson, S., Bloomfield, A., Aghajanian-Stewart, K., & Kim, S. (2016a). *The development of the language difficulty categorization framework.* College Park, MD: University of Maryland Center for Advanced Study of Language.

Clark, M., Ross, S., Jackson, S., Kim, S., O'Rourke, P., & Aghajanian-Stewart, K. (2016b). *Empirical investigation of language difficulty categories.* College Park, MD: University of Maryland Center for Advanced Study of Language.

Clark, M., Ross, S., Jackson, S., Kim, S., O'Rourke, P., & Aghajanian-Stewart, K. (2016c). *Empirical investigation of language difficulty categorization: Examining within difficulty category variation.* College Park, MD: University of Maryland Center for Advanced Study of Language.

Cysouw, M. (2013). Predicting language–learning difficulty. In Borin, L. & Saxena, A. (Eds.), *Approaches to measuring linguistic differences* (pp. 57–82). Berlin: Walter de Gruyter.

Frechtling, J. A. (2007). *Logic modeling methods in program evaluation.* San Francisco, CA: Jossey-Bass.

Hancock, G. (2011). *Structural equation modeling.* Workshop given at the University of Maryland Center for Advanced Study of Language, June 1–3, 6–7.

Hart-Gonzalez, L., & Lindemann, S. (1993). *Expected achievement in speaking proficiency.* Washington, DC: School of Language Studies, Foreign Service Institute, Department of State.

Jackson, F. H., & Kaplan, M. A. (2001). Fifty years of theory and practice in government language teaching. In J. Alatis & A. Hui Tan (Eds.), *1999 Georgetown University round table on languages and linguistics* (pp. 71–87). Washington, DC: Georgetown University Press.

Koch, A., & McCloy, R. (2015). *Language difficulty categorization in the Defense Language Testing Program.* Alexandria, VA: Human Resources Research Organization.

Lett, J. A. (n.d.). DLIFLC student profiles. Retrieved from www.utexas.edu/cola/centers/tlc/_files/proficiencyconference/presentations/DLI/2.pdf on February 23, 2015.

Lett, J. A., & O'Mara, F. E. (1990). Predictors of success in an intensive foreign language-learning context: Correlates of language-learning at the Defense Language Institute Foreign Language Center. In Parry, T. & Stansfield, C. (Eds.), *Language aptitude reconsidered* (pp. 222–260). Englewood Cliffs, NJ: Prentice Hall.

Lowe, P. Jr. (1998). Zero-based language aptitude test design: Where's the focus for the test? *Applied Language Learning, 9*(1–2), 11–30.

Mackey, B. (2014). *Aptitude as a predictor of individual differences in language proficiency growth.* College Park, MD: School of Language, Literatures and Cultures.

Masters, M. C. (2016). *Pathways to proficiency: An exploration of how cognitive and non-cognitive variables contribute to the development of achievement and proficiency outcomes.* College Park, MD: School of Language, Literatures and Cultures.

Norris, J. M. (2016). Language program evaluation. *The Modern Language Journal, 100,* 169–189.

Renger, R., & Titcomb, A. (2002). A three-step approach to teaching logic models. *American Journal of Evaluation, 23*(4), 493–503. https://doi.org/10.1177/109821400202300409

Ross, S. J., Bloomfield, A., Masters, M., Nielson, K., Kramasz, D., O'Connell, S., & Gynther, K. (2011). *How does foreign language proficiency change over time?* College Park, MD: University of Maryland Center for Advanced Study of Language.

Wagner, T. (2014). *Aptitude and achievement measures as predictors of growth in second language proficiency.* College Park, MD: School of Language, Literatures and Cultures.

Weiss, C. H. (1997). How can theory-based evaluation make greater headway? Evaluation Review, 21, 501–524.

6

MODELING LONGITUDINAL COHERENCE IN A FOREIGN LANGUAGE PROGRAM

Leslie N. Ono and Steven J. Ross

Introduction

Foreign language programs are most commonly organized around a skill-based curriculum. Depending on the size of the program, and its duration, instruction is provided to class sections that are streamed by ability levels or may simply be based on non-systematic assignment. When multiple sections of a skills-based language course are required, program administrators can opt for a *laissez-faire* approach, leaving the syllabus content, instructional methods, and assessment criteria primarily up to individual instructors. Alternatively, and relevant to the notion of *coherence*, is the practice of course coordination by convening organizational meetings among instructors who are assigned to teach different sections of the same course. Organized courses of instruction, to some degree, imply standardization of the instructional syllabus, learning materials and tasks, and assessment criteria. The rationale for course standardization is essentially that the quality of instruction and learning outcomes will be observably consistent across multiple cohorts of learners. Evidence that they in fact do so requires longitudinal data collection and cumulative analysis of each language-learning cohort.

Achievement Coherence

A research question that arises from instructional coherence within an English as a foreign language (EFL) program context is whether student achievement outcomes, in the form of course grades awarded to learners within a cohort, cohere concurrently with other achievements, and whether they maintain coherence over time. A core assumption of assessment coherence pertains to how achievements are operationalized. In a coordinated program, the criteria for

DOI: 10.4324/9781003087939-7

defining learning outcomes are pre-set, with the expectation that each instructor within a skill, domain will deliver the standardized curriculum and use the agreed-upon assessment criteria. In programs with a division of labor in teaching separate language skills, such as reading, writing, listening, and speaking, learner achievement outcomes can be tested for coherence by correlating achievements from previous courses with latter outcomes in the same domain.

Figure 6.1 illustrates the logic model for program achievement coherence, inclusive of the cross-sectional, concurrent-course, sequential diachronic, and predictive representations of coherence within a program. For a multi-sectional course, cross-sectional coherence can be evaluated by conducting linear regression analyses with prior measures of proficiency and learner achievements from previous courses to predict the grades awarded in a particular skill domain. The generated residuals, indicating the difference between the predicted and observed grades, can be standardized and plotted for a visual display (Ross, 2009; Ono, 2018). The diagram under Cross-Sectional Coherence in Figure 6.1 represents one foreign language course with ten class sections. The horizontal lines depict the plotted residuals for each class section derived from a linear regression model relative to a standardized mid-point of zero difference between predicted and observed grades, represented by the vertical line. Class sections with residuals mostly positioned to the left or right of the mid-point suggest achievement residuals resulting from instructors awarding grades well above or below what would have been predicted from learners' previous records of achievement and demonstrated proficiency. Such a finding could be indicative of course assessment rubrics not being applied consistently, or instructors systematically inflating or deflating student grades. Large heterogeneity of residuals may be the first indication of programmatic incoherence and would suggest that grading criteria vary across class sections even within one skill domain.

After the confirmation of cross-sectional coherence for each multi-section skill course, namely that class sections are not associated with significantly outlying residuals, concurrent coherence can be examined through analyses of inter-correlations and dimensionality of achievements within each term or year. As achievements, R1, W1, L1, etc. for skill-focused courses, are the final course grades awarded by instructors to individual language learners, one assumption would be that an achievement in language learning is not narrowly skill-dependent. That is, learners who receive relatively high or low assessments in one skill domain would be expected to do so in other domains if ability, motivation, and aptitude generally influence achievement.

The diagram under Concurrent Coherence in Figure 6.1 represents a confirmatory factor analysis model with the anticipated unidimensional latent achievement factor (A1) representing the expected single dimension of learner achievement across the four skills (reading, writing, listening, and speaking) taught in different class sections during the same academic term. To the extent that there are strong inter-correlations among the four skill domains taught concurrently,

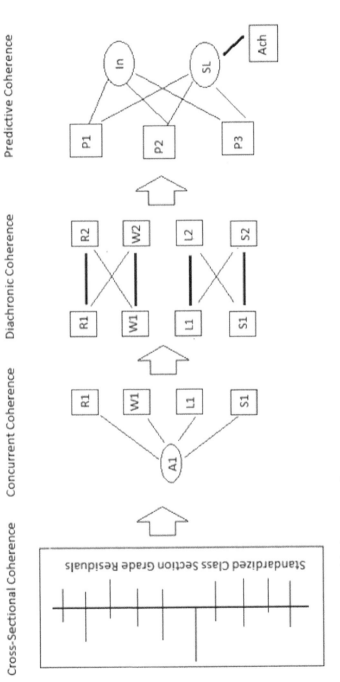

FIGURE 6.1 Logic model of program coherence.

implying a single dimension of achievement, the second criterion for coherence would be met.

Most language-learning programs, especially those for foreign language majors and training linguists in the military, involve several contiguous terms of instruction. When achievement data are archived across those terms, the question of coherence over time, or diachronic coherence (Ross, 2003), arises. Essentially, the anticipated inter-relatedness of achievement outcomes would reveal carry-over effects from achievements in the same skill domains over time.

The diagram under the Diachronic Coherence panel in Figure 6.1 shows a path analysis model in which the dark paths are predicted to yield larger standardized regression coefficients between the same skill domains over time (e.g., R1 → R2), to denote an expected path from first-semester reading to second-semester reading) compared to paths from different skill domains. Furthermore, achievement outcomes in foreign language literacy (i.e., W and R) and oral skills (i.e., L and S) would be expected to be more inter-related than cross-over effects between the two domains (e.g., W and L). Insignificant or small carry-over effects within skill domains may provoke investigation into the factors that cause the unexpected discontinuity of achievement coherence over continuous terms. Similarly, unanticipated cross-over effects between skill domains might reveal indirect effects on one skill domain owing to the reliance on a particular skill, for instance, listening as a condition for success in a different skill domain such as writing. Such cross-over effects can reveal the complexity of influences on language learning and the effects of direct method instruction, in which the target language is both the object and the medium of instruction.

The right-most panel of Figure 6.1 represents the predictive coherence of achievement, which is synonymous with its predictive validity. The individual differences in the proficiency growth latent factor, defined by periodic proficiency over the course of instruction, would serve as the outcome of interest and basis for validation. The cumulative measure of achievement (Ach), either as a final program grade point average (GPA) or as a latent factor, serves as a growth predictor in the validation phase of the program coherence model. The diagram under Predictive Coherence depicts a growth prediction model based on three repeated measures of proficiency (P1–P3), with the measures before instruction, after two semesters, and again after four semesters, to assess learners' initial starting proficiency and subsequent gains as they progress through the program. The proficiency measures can be skill domain-specific such as repeated oral proficiency interviews, or subtest scores from standardized measures. The ovals represent latent variables, with the In oval revealing the latent intercept or starting point for individual differences in proficiency, and the SL oval representing the slope or growth trajectory at the individual learner level. The path from the cumulative measure of achievement Ach to SL is predicted to show a large, standardized coefficient, which would support the claim that variation in cumulative achievement within the program of instruction accounts for variation in proficiency growth over the longitudinal period of instruction. A large, standardized coefficient from Ach to SL would imply that variation in proficiency gains is predicted by achievement in the program of instruction.

A Closer Look at Program Diachronic Coherence

One research question arising from analyses of multiple cohorts within a language instruction program is how variation in diachronic coherence affects cross-cohort comparisons in proficiency gains. To this end, two non-contiguous cohorts of EFL learners are compared. The focus is on what can generally be called *instructional program coherence*, characterized by Newmann et al. (2001) as a highly organized and coordinated educational context guided by a common framework, which, in this case, leads to coherent EFL course achievement records. The achievement outcomes, in turn, can co-vary with or mediate EFL proficiency gains. The assumption is that highly organized language programs would offer a comparatively more coordinated, inter-related, and effective foreign language curriculum.

Most of the analyses presented in this chapter were part of a longitudinal program evaluation study taking place within a Japanese university two-year EFL program context (Ono, 2018). The program was highly coordinated in that the multi-sectional skills-based courses were all taught from a common syllabus based on clear learning objectives with standardized lessons, materials, and assessments to suit. The EFL learners completed four skills-based courses every term, for a total of four terms over the two-year program. At the end of each term, students received a final course grade in each of the four courses, which was then averaged to yield their EFL GPA for that term. The four EFL term GPAs were then averaged to yield the final program achievement EFL GPA for each student, shown as Ach in the right-most panel of Figure 6.1.

The Test of English as a Foreign Language Institutional Testing Program (TOEFL ITP) exam was administered to students as the standardized proficiency measure at three set times during the program—upon entrance, after the first year, and at the end of the second year. The TOEFL ITP is comprised of three subsections designed to measure academic listening comprehension, grammar knowledge, and reading comprehension. For the achievement coherence analysis in this study, only the Listening Comprehension (LC) and Reading Comprehension (RC) subsection measures were used and modeled separately as these academic proficiency domains were most relevant to the focus of the program's skills-based curriculum. Each of the LC and RC three repeated proficiency measures is represented as P1, P2, and P3 in the right-most panel of Figure 6.1.

Recursive Path Analysis

The cohort-level recursive path model for the present study utilized a regression impact analysis approach to assessing outcomes (Mohr, 1995). A recursive path model is a series of time-ordered unidirectional linear regression analyses designed to investigate the influence of antecedent-independent variables on an outcome-dependent variable. In this approach, the achievements, final course grades given in two contiguous academic terms (i.e., the panel under Diachronic Coherence in Figure 6.1), are expanded to the third and fourth academic terms. As each cohort of foreign language learners progresses through the four-term program, 16 sets of grades are archived for each learner in each cohort. The longitudinal research focus can thus be cohort-specific, involving 16 achievements and three repeated measures of proficiency (TOEFL ITP), or can be a cross-cohort longitudinal design, comparing cohorts in the same program sampled over the life of the program.

The cohort-specific recursive path model featured in this chapter represented a two-year program of instruction, inclusive of four academic terms of 16 course achievement indicators and two of the TOEFL ITP subsections (LC3 and RC3) as the third and final program proficiency measure. The regression model can be dissected into four waves—Wave 1, Wave 2, Wave 3, Wave 4—each representing the cumulative addition of successive terms during the two-year program when proficiency testing and achievement outcomes were conducted. Because a singular and fully saturated path model would make visual interpretation difficult, the dissection of the model depicting Wave 1 and Wave 2 is presented in Figures 6.2 and 6.3, respectively. Figure 6.2 illustrates the two-year recursive path model for Wave 1 with second-term achievement outcome paths indicated by gray lines. To conduct the Wave 1 analyses, four first-semester achievement indicators—i.e., the final course grades for W1, S1, L1, and R1—were simultaneously entered as independent variables, or predictors, in separate regression analyses with each of the second-term achievement indicators as the dependent variable, or outcome. As an example of one Wave 1 regression, W1, S1, L1, and R1 final course grades were entered as predictors for the W2 final course grade. The resulting paths indicated the extent that each of the first-term courses accounted for variation in the second-term writing course outcome. This regression was repeated with each of the second-term courses as the dependent variable. Significant positive path coefficients ($p < 0.05$) provided evidence of course relatedness, whereas insignificant and/or negative paths indicated a lack of predictive validity. The four Wave 1 regression analyses conducted generated 16 possible paths.

Figure 6.3 illustrates the two-year recursive path model for Wave 2 with third-term achievement outcome paths indicated by dashed lines. For ease of interpretation, only the paths between the second- and third-term achievement indicators are shown, although the first-term achievement indicators were also included as Wave 2 predictors for the third-term outcomes. To conduct the Wave 2 analyses, the eight first-year achievement indicators—i.e., the final course grades for W1, S1, L1, R1, W2, S2, L2, and P2—were simultaneously entered as predictors in separate regression analyses for each of the third-term achievement indicator outcomes (W3, S3, etc., as the outcome measure). As an example of one Wave 2

WAVE 1 – Second-term achievement outcomes

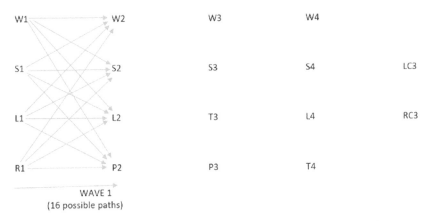

FIGURE 6.2 The recursive path model indicating the Wave 1 second-term achievement outcome paths. W1 = first-term writing course; S1 = first-term speaking course; L1 = first-term listening course; R1 = first-term reading course; W2 = second-term writing course; S2 = second-term speaking course; L2 = second-term listening course; P2 = second-term presentation course; W3 = third-term writing course; S3 = third-term speaking course; T3 = third-term topics course (content-based); P3 = third-term presentation course; W4 = fourth-term writing course; S4 = fourth-term speaking course; L4 = fourth-term listening course; T4 = fourth-term topics course (content-based); LC3 = Test of English as a Foreign Language Institutional Testing Program (TOEFL ITP) Listening Comprehension subsection test 3; RC3 = TOEFL ITP Reading Comprehension subsection test 3.

regression, the eight first- and second-term final course grades were entered as predictors for the W3 final course grade. The resulting paths indicated the extent that each of the first-year courses accounted for variation in the third-term writing course outcome. This regression was repeated with each of the third-term courses as the dependent variable. Significant positive path coefficients ($p < 0.05$) provided evidence of course relatedness, whereas insignificant and/or negative path coefficients indicated a lack of interconnectivity. The four Wave 2 regression analyses, utilizing eight independent variables, generated 32 possible paths.

At the end of each term of instruction, another wave of achievements is added to the cumulative regression model, and each achievement, in turn, is tested as the outcome in a series of regressions. The path diagrams for Waves 3 and 4 are available in the online resources associated with this chapter and indicate which preceding achievements carry over or cross over to influence the right-most or most recent achievement and proficiency outcomes. The complete program yields a cumulative total of 112 possible paths for each cohort.

WAVE 2 – Third-term achievement outcomes

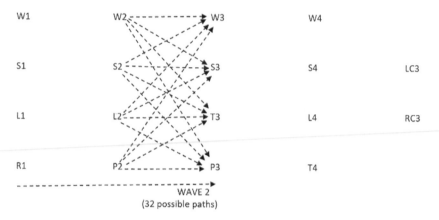

FIGURE 6.3 The recursive path model indicating the Wave 2 third-term achievement outcome paths. W1 = first-term writing course; S1 = first-term speaking course; L1 = first-term listening course; R1 = first-term reading course; W2 = second-term writing course; S2 = second-term speaking course; L2 = second-term listening course; P2 = second-term presentation course; W3 = third-term writing course; S3 = third-term speaking course; T3 = third-term topics course (content-based); P3 = third-term presentation course; W4 = fourth-term writing course; S4 = fourth-term speaking course; L4 = fourth-term listening course; T4 = fourth-term topics course (content-based); LC3 = Test of English as a Foreign Language Institutional Testing Program (TOEFL ITP) Listening Comprehension subsection test 3; RC3 = TOEFL ITP Reading Comprehension subsection test 3.

Coherence Metrics

As coherence is operationalized as the predictability of the most recent achievement outcomes based on all the preceding achievements, three metrics are of interest as potentially useful for comparing different cohorts longitudinally within the same foreign language program. A comparison of cohorts on cohesion metrics affords an opportunity to assess intended or incidental changes in the relationship between achievement outcomes and proficiency gains over time and across cohorts.

The first measure is a simple tally of the number of paths significant at $p <$ 0.05 out of the total 112 possible paths in a two-year assembly of achievements and proficiency measures for each cohort. A cohort demonstrating strong course interrelatedness would presumably yield a greater number of significant paths between achievement outcomes and proficiency measures, which would provide stronger evidence of overall diachronic cohesion for a particular cohort; fewer significant paths would be indicative of less interrelatedness, suggestive of weaker achievement coherence.

The second measure of interest is the full model R^2 generated by regressing the final program-end listening or reading proficiency measure as the outcome. This

R^2 represents the percentage of variance in the outcome proficiency measures accounted for in the final path model with insignificant paths deleted. A higher value for the model R^2 would indicate that the antecedent achievement metrics in the model were cumulatively predictive of the final proficiency outcome; if the achievement indicators were more sparse and less correlated with the proficiency outcome, a smaller R^2 value in the final model would be expected.

The third potentially useful metric is the most general indicator of achievement in foreign language courses and is used to predict growth in proficiency. As indicated in the right-most part of Figure 6.1, achievement is operationalized as the cumulative GPA of all 16 foreign language courses taken, and functions as the predictor of individual differences in proficiency growth as measured by the three TOEFL ITP administrations for each cohort.

Testing Cross-Cohort Differences in Coherence

Contrastive Cohort Analyses

Cohorts within a program of instruction can experience some variation, particularly if instructors, syllabi, and curriculum are in flux from term to term. However, when there is an effort to establish and maintain long-term program instructional coordination, such as in the case of the EFL program featured here, there is an expectation that language-learning processes are stable and generally lead to similar outcomes across cohorts. The research question is whether this expectation is supported with longitudinal evidence when cohorts separated by a few years show diachronic coherence in achievements, and whether those achievements yield similar co-variances with end-of-program gains in proficiency.

The three coherence criteria outlined above provide a framework for cross-cohort comparisons aiming to identify the mediating impact of achievement coherence on proficiency change. To this end, cohorts in the continuous program of instruction can be selected for comparison. One criterion for a contrastive comparison can be based on paired-sample t-tests to identify cohorts that differ significantly on the first and final administrations of the standardized proficiency measures, for instance, the TOEFL ITP listening and reading subsection measures (i.e., LC3 minus LC1, and RC3 minus RC1). For the program featured in this study, 20 cohorts of learners were tested to select two pairs of listening and reading contrastive-proficiency gain cohorts, one of each having attained: (1) the highest listening gain (LC High); (2) the lowest listening gain (LC Low); (3) the highest reading gain (RC High); and (4) the lowest reading gain (RC Low) by the completion of the instructional program. All high- versus low-cohort mean gain contrasts were statistically significant. The contrast of high- versus low-gaining cohorts provides the basis for testing whether the proposed coherence metrics—the sum of significant path coefficients, the cumulative coefficient of determination (R^2), or the magnitude of the standardized path from achievement

GPA in the EFL program to variation in growth in proficiency—as modeled in contrastive growth prediction models, serves to differentiate higher- versus lower-gaining cohorts.

The first measure of interest generated by the recursive path analysis is the summation of the total number of significant paths ($p < 0.05$) in the model. For each contrasted pair of cohorts, the four waves of path analyses produce a total number of significant paths out of the 112 paths possible in the model. A Pearson's chi-square test can be used to assess if any meaningful relationship exists between the number of significant versus insignificant paths for the high- and low-gain cohorts within each proficiency domain. If asymptotic significance of $p < 0.05$ is found, then the null hypothesis, which implies that the variables are independent, would be rejected. A rejection of the null hypothesis indicates the existence of a relationship between the categorization of high- or low-proficiency gain cohorts and the number of significant paths in the model. The expectation is that high-gain cohorts benefit from stronger course inter-relatedness, which would be indicated by a greater number of significant paths.

Following the guidelines outlined in Field (2009), the Pearson's chi-square test assumptions need to be checked and met in that: (1) the data used are independent, meaning that each datum occurrence was represented only once in the analysis; and (2) the expected frequency for each cell in the two-by-two contingency table is greater than five instances of occurrence. Furthermore, the conservative Yate's continuity correction should be used, as this was a two-by-two categorical data design, to adjust for the one degree of freedom and correct for the possibility of a type 1 error.

The second measure of interest generated by the recursive path analysis is the final model R^2 value. The R^2 represented the total amount of variance in each of the final listening and reading proficiency outcomes that is accounted for by all 16 antecedent achievement indicators. This component of the analysis aims to assess if there were significant differences between final model R^2 values for the contrastive gain cohorts within each of the listening and reading proficiency domains. To compare correlation coefficients, it is necessary to transform r coefficients, derived from independent populations that are not normally distributed, to z-scores corresponding to a normal distribution (Field, 2009). The first step of this process involved applying the square root to the R^2 values to transform them to r correlation coefficients. Fisher's z transformation was then applied to the r coefficients as follows to ensure normal sampling distributions (Fisher, 1921; Field, 2009):

(1) $z_r = 0.5\log[(1 + r) / (1 - r)]$

The resulting standard error for z is calculated as follows:

(2) $\text{SE}_{z_r} = 1 / \text{sqrt}(N - 3)$

Using the resulting z-scores, z standard error values, and n-sizes for each of the two independent target cohort populations within each proficiency domain, the difference between z scores, also referred to as the z-statistic, was calculated as follows:

(3) $z_{statistic} = (z_{r1} - z_{r2})$ / sqrt$\{[1 \ / \ (N_1 - 3)] + [1 \ / \ (N_2 - 3)]\}$

Using equation 3, z-statistics were calculated for the two contrastive listening gain cohort pairs and two contrastive reading gain cohorts. The resulting listening and reading z-statistic values were cross-checked with the z table of standard normal probabilities to determine if significant differences existed for the target contrastive cohort proficiency domains at $p < 0.05$.

The third measure of program impact on relative growth in proficiency involves a growth prediction model in which individual trajectories of growth in reading and listening proficiency are modeled before the path from the cumulative GPA in the EFL courses is tested for its influence on the variation in growth trajectories. The paths from the GPA to the growth indicator are then compared across the contrasted cohorts.

Contrastive Cohort Coherence Results

To test the first two coherence metrics, recursive path analyses are conducted with each of the four target contrastive gain cohorts, that is, high- versus low-gaining cohorts in listening comprehension, and a different pair contrasted in reading comprehension. As previously described, the cohort-specific model for the current study includes the time-ordered 16 achievement indicators for the core EFL curriculum completed over the four program terms. The final listening or reading proficiency outcome measures are taken at the end of instruction. The recursive path model posited is dissected into four waves of simultaneous multiple regression analyses conducted to examine course interrelatedness and the impact of the cumulative achievement indicators on the third and final proficiency exam.

The number of significant paths ($p < 0.05$) is tallied for each wave, with the total summation value used as one measure of comparison between the target cohorts. The second measure for comparison is the final R^2 generated with all prior achievements as predictors of the proficiency outcomes, with the third and last proficiency measure as the final program outcome.

Figure 6.4 illustrates the recursive path results for the LC High target cohort ($n = 268$). The total summation of significant paths for the final model was 41 out of the 112 paths possible, including 11 Wave 1, 14 Wave 2, 12 Wave 3, and 4 Wave 4 significant paths. The figure illustrates—with gray, dashed, solid, and bold lines—the significant paths ($p < 0.05$) between antecedent achievement indicators and a subsequent achievement outcome for each of the four waves. Non-significant paths are not shown. For this cohort with relatively higher listening proficiency

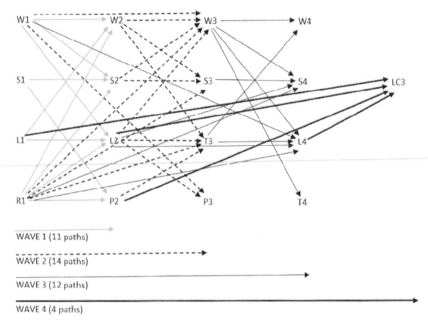

FIGURE 6.4 Highest listening comprehension gain (LC High) cohort recursive path model results. $n = 268$; final model LC3 $R^2 = 0.342$; total significant paths for complete model = 41 paths ($p < 0.05$); W1 = first-term writing course; S1 = first-term speaking course; L1 = first-term listening course; R1 = first-term reading course; W2 = second-term writing course; S2 = second-term speaking course; L2 = second-term listening course; P2 = second-term presentation course; W3 = third-term writing course; S3 = third-term speaking course; T3 = third-term topics course (content-based); P3 = third-term presentation course; W4 = fourth-term writing course; S4 = fourth-term speaking course; L4 = fourth-term listening course; T4 = fourth-term topics course (content-based); LC3 = Test of English as a Foreign Language Institutional Testing Program (TOEFL ITP) Listening Comprehension subsection test 3.

gains, the final model with LC3 as the outcome produced an R^2 of 0.342 ($p < 0.05$), indicating that 34% of the variance in the cohort's final listening proficiency measure was accounted for by the 16 achievement indicators.

The path diagrams for the low-gaining listening comprehension cohort and the high and low reading comprehension cohorts are in the online resources associated with this chapter.

If the first two metrics of interest, the sum of significant paths and the model coefficient of determination, are valid indicators of coherence, then they would be hypothesized to differentiate the high- versus low-gaining cohorts. The Pearson's chi-square test is first used to assess if any difference exists between the number of significant versus insignificant paths for the high- and low-gain cohorts within each proficiency domain. The conservative Yate's continuity correction is used given the one degree of freedom for this two-by-two design.

Table 6.1 is the two-by-two cross-tabulation contingency table showing the number of significant and non-significant paths generated by the complete models, inclusive of the four waves of regressions, for the high and low listening proficiency gain cohorts. The results indicate that the LC High cohort had slightly more significant paths in the recursive path model compared with the LC Low cohort. However, the results for the Pearson's chi-squared test of the cross-tabulations in Table 6.1 indicate that the expected difference was not found (chi-square with Yate's correction = 0.50; $p = 0.48$). Simply put, there is, for this cohort contrast, no significant association found between high or low listening gain cohort categorization and the frequency of significant paths in the regression model.

TABLE 6.1 Frequency of significant and non-significant paths in the complete models for the contrastive listening gain cohorts

	LC High cohort	LC Low cohort	Path total
Number of significant paths	41	35	76
Number of non-significant paths	71	77	148
Path total	112	112	224

LC High = cohort with high gain from Test of English as a Foreign Language Institutional Testing Program (TOEFL ITP) Listening Comprehension subsection test 1 to test 3; LC Low = cohort with low gain from TOEFL ITP Listening Comprehension subsection test 1 to test 3.

A similar result is found for the contrast between the high reading proficiency gain cohort and the low gain in reading cohort.

The second coherence metric generated by the recursive path models for the target contrastive gain cohorts was the final model R^2. Recall that the Wave 4 analysis was the final segment of the path model that utilized all 16 achievement indicators from the two years of EFL coursework as predictors for the final listening and reading proficiency outcomes. The resulting R^2 value indicates the amount of variance in the final proficiency outcome that was accounted for by all previous achievement indicators and represents a potential measure of cohort-level achievement coherence. Any significant differences for this measure between the contrastive proficiency gain cohorts would be indicative of possible differences in the impact of a particular cohort's EFL coursework, or achievement measures, to lead to proficiency gain.

As noted above, R^2 values for LC High, LC Low, RC High, and RC Low gain cohorts were transformed to z-scores. These values were then used to calculate z-statistics to determine if there were significant differences ($p < 0.05$) between the contrastive gain cohort pair correlation coefficients.

The resulting z-statistic was then cross-checked with the z table of standard normal probabilities to determine if significant differences existed between each of the contrastive gain cohort proficiency domains at $p < 0.05$.

Table 6.2 shows the results of these R^2 transformations and calculations for the four target cohorts. The R^2 values for the LC High and LC Low multiple regression analyses were 0.342 and 0.383, respectively ($p < 0.05$). The square root of these values resulted in r correlation coefficients of 0.585 for LC High and 0.619 for LC Low. Following z-score transformation, the z-statistic for the listening proficiency cohorts was calculated to be 0.666, indicating that no significant difference existed. Regarding the reading proficiency domain, the R^2 values for the RC High and RC Low multiple regression analyses were 0.151 and 0.118, respectively. The square root of these values resulted in r correlation coefficients of 0.389 for RC High and 0.344 for RC Low. Following z-score transformation, the z-statistic for the contrastive reading proficiency cohorts was 0.721, indicating a non-significant finding.

TABLE 6.2 Results for the target cohort Wave 4 R^2 value transformations, calculations, and z-statistic tests

Cohort	N-size	Wave 4 R2	r correlation coefficient	z-score	z-score se	z-statistic	p
LC High	268	0.342	0.585	0.670	0.061	0.666	0.253
LC Low	380	0.383	0.619	0.723	0.052		
RC High	384	0.151	0.389	0.411	0.051	0.721	0.235
RC Low	392	0.118	0.344	0.359	0.051		

LC = Test of English as a Foreign Language Institutional Testing Program (TOEFL ITP) Listening Comprehension subsection; RC = TOEFL ITP Reading Comprehension subsection.

Neither of the two coherence metrics generated from the carry-over and cross-over effects in the semester to semester and total array of 16 achievements in courses differentiated the high- versus low-gain cohorts in listening and reading. In this case, the path analytic approach did not yield the expected discriminating effect.

Program GPA Mediation of Learner Proficiency Growth for Target Cohorts

We now outline the third method, which is based on the average of all grades in the foreign language program. As each term grade is the average of the four course grades, the four term grades are averaged to compute the student's final program GPA. The third approach differs in that, instead of the correlations among the grades as the basis for cohesion, the proficiency growth trajectories of individual learners within each cohort are modeled as latent growth differences. As in the right side of Figure 6.1, the sole predictor of the latent growth, defined as the slope of change or growth (Duncan, Duncan, and Strycker, 2011; Little, 2013), varies across learners within each cohort. Their individual cumulative GPA is then used to predict the variation in proficiency growth.

The latent growth curve model for the four cohorts featured here, a contrast between high and low gains in listening, and another pair with contrasting gains in reading, were each in turn tested with the growth prediction model as shown in Figure 6.5. Table 6.3 summarizes the results.

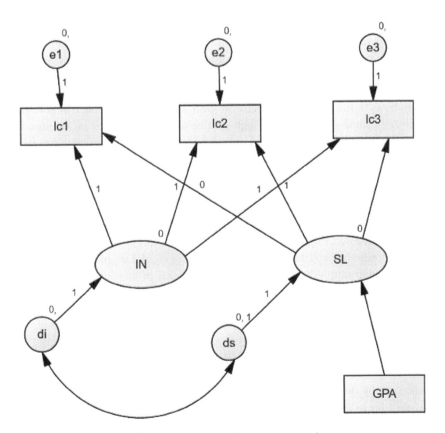

FIGURE 6.5 Growth prediction model for cohort contrast analysis.

TABLE 6.3 Growth prediction models for contrastive gain cohorts

Cohort	N-size	CFI	GPA→slope	p
LC High	268	0.957	0.431	<0.01
LC Low	380	0.935	0.569	<0.01
RC High	384	0.968	0.618	<0.01
RC Low	392	0.999	0.064	=0.07

CFI = comparative fit index; GPA = grade point average; LC = repeated measures of Test of English as a Foreign Language Institutional Testing Program (TOEFL ITP) Listening Comprehension subsection; RC = repeated Measures of TOEFL ITP Reading Comprehension subsection.

Noteworthy in the growth prediction models is the lack of the predicted difference in the magnitude of the standardized path from cumulative achievement to variation in growth for listening. Counter-intuitively, the lower-gain cohort's (0.569) individual differences in foreign language achievement show a stronger relation to variation in listening growth compared to the higher-gaining cohort (0.431). In contrast, the size of the path from GPA to growth for the low reading gain cohort (0.064) compared to the high reading gain cohort (0.618) is strikingly different. The cumulative achievement GPA in the 16 foreign language courses here shows a strong predictive relation with individual differences in foreign language reading growth for the high-gain cohort, while there is no significant relation between achievement and growth in reading for the low reading gain cohort. In Chapter 7 of this volume, Ono, using a time series analysis, shows that growth in listening happens symmetrically in every cohort, suggesting that intensive exposure to direct method instruction has an effect on proficiency growth in listening in spite of variation in GPAs. It would appear then, that achievement as indicated by a global cumulative GPA has predictive validity in the reading domain. This result might be indicative of the fact that grades are often contingent on homework, collaborative group work, projects, and assignments. Listening might develop simply by exposure to large amounts of focused input, even for learners with average or even below-average patterns of achievement.

Summary and Conclusion

The three indicators of cohesion, including the summation of non-random path coefficients, the coefficient of determination (R^2) for the pairs of cohorts contrasted by the relative magnitude of gains, and the predictive path from GPA to variation in growth at the individual learner level, did not serve to systematically differentiate between the high- and low-coherence cohorts. A few caveats are, however, in order. First, while statistically significant, the proficiency gain differences between the contrastive cohort pairs were relatively small, given the fact that the EFL program provided roughly the same 336 hours of instruction for all of the cohorts tested. Furthermore, the two coherence metrics based on the inter-relation among the course grade outcomes, hypothesized to indicate predictive coherence, were likely too gross to discriminate between relatively high- and low-gaining cohorts. Because the two grade cohesion metrics were at the cohort level, rather than at the individual learner level, they might have been too approximate to detect gain differences between cohorts. With that said, the third metric, the foreign language GPA measured at the individual person level, did show predictive validity for reading growth.

As noted earlier, foreign language instruction organized around skill domains presents opportunities to test carry-over effects from term to term. A narrower focus on only carry-over path magnitudes remains a coherence criterion to be explored. Further, as foreign language curricula evolve over time, there is often a drift from conventional skills-based instruction to more multi-skill content instruction. The emergence of content-based instruction in foreign language education can be expected to make achievement, as manifested in course grades awarded, multi-dimensional and inclusive of criteria not as limited to a narrowly focused skills-based course design and syllabus (see Brown, Plonsky, and Teimouri, 2018, for a review).

The larger implication of the foregoing analyses of program coherence is whether foreign language programs benefit from a coordinated curriculum design wherein multi-section courses share common materials, assessment criteria, and instructional techniques. The cohorts contrasted in this chapter were all taught in a systematically coordinated foreign language curriculum, and thus the program design and organization present minimal variation across time and outcomes. What remains to be seen is a comparison of the coherence of instructional programs organized around the coordinated curriculum model with more *laissez-faire* models having minimal coordination among instructors, sections, materials, and achievement indicators. Our prediction is that foreign language learners will show systematic growth in listening and speaking proficiency as long as there is any kind of sustained target language input, whether the curriculum is coordinated or not. Future longitudinal research will be needed to test whether curricular coherence provides the basis for differential growth in foreign language reading and writing. If there is no difference in language-learning outcomes on standardized foreign language tests, the inference would be that gains in proficiency are the result of cumulative maturation accruing from exposure to a foreign language, even if such exposure is loosely organized. Such a longitudinal study remains to be undertaken.

References

Brown, A. V., Plonsky, L., & Teimouri, Y. (2018). The use of course grades as metrics in L2 research: A systematic review. *Foreign Language Annals, 51*, 763–778.

Duncan, T. E., Duncan, S. C., & Strycker, L. A. (2011). *An Introduction to Latent Variable Growth Curve Modeling* (2nd ed.). New York: Lawrence Erlbaum.

Field, A. (2009). *Discovering Statistics Using SPSS* (3rd ed.). London: Sage.

Fisher, R. A. (1921). On the probable error of a coefficient of correlation deduced from a small sample. *Metron*, 1, 3–32.

Little, T. D. (2013). *Longitudinal Structural Equation Modeling*. New York, NY: Guilford Press.

Mohr, L. (1995). *Impact Analysis for Program Evaluation* (2nd ed.). Thousand Oaks, CA: Sage.

Newmann, F. M., Smith, B., Allensworth, E., & Bryk, A. S. (2001). Instructional program coherence: What it is and why it should guide school improvement policy. *Educational Evaluation and Policy Analysis*, 23(4), 297–321. doi:10.3102/01623737023004297

Ono, L. (2018). *Coherence in quantitative longitudinal language program evaluation* [Doctoral dissertation, Temple University]. Temple University Electronic Theses and Dissertations.

Ross, S. J. (2003). A diachronic coherence model for language program evaluation. *Language Learning*, 53(1), 1–33. doi:10.1111/1467-9922.00209

Ross, S. J. (2009). Program evaluation. In M. H. Long & C. J. Doughty (Eds.), *The Handbook of Language Teaching* (pp. 756–778). Malden, MA: Wiley-Blackwell.

7

FACTORS AFFECTING PROFICIENCY OUTCOMES IN A FOREIGN LANGUAGE PROGRAM OVER 20 YEARS

Leslie N. Ono

Introduction

In recent years, the topic of foreign language program evaluation has garnered greater attention among language educators and evaluators. This is largely a result of increased external pressures stemming from institutional accreditation interests and calls for greater quality control (Norris, 2009). Despite this movement toward greater accountability, there remain few published examples of longitudinal program evaluation across the foreign language education discipline. Furthermore, when they do exist, studies intended to longitudinally examine foreign language program impact are often limited to the inclusion of one or two student cohorts. Such limited longitudinal studies are not without their merits, and understandably time and resource constraints often play key roles in preventing the implementation of extended longitudinal designs. However, for long-term program evaluation and monitoring purposes, it is important to consider that foreign language programs are dynamic institutional contexts, potentially influenced by a variety of social, economic, political, and demographic factors over time. For example, institutional internal factors, such as decisions to reform the program curriculum or revise admissions procedures, could ultimately influence program outcomes over time. Additionally, external factors beyond the control of the institution, such as increases in competition with other institutions or changes to national-level educational policy, could lead to gradual changes in the types of students entering the program, which can in turn influence program outcomes over time. Expanding evaluation to include multiple cohorts spanning an extended period can provide the opportunity to identify and assess long-term trends in program implementation and effectiveness. This type of expansive longitudinal design would also allow

DOI: 10.4324/9781003087939-8

for further subsequent research focused on target cohorts, yielding results which could be situated and interpreted within the historical program context.

Time series regression analysis (Mohr, 1995) is a useful analytical approach to account for the changes in a series of repeated measures over a period during which planned and unplanned events may have an impact. For language program evaluation, curricular innovations and factors hypothesized to influence the series can be empirically tested. Examples of such factors are macro-level curricular policies in secondary schools, which eventually affect the starting proficiency levels of incoming college students, and within-institution policy changes, such as initiation of novel majors requiring higher foreign language proficiency. A time series analysis can graphically represent and statistically test the effect of such changes.

The English as a Foreign Language (EFL) Program Context

As part of a larger longitudinal program evaluation study (Ono, 2018), the line of research inquiry provided in this chapter examined the patterns and growth trajectories of English proficiency outcomes of a Japanese university undergraduate EFL program over a 20-year period. The participants were 7,541 first- and second-year Japanese students who were enrolled in the university's policy studies department and completed a required two-year EFL program between 1995 and 2015. Student cohorts were predominantly Japanese, had a balanced percentage of females and males, and typically ranged from 18 through 20 years of age. In addition to their academic major coursework and as part of the department's matriculation requirements, students participated in four weekly 90-minute English skills-based courses (e.g., reading, writing, discussion, presentation) each semester over four semesters, resulting in approximately 336 hours of in-class study. The EFL program curriculum was demanding and highly coordinated, meaning that each course was taught from a common syllabus designed to achieve set learning objectives, and the course materials, lessons, and assessments were standardized and delivered uniformly by all teachers across course sections.

The Test of English as a Foreign Language Institutional Testing Program (TOEFL ITP) was used as the program's proficiency measure for student placement and program evaluation purposes. The TOEFL ITP is a standardized paper-based academic English proficiency exam designed to measure listening comprehension, grammar and written expression, and reading comprehension. The test also provides an overall composite proficiency score. Parallel forms of the TOEFL ITP were administered to each student cohort on three different occasions throughout the two-year program:

1. Upon entering for initial placement purposes (ITP1)
2. At the end of the first year to measure proficiency change and determine appropriate second-year course placement (ITP2)
3. At the end of the second year as the final exiting proficiency measure (ITP3)

The three TOEFL ITP administrations for each of the 20 cohorts yielded 60 time-separated repeated proficiency measures across the 20-year period—data that represented the program outcome of interest in this study.

Given the expansive longitudinal design of this research, there were several historical factors hypothesized to have potentially influenced the EFL program's proficiency outcomes over the 20-year span. The first event was internal to the university and involved the addition of a new academic major within the department's undergraduate degree program in 2002. Unlike the other existing departmental majors emphasizing social policy studies, this new specialization offered a course of study covering different forms of media and technical skills for working with information systems. The start of the new major impacted the department's EFL program in two important ways. First, the department's expansion resulted in larger cohorts of students entering the program. In order to accommodate the larger program cohorts, course sections were added, and the number of instructors was increased. The second impact was hypothesized to be an influence on the student demographic, mainly the academic profiles and interests of students entering the program. Because the new major focused on information systems, it was speculated that it might have appealed to students who were less interested and proficient in English compared with those drawn to the other social policies departmental majors offered.

The second event of interest was external to the university and involved the implementation of new national educational reforms implemented in Japanese junior high schools from 2002 and in senior high schools from 2003, thereby affecting university entrants from 2006. These new policies, known as *relaxed education*, or *yutori kyouiku* in Japanese, were mandated by the Japanese ministry with the aim of integrating flexibility into the curriculum by offering students a more diversified education (Butler & Iino, 2005). To do so, the measures effectively reduced the number of school hours through eliminating Saturday classes, reducing the number of hours focused on academic subjects, and reducing the amount of curriculum content covered. For English education, specifically, the relaxed education reforms entailed reductions in English study class time, the amount of English textbook content, and the quantity of English vocabulary studied (Shite, 2007). Furthermore, these reforms involved a considerable change in English teaching methodology. Prior to the introduction of the new policies, English pedagogical practices were mainly characterized by a focus on reading, writing, and grammar study, also referred to as a traditional *grammar translation approach*. However, the relaxed education measures introduced and emphasized a more *communicative approach* to English teaching and learning, with a clear shift in focus on literacy skills to the development of students' listening and speaking abilities (Shite, 2007). The impact of the relaxed education reforms has been a source of heated debate and is often cited as a potential cause for observed trends in declining Japanese academic ability (Butler & Iino, 2005). Therefore, this study included an investigation of the influence of these reforms on incoming program cohort proficiency levels and outcomes, starting with the first relaxed education university entrants in 2006.

The third historical factor of interest was external to the university and not limited to one event, but rather stemmed from the gradual effects of the declining Japanese birth rate over recent decades. More specifically, Japan's falling birth rate has resulted in a steady decrease in the number of 18-year-olds, a population which comprises approximately 95% of Japanese university new entrants (Goodman, 2010). According to the Ministry of Education, Culture, Sports, and Science and Technology (MEXT; 2017), the population of Japanese 18-year-olds reached 2.05 million in 1992, but experienced a continuous decline from that point onward, falling to 1.19 million in 2014, constituting a 42% decline over the 22-year period.

This population trend has had important implications for both Japanese universities, as well as the students they serve. For larger universities, it has inevitably fueled an increase in competition for new students as they struggle to meet enrollment capacities. Efforts to attract and retain students often take the form of renewed public relations, revised curriculum, the establishment of new programs, and increases in the acceptance of applicants through various methods of admissions (Goodman, 2010). As the population of Japanese 18-year-olds has steadily dwindled, the balance of supply and demand between university admission capacities and applicants has been approaching an equilibrium. In 1992, approximately 27% of the 18-year-old population entered universities with a 59% applicant acceptance rate, while in 2011, 51% entered universities with a 91% applicant acceptance rate (Ministry of Education, Culture, Sports, Science and Technology, 2012). These figures, indicating the growing number of applicants entering with increasingly high acceptance rates, suggest that universities have had to adjust to population trends by becoming less selective in their admissions procedures. Such changes over time have likely influenced the demographics and academic profiles of university entrants, particularly in terms of their high school educational background (e.g., having graduated from academically top-, mid-, or lower-level high schools), academic interests and abilities, motivations for entering university, and career aspirations. Of specific interest in this study was the extent to which such changes in cohort student demographics might be reflected in the emerging English proficiency patterns and program outcomes over time.

The Aims of this Study

Using a time series linear regression approach, there were three primary aims of this expansive longitudinal program evaluation study. The first was to investigate the emerging trends for each of the three proficiency domains utilizing the 20 cohorts of 60 chronically charted TOEFL ITP administrations across the program's 20-year history. The examination of proficiency-specific trends within a wider historical context could help administrators to better evaluate long-term program performance and address potential curriculum development needs. A second aim was to investigate the impact of the two-year program on proficiency gains by examining the possible emerging cohort-specific and between-group proficiency patterns. This would allow an examination of growth trajectories for the proficiency domains at different points in the two-year program, both within and between cohorts. Lastly, considering the historical context of this longitudinal program evaluation research, the third aim of this study was to investigate the potential impact of historical events on the program's proficiency trends, including the start of the new department major from 2002, the new secondary educational policies affecting university entrants from 2006, and the declining birth rate resulting in the steady decrease in the 18-year-old population over time. Larger external influences as well as internal institutional changes can yield unplanned consequences for language programs, affecting outcomes and leading to possible misinterpretations about true program effectiveness. Considering these study aims, the three research questions under investigation were:

> Research Question 1 (RQ1): What general patterns of proficiency growth emerge from charting and testing changes in the three TOEFL ITP proficiency domains across the 20-year span of an EFL program?
>
> Research Question 2 (RQ2): What impact does the two-year EFL program have on cohort-specific growth trajectories for the three proficiency domains during the 20-year span?
>
> Research Question 3 (RQ3): What was the initial impact and subsequent effect of specific program-internal and -external events on patterns of proficiency growth over the 20-year period?

Methodology

Data Compilation, Screening, and Imputation

The TOEFL ITP data for the 20 cohorts included in this study had been archived in various electronic forms and files since the program's inception in 1995. Following Tabachnick and Fidell's (2013) recommendations, prior to conducting analyses, careful screening procedures were implemented in the collation of the extensive TOEFL ITP data set used in this study. First, the archived TOEFL ITP data files from 1995 through 2015 were retrieved, compiled, and both visually and analytically scrutinized for anomalies—such as input errors or implausible values—which, if found, were then deleted. Additionally, while sitting the three exam administrations was a program requirement resulting in largely complete cohort TOEFL ITP data sets, there were inevitably student absences reflected in the records to address. Given that proficiency change was of primary interest, it was deemed important for students to have at least two of the three TOEFL ITP repeated measures on record to be included in this study. Thus, individual student cases that had only one of three TOEFL ITP recorded were considered critically incomplete and removed from the data set.

As a final step, the cumulative data set was examined for student cases that had only one missing TOEFL ITP data value. When conducting longitudinal research, missing data is a pervasive issue with potentially consequential impact, and one that requires thorough consideration prior to conducting any analyses (Barkaoui, 2014; Ross, 2005; Singer & Willet, 2003). One common approach to dealing with missing data is to remove participants with missing values through listwise and pairwise deletion. Although easy to implement, listwise deletion can result in the exclusion of vital data, whereas pairwise deletion can introduce asymmetry into the analyses and therefore bias the outcome (Ross, 2005). An important assumption when employing deletion methods is that data values are missing completely at random, which is often not the case. The removal of participants exhibiting systematic missingness can ultimately invalidate inferences (Singer & Willett, 2003), undermine internal validity (Barkaoui, 2014), inject bias and complicate interpretation, as well as impact the generalizability of the outcome (Ross, 2005). For instance, in the present study, student absence from ITP3—the final administration given at the conclusion of the program—was more frequent compared with ITP1 and ITP2 attendance. Without a concrete incentive to sit the final exam, waning motivation and selective avoidance, particularly among the less successful English learners, were presumed to be factors contributing to increased ITP3 absence. The deletion of these cases could therefore skew the participant population by underrepresenting less proficient students, thereby biasing the outcome by inflating the ITP results.

A more recent strategy for addressing the issue of data missingness in social science research is to employ multiple imputation methods (Ross, 2005; Singer & Willett, 2003). Multiple imputation software applies expected maximum likelihood algorithms with the existing data to generate the most plausible values to replace the missing data points within a data set (Nunnery, Ross, & McDonald, 2006). The resulting imputed value represents the most likely substitute for the missing datum according to the data profile generated using the existing data inclusive of all measures. In the present study, the NORM multiple imputation software program (Schafer, 1997) was used to impute any singular missing ITP1, ITP2, or ITP3 value for participants within the cumulative data set.

Time Series Analyses

Following imputation procedures, the final data set was complete and time series analyses with a linear regression approach were used to investigate patterns of proficiency growth over the 60 TOEFL ITP exam administrations. This involved using the aggregate mean scores for the 20 cohorts of students on the three proficiency domains as measured by the subsections of the TOEFL ITP, including Listening Comprehension (LC), Structure (ST), and Reading Comprehension (RC).

According to Tabachnick and Fidell (2013), time series analyses are often used with a sequence of repeated measures, typically involving 50 observations or more, collected over a period of time. The observations can be on one individual or involve aggregate scores of a group of participants. One primary goal of time series analyses is to identify and examine patterns of change over a sequence of many observations, while accounting for the likely existence of correlated residual terms. Due to the nature of utilizing an extensive number of repeated measures, with the primary distinguishing factor being time, there is the strong likelihood of the existence of highly correlated residuals, also known as autocorrelation. For this reason, a time series approach is more appropriate than multiple regression analysis because there is an expectation that the assumption of independence will be violated and there are procedures in place to account for this violation. A second goal of time series can be to test an intervention or the impact of a specific event that has taken place at a certain point in the series sequence. This approach, often referred to as an interrupted time series, allows for the examination of the immediate impact, or shock, to the series as well as any subsequent changes to the observed patterns following the event.

A useful first step in conducting time series analyses is to graphically chart the raw series data to visually inspect the possible existence of trends, as well as the magnitude and nature of change across the observations of time (Mohr, 1995). Therefore, as an initial step, the aggregate means for each of the proficiency domains were chronologically charted for the 20 cohorts, inclusive of the three exam sittings for each cohort (i.e., ITP1, ITP2, and ITP3), for a total of 60 exam administrations. This allowed for the visual inspection of overall trends and cohort-specific cycles in English proficiency changes across the span of the program. For ease of interpretation, Figure 7.1 provides the plotted mean results for only two of the TOEFL ITP subsections—LC and RC. The y-axis indicates the TOEFL ITP score value scale for these two components of the exam. The 60 exam administrations are represented by the variable Time and ordered sequentially along the x-axis; for example, Cohort 1 (1995) results are plotted at Time 1 (ITP1), Time 2, (ITP2), and Time 3 (ITP3); Cohort 2 (1996) results are plotted at Time 4 (ITP1), Time 5 (ITP2), and Time 6 (ITP3), and so on.

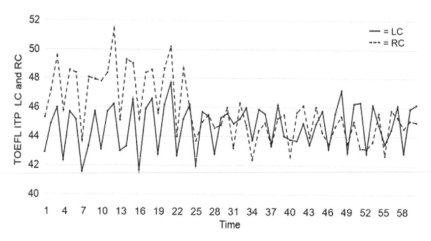

FIGURE 7.1 Test of English as a Foreign Language Institutional Testing Program (TOEFL ITP) subsection results charted sequentially for 20 program cohorts. LC = Listening Comprehension subsection; RC = Reading Comprehension subsection.

Figure 7.1 provides evidence of a cyclical proficiency pattern for the cohorts across time. For example, in looking at the LC results for Cohort 1 plotted at Times 1, 2, and 3, there is a progressive increase, which can be interpreted as gains in listening proficiency, as students progressed through the two-year program. Subsequently, at Time 4 there is a sharp decrease, as this plot represents the first LC mean score for Cohort 2, followed by a similar gain pattern over the next two exam administrations, Times 5 and 6, suggesting evidence of a cyclical pattern as a new cohort enters the series every fourth Time.

Furthermore, the three exam administrations appear to yield similar patterns of proficiency growth trajectories for all cohorts. As illustrated in the listening pattern for Cohort 1, the sharpest increase was achieved between Time 1 to Time 2 (i.e., ITP1 and ITP2), representing the proficiency gain attained during the first year in the program. This was followed by a modest increase from Time 2 to Time 3 (i.e., ITP2 to ITP3), indicating the amount of proficiency gain attained in the second year in the program. For most cohorts, the pattern for the second year indicates a minimal gain, no gain, or in some instances, a decrease in proficiency between ITP2 and ITP3, as is the case for Cohort 2's listening trend from Time 5 to Time 6. These mixed results for the second year are largely due to factors affecting the third administration of the exam, which will be discussed later.

In addition to cyclical cohort-specific trends, Figure 7.1 indicates the existence of general trends for the different proficiency domains across the 20 years. For example, the reading proficiency series is characterized by cohorts entering with noticeably higher reading proficiency levels and achieving greater gains earlier compared to later in the program history, resulting in what visually appears to be a gradual downward trend across the 20 years. In contrast, the overall proficiency trend for listening appears to hold steady across time, with most cohorts having comparable entering levels and achieving comparable gains.

Following visual inspection and to address the three research questions under investigation, separate time series analyses were conducted for each of the three proficiency domains to assess the general patterns of proficiency growth, cohort-specific patterns and proficiency growth trajectories, and the impact of historical events on program proficiency trends. To address RQ1, an initial time series linear regression analysis, referred to as Model 1, was conducted for each proficiency domain to investigate the overall proficiency trend across Time. Model 1 for listening proficiency is represented as:

$$LC = B0 + B(Time) + e$$

In this Model 1 equation, listening proficiency changes and patterns over the 60 repeated-measures observations is the outcome of interest. B0 represents the intercept, or baseline starting listening proficiency for participants on each of the 60 exam administrations. The inclusion of the independent variable Time tests the extent that the sequentially ordered repeated measures yield significant patterns of listening proficiency change across the 60 exam administrations.

To address RQ2, Model 2 was tested to examine program impact and between-group differences in proficiency patterns for the 20 program cohorts. As observed in Figure 7.1, a cyclical pattern emerges among the 60 exam administrations represented by the variable Time. These cycles appear to reflect the timing of the exam for each cohort, specifically the pre-, mid-, and post-program administrations, labeled ITP1, ITP2, and ITP3, respectively. To account for and investigate this cyclical pattern in the series, a dummy code was entered to capture the mid- and post-program administrations of the exam for each cohort, ITP2 and ITP3. Note that the first pre-program administration of the exam, ITP1, was not entered as it was the reference period already captured in the variable Time. Model 2 for the listening proficiency domain is represented as:

$$LC = B0 + B(Time) + B(ITP2) 10+ B(ITP3) + e$$

In the Model 2 equation above, B0 represents the baseline starting listening proficiency and Time represents the 60 sequentially ordered exam administrations. The inclusion of the ITP2 and ITP3 dummy coded variables tested the potential cyclical pattern of proficiency changes for the pre-, mid-, and post-program sequencing (i.e., ITP1 to ITP2 to ITP3) for the 20 cohorts. In the program of interest, there were over 160 hours of English instruction each year between proficiency exam administrations. Model 2 examined the extent that instruction led to proficiency gain for each program year, and the extent that there was any variation in this growth across the 20 cohorts.

Lastly, to investigate RQ3, Model 3 tested the impact of two specific events that occurred during the program's 20-year history on proficiency patterns. The first event, considered institutional internal, was the start of a new undergraduate major within the department in 2002. The second event, considered institutional external, involved changes to the national English education policies in secondary education affecting university entrants from 2006 onward. Based on the department's historical records, these events were identified and selected according to their potential influence on the number, academic orientation, and English interest and ability of students entering the department over the years. It was hypothesized that events leading to changes in such student demographics could potentially affect program proficiency trends. For this investigation, an interrupted time series approach was used to separately test the influence of these events on the initial shock to proficiency trends, as well as any subsequent change in proficiency patterns following each event. The two interrupted time series models for the listening proficiency domain are represented as:

Model 3A:

$$LC = B0 + B(Time) + B(ITP2) + B(ITP3) + B(Major\ Event) + B(Major\ Slope) + e$$

Model 3B:

$$LC = B0 + B(Time) + B(ITP2) + B(ITP3) + B(Policy\ Event) + B(Policy\ Slope) + e$$

In the above equations, Model 3A examined the impact of the start of a new undergraduate major in 2002, referred to as Major Event, and Model 3B examined the impact of secondary school relaxed education graduations first entering the program from 2006, referred to as Policy Event. In these models, B0 represents the baseline starting listening proficiency, Time represents the 60 sequentially ordered exam administrations, and the ITP2 and ITP3 dummy coded variables modeled the cyclical pre-, mid-, and post-program sequencing of exam administrations for each cohort. In addition, dummy codes were used to test the impact of the specified event on the series at a particular time (e.g., Major Event, dummy coded from 2002 onward), as well as capture any subsequent change in the trend from the start of the specified event (e.g., Major Slope, dummy coded from 2002 onward).

In addition to these two events, the impact of another external influence on proficiency changes was of interest; that is, the declining Japanese birth rate which has led to competition for university applicants and increased rates of acceptances. While this factor cannot be tested at one point in time in the series, it was hypothesized that any potential influences might be reflected and observed in emerging gradual changes of the program's general proficiency trends over time.

Prior to conducting all analyses, the assumptions for time series were checked and confirmed (Field, 2009; Tabachnick & Fidell, 2013). Scatterplots were generated to examine the distribution of the dependent variable, in this case the TOEFL ITP outcome measures, in relation to the residuals, or errors of prediction. Normality, linearity, and homoscedasticity of distribution were all satisfied. The collinearity statistics were examined and within range, with the variance inflation factor well below 10 and the tolerance statistic above 0.2, thus meeting the assumption of no multicollinearity (Field, 2009).

Furthermore, diagnostics were conducted to determine the independence of residuals for each series. This is one of the more important assumptions for time series analysis, and one that is not likely to be met when using serially ordered time series data. With time series data, there is an expectation of a violation of independent residuals, as error terms are likely to be correlated due to patterns over time (Tabachnick & Fidell, 2013). Autocorrelated residuals can result in bias in the observed regression coefficients, so they should be corrected if found. To address this issue, Durbin–Watson diagnostics were used for each series to confirm the independence of the residuals. If the assumption was violated, then the Cochrane–Orcutt estimation, a procedure that adjusts the serial correlation in the error term for linear models, was entered as a syntax function prior to rerunning the analysis. This procedure effectively adjusted any initially correlated residuals and transformed the Durbin–Watson to an acceptable range.

Results

RQ1: General Proficiency Trends

RQ1 asked: What general patterns of proficiency growth emerge from charting and testing changes in the three TOEFL ITP proficiency domains across the 20-year span of an EFL program? To address this question, first the mean scores of the three exam sittings for each cohort (pre-, mid-, and post-program) were chronologically charted to visually inspect patterns of growth for each proficiency domain across the 20 years (provided separately in Figures 7.2, 7.3, and 7.4 below for ease of interpretation). Model 1 was then tested using separate time series regression analyses for each of the listening, grammar, and reading TOEFL ITP subsections to evaluate the overall trends across the variable Time, represented by the 60 exam administrations. The results for Model 1 for each proficiency domain are provided in Table 7.1.

TABLE 7.1 Time series results for Model 1: general proficiency trends

	B	$se\ B$	β	R^2
Listening				0.02
Constant	44.36★★★	0.40		
Time	0.01	0.01	0.14	
Grammar				0.52★★★
Constant	47.87★★★	0.39		
Time	−0.09★★★	0.01	−0.72	
Reading				0.35★★★
Constant	47.94★★★	0.45		
Time	−0.07★★★	0.01	−0.59	

$n = 7,541$; Constant = average baseline proficiency as measured by the Test of English as a Foreign Language Institutional Testing Program (TOEFL ITP) subsection; Time = proficiency trend across the 60 exam administrations.

★$p < 0.05$; ★★ $p < 0.01$; ★★★ $p < 0.001$.

As indicated in Table 7.1, the baseline average for the listening subsection score was significant at B = 44.36, $p < 0.001$ across the 60 exam administrations. However, the listening model as a whole was not significant ($R^2 = 0.02$, $F(1, 58) = 1.10$, $p = 0.39$), indicating that there was no cross-cohort variation in listening proficiency change. In other words, the overall pattern for listening proficiency across the 20 years was not characterized by any meaningful downward or upward trends. This finding was also supported by visual inspection of the plotted means in Figure 7.2.

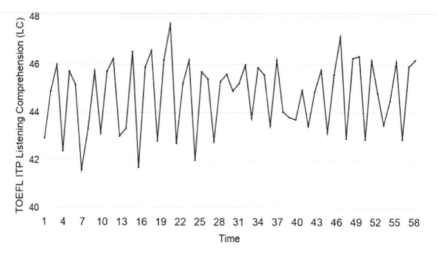

FIGURE 7.2 The means for the Test of English as a Foreign Language Institutional Testing Program (TOEFL ITP) Listening Comprehension (LC) subsection across time.

As illustrated in Figure 7.2, overall, cohorts tended to enter the program and make comparable gains over the 20-year period. Apart from several cohorts having relatively low entering listening averages in the early years of the program (e.g., Times 7, 16, and 25), and a few with notable exiting gains (e.g., Times 21 and 48), the general listening growth pattern across the life of the program appears consistent. With a few exceptions, the gains were relatively uniform, with most cohorts exiting the program within a similarly comparable range, regardless of their entering listening score averages.

The Model 1 overall trend for grammar proficiency across variable Time was significant ($R^2 = 0.52$, $F(1, 58) = 63.62$, $p < 0.001$), indicating that 52% of the variation in grammar proficiency change was accounted for in this model. The baseline intercept was significant at B = 47.87, $p < 0.001$ and there was a significant downward trend for grammar proficiency across the 60 TOEFL tests indicated by Time, (B = −0.09, $p < 0.001$). This means that the average cohort starting grammar proficiency was 47.87, and for every successive TOEFL pre-test administration in the series, there was a 0.09 of a TOEFL ITP Structure subsection point decline. This general downward trend is also reflected in Figure 7.3, illustrating the grammar proficiency mean plots over the 20-year period.

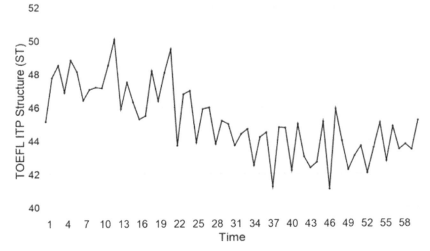

FIGURE 7.3 The means for the Test of English as a Foreign Language Institutional Testing Program (TOEFL ITP) Structure (ST) subsection across time.

While the individual cohorts appear to demonstrate varying degrees of grammar proficiency gains through their respective pre-, mid-, and post-program exam administrations, the overall trend indicates a gradual, yet notable, decline in student grammar proficiency across the 20 cohorts. Cohorts earlier in the program's history (e.g., Time 1 through 31) entered with relatively high grammar proficiency levels compared with those entering later. Furthermore, despite the higher starting points, most earlier cohorts show evidence of demonstrating considerable grammar proficiency gains, with particularly high program exit averages at Time 12 and Time 21. In contrast, there appears to be a shift in the grammar levels of students entering from Time 34, with relatively constricted grammar proficiency gains made from that point onward.

As indicated in Table 7.1, the overall trend for reading proficiency across the variable Time was significant ($R^2 = 0.35$, $F(1, 58) = 31.47$, $p < 0.001$), indicating that only 35% of the variation in reading proficiency change was accounted for by this model. The baseline intercept for reading proficiency was significant at $B = 47.94$, $p < 0.001$ and there was a significant overall downward trend across time with $B = -0.07$, $p < 0.001$. In other words, the average cohort entering reading proficiency baseline was 47.87, and for every successive exam administration in the proficiency series, there was a 0.07 of a TOEFL ITP reading point decline in the pre-instruction test means. This finding is also visually demonstrated in Figure 7.4 with the observed general downward trend of the reading proficiency mean plots across the life of the program.

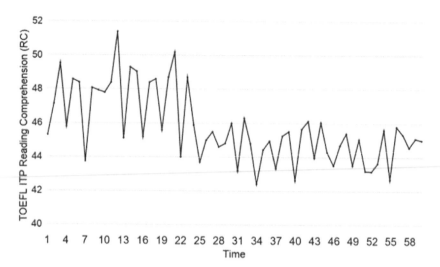

FIGURE 7.4 The means for the Test of English as a Foreign Language Institutional Testing Program (TOEFL ITP) Reading Comprehension (RC) subsection across time.

Similar to the grammar trend, the individual cohorts appear to achieve reading proficiency gains as they progress through the two-year program; however, there is an overall negative trend across the 60 exams. Apart from Cohort 3's entering reading proficiency at Time 7, the plotted reading mean results for the earlier years of the program indicate that cohorts were entering with relatively higher levels of reading proficiency and were able to achieve considerable gains. However, there was a somewhat dramatic change for the cohort entering at Time 25, where the entering reading proficiency levels were comparatively low and the cohort's reading gains were noticeably constricted—a trend which appears to continue from that point forward.

RQ2: Cohort-Specific Proficiency Trends

RQ2 asked: What impact does the two-year EFL program have on cohort-specific growth trajectories for the three proficiency domains during the 20-year span? To address this question, Model 2 was tested to examine the cyclical pre-, mid-, post-program exam administrations for each proficiency domain across the 20 cohorts. The aim of this analysis was to investigate the impact of program instruction on proficiency gains between the ITP1–ITP2–ITP3 administrations, and the extent that there might be variation in growth trajectories for the different proficiency domains across cohorts. The results for Model 2 are provided in Table 7.2.

TABLE 7.2 Time series results for Model 2: cohort-specific proficiency trends

	B	$se\ B$	β	R^2
Listening				0.71★★★
Constant	42.73★★★	0.26		
Time	0.01	0.01	0.10	
ITP2	2.29★★★	0.26	0.72	
ITP3	2.91★★★	0.26	0.91	
Grammar				0.69★★★
Constant	42.71★★★	0.26		
Time	0.01	0.01	0.12	
ITP2	2.30★★★	0.29	0.71	
ITP3	2.92★★★	0.29	0.91	
Reading				0.66★★★
Constant	46.50★★★	0.48		
Time	−0.08★★★	0.01	−0.50	
ITP2	2.29★★★	0.35	0.61	
ITP3	2.54★★★	0.35	0.68	

n = 7,541; Constant = average baseline proficiency as measured by the Test of English as a Foreign Language Institutional Testing Program (TOEFL ITP) subsection; Time = proficiency trend across the 60 exam administrations; ITP2 = average gain from the first to the second administration of the TOEFL ITP subsection; ITP3 = average gain from the first to the third administration of the TOEFL ITP subsection.

★$p < 0.05$; ★★ $p < 0.01$; ★★★ $p < 0.001$.

Model 2 was significant for the three proficiency domains, confirming growth trajectories resulting from the two-year program impact across all cohorts. For listening proficiency, $R^2 = 0.71$, $F(3, 56) = 46.18$, $p < 0.001$, indicating that 71% of the variation in listening proficiency change was accounted for by the ITP cycle. While Time remained insignificant, the listening proficiency constant (B = 42.72), ITP2 (B = 2.29), and ITP3 (B = 2.91) were all found to be significant at $p < 0.001$. In other words, participants started the program with an average listening proficiency baseline of 42.73 on ITP1, subsequently gaining an average of 2.29 points on ITP2 and 2.91 points on ITP3 as they progressed through the program. This finding confirmed that there was a meaningful growth in listening pattern within the cohorts, captured by the sequential ordering of the ITP1–ITP2–ITP3 exam cycle.

For grammar proficiency, Model 2 was significant at $R^2 = 0.69$, $F(3, 54) = 51.48$, $p < 0.001$, indicating that 69% of the variation in grammar proficiency change was accounted for by the ITP cycle. While the variable Time was insignificant, the grammar proficiency constant (B = 42.71), ITP2 (B = 2.30), and ITP3 (B = 2.92) were all significant at $p < 0.01$. This means that participants started with an average grammar proficiency baseline of 42.71 on ITP1, and then gained an average of 2.30 points on ITP2 and 2.92 points on ITP3. Furthermore, this positive grammar proficiency growth trajectory for the cohorts seemingly negated the gradual significant downward trend in the overall grammar proficiency pattern observed across all exam administrations in Model 1.

For reading proficiency, Model 2 was significant at $R^2 = 0.66$, $F(3, 54) = 37.16$, $p < 0.001$, indicating that 66% of the variation in reading proficiency change was accounted for by the ITP cycle. Specifically, the constant (B = 46.50), variable Time (B = −0.08), and cycle variables of ITP2 (B = 2.29) and ITP3 (B = 2.54) were all significant at $p < 0.001$. In other words, the average reading proficiency baseline for entering cohorts was 46.50 on ITP1, followed by an average gain of 2.29 points on ITP2 and 2.54 points on ITP3. However, despite this growth trajectory for the cohorts, there remained a significant overall negative trend for reading proficiency across Time. Specifically, for every successive administration of the 60 exams, there was a 0.08 of a TOEFL ITP reading point decline, indicating an overall downward reading proficiency trend over the 20-year period.

RQ3: Event Impact on Proficiency Trends

RQ3 asked: What was the initial impact and subsequent effect of specific program-internal and -external events on patterns of proficiency growth over the 20-year period? To address this question, Model 3 used an interrupted time series approach to test and examine two potentially influential events in the program's history. Specifically, Model 3A examined the impact of the start of a new departmental undergraduate major in 2002, starting at Time 22 within the series of 60 exam administrations represented in Figures 7.2, 7.3, and 7.4. Model 3B examined the impact of national policies, referred to as *relaxed education*, that took place at the secondary education level and affected university entrants from 2006, starting at Time 34 in the proficiency series. The results for Model 3A investigating the new undergraduate Major Event are provided in Table 7.3.

Model 3A for listening proficiency was significant ($R^2 = 0.73$, $F(5, 54) = 28.76$, $p < 0.001$), indicating that the significant Constant and ITP cycle variables accounted for 73% of the variation in listening proficiency change in this model. However, the inclusion of the Major Event and Major Slope variables from Time 22 were not significant predictors in the model. Thus, the start of the new academic major in 2002 did not have any immediate impact on the listening series, nor did it significantly influence the series trend following the event.

Model 3A for grammar proficiency was significant ($R^2 = 0.79$, $F(5, 52) = 44.22$, $p < 0.001$), indicating that 79% of the variation in grammar proficiency change was accounted for by this model. Similar to Model 2, the cyclical proficiency growth pattern for the cohorts remained significant while the trend captured by Time

TABLE 7.3 Time series results for Model 3A: new major event impact

	B	se B	β	R^2
Listening				0.73★★★
Constant	42.24★★★	0.40		
Time	0.06	0.03	0.68	
ITP2	2.27★★★	0.26	0.71	
ITP3	2.87★★★	0.26	0.90	
Major event	−0.50	0.44	−0.16	
Major slope	−0.05	0.03	−0.46	
Grammar				0.79★★★
Constant	46.52★★★	0.59		
Time	−0.03	0.04	−0.22	
ITP2	1.70★★★	0.30	0.43	
ITP3	2.06★★★	0.30	0.52	
Major Event	−2.21★★★	0.59	−0.46	
Major Slope	−0.02	0.05	−0.11	
Reading				0.79★★★
Constant	45.59★★★	0.48		
Time	0.05	0.04	0.43	
ITP2	2.26★★★	0.32	0.51	
ITP3	2.44★★★	0.32	0.55	
Major Event	−3.00★★★	0.54	−0.69	
Major Slope	−0.08★	0.04	−0.50	

$n = 7,541$; Constant = average baseline proficiency as measured by the Test of English as a Foreign Language Institutional Testing Program (TOEFL ITP) subsection; Time = proficiency trend across the 60 exam administrations; ITP2 = average gain from the first to the second administration of the TOEFL ITP subsection; ITP3 = average gain from the first to the third administration of the TOEFL ITP subsection; Major Event = impact of the start of the new academic major specialization in 2002 on proficiency; Major Slope = proficiency trend captured from the start of the new major in 2002.

★$p < 0.05$, ★★ $p < 0.01$, ★★★ $p < 0.001$.

across the 60 administrations was not significant. Importantly, the addition of the Major Event at Time 22 had a significant negative impact on the grammar proficiency series (B = −2.21, $p < 0.001$), while the Major Slope variable entered to capture any meaningful subsequent change to the trend was not significant. That is, at the start of the new major in 2002, the average grammar proficiency baseline for entering cohorts was significantly reduced by 2.21 points. Although this represented a clear shock to the grammar series at the intercept, it did not yield any lasting negative effects on the grammar proficiency trend from that point forward.

Model 3A for reading proficiency was significant ($R^2 = 0.79$, $F(5, 54) = 40.10$, $p < 0.001$), indicating that 79% of the variation in reading proficiency change was accounted for by this model. While the 20-year trend captured by Time was not significant, the cohort-specific growth patterns based on the ITP cycles remained statistically significant. Most notable, however, is the finding that the addition of the Major Event at Time 22 had a significant negative impact on the baseline reading proficiency level (B = −3.00, $p < 0.001$), as well as the subsequent reading proficiency trend captured by Major Slope (B = −0.08, $p < 0.001$). In other words, at the start of the new major in 2002, the reading proficiency baseline experienced a clear negative shock to the series of a 3.00-point reduction. Moreover, the significant negative finding for Major Slope indicates that, following the start of the new major and for every successive exam administration onward, there was 0.08 of a TOEFL ITP reading point decline.

Next, interrupted time series analyses were conducted to test Model 3B and examine the potential influence of the relaxed education reforms on program proficiency trends for incoming cohorts from 2006, represented by Time 34 in the series. The results for Model 3B are provided in Table 7.4.

TABLE 7.4 Time series results for Model 3B: national policy event impact

	B	se B	β	R^2
Listening				0.72★★★
Constant	42.51★★★	0.31		
Time	0.03	0.02	0.29	
ITP2	2.28★★★	0.27	0.72	
ITP3	2.89★★★	0.27	0.91	
Policy event	−0.32	0.44	−0.12	
Policy slope	−0.02	0.03	−0.11	
Grammar				0.80★★★
Constant	47.09★★★	0.39		
Time	−0.11★★★	0.02	−0.92	
ITP2	1.79★★★	0.31	0.40	
ITP3	2.16★★★	0.31	0.48	
Policy Event	−1.29★★★	0.52	−0.31	
Policy Slope	0.12★★★	0.03	0.50	
Reading				0.71★★★
Constant	46.89★★★	0.46		
Time	−0.10★★★	0.02	−0.83	
ITP2	2.32★★★	0.37	0.53	
ITP3	2.55★★★	0.37	0.58	
Policy Event	−0.77	0.62	−0.19	
Policy Slope	0.10★★	0.04	0.43	

$n = 7{,}541$; Constant = average baseline proficiency as measured by the Test of English as a Foreign Language Institutional Testing Program (TOEFL ITP) subsection; Time = proficiency trend across the 60 exam administrations; ITP2 = average gain from the first to the second administration of the TOEFL ITP subsection; ITP3 = average gain from the first to the third administration of the TOEFL ITP subsection; Policy Event = impact of the start of the entrance of the relaxed education generation from 2006 on proficiency; Policy Slope = the proficiency trend captured from the start of the entrance of the relaxed generation in 2006.

★$p < 0.05$; ★★ $p < 0.01$; ★★★ $p < 0.001$.

As indicated in Table 7.4, Model 3B for listening proficiency was significant ($R^2 = 0.72$, $F(5, 54) = 27.64$, $p < 0.001$) for the cohort growth patterns resulting from the three ITP administrations. However, Policy Event and Policy Slope were not significant, confirming that the entrance of the relaxed education generation from 2006 had no discernible effect on the program's listening proficiency patterns.

Model 3B for grammar proficiency was also found to be significant ($R^2 = 0.80$, $F(5, 54) = 44.02$, $p < 0.001$). There was a slight downward trend for the overall grammar trend captured by Time, and the cohort-specific ITP cycle growth patterns remained significant. Furthermore, the entrance of the first relaxed education generation had a significant negative impact on the grammar proficiency trend, yielding a decrease of 1.29 points on the grammar baseline measure. Despite the initial negative impact, interestingly, a slight but significant positive trend captured by Policy Slope (B = 0.12, $p < 0.001$) emerged, revealing growth in grammar proficiency by 0.12 points for each subsequent exam in the series.

Lastly, Model 3B for reading proficiency was found to be significant ($R^2 = 0.71$, $F(5, 54) = 26.63$, $p < 0.001$). Similar to the grammar series, the cyclical ITP growth pattern for the cohorts as well as the downward trend across the 20 years remained significant. Moreover, while the relaxed education entrants did not have a meaningful initial impact on the reading series, a significant positive reading trend emerged from that point onward (B = 0.10, $p < 0.01$). Like grammar, this shows that cohorts entering the program from 2006 demonstrated a modest increase on each subsequent administration of the exam in the reading series.

Discussion

General Proficiency Trends

The expansive longitudinal design of this time series examination of EFL program proficiency outcomes revealed several key findings, which may be of particular interest to program administrators and evaluators. First, if language proficiency development is the program outcome of interest, then the results of this study indicate the value of monitoring changes for the different proficiency domains separately. While it might be more common practice to utilize exam composite scores for program-related benchmarks and decision making—for example, for program entrance, progression to next levels, and graduation—this study has demonstrated that domain-specific proficiency measures can offer more precise and useful information for formative evaluation purposes. Specifically, by utilizing the listening, grammar, and reading subsection measures of the TOEFL ITP exam, the results of this study revealed the different emerging trends for the three proficiency domains. Although all 20 cohorts experienced development in these proficiencies by the end of the two-year program, there were differences in entering proficiency levels, the extent of gains achieved, and exiting proficiency levels across cohorts. Monitoring skill-specific proficiency development would allow evaluators and administrators to have a better understanding of program curricular impact on the different domain outcomes.

Furthermore, investigating the three proficiency domains separately allowed for a clearer investigation of how emerging trends might be differentially affected by program impact and other influential factors over time. Notably, the overall grammar and reading trends were characterized by student cohorts entering and exiting the program with less proficiency over the 20 years, resulting in significant gradual decline for these two proficiency domains. This finding provides some evidence of the potential influence of changing demographics for students entering the program. In fact, the interrupted time series event impact analyses revealed that the start of the new academic major from 2002 and relaxed education entrants from 2006 significantly contributed to the initial negative impact on the reading and grammar trends. It was speculated that the new academic major might have attracted a student population with comparatively less interest and ability in English, while the relaxed education policy measures in secondary schools emphasized a shift from a literacy-based approach to a communicative approach in English instruction. Moreover, the impact of these events was likely compounded by the largest external factor influencing Japanese university student demographics—that is, the declining birth rate resulting in the shrinking population of 18-year-olds. This phenomenon has forced competition among universities to meet enrollment capacities, expanded methods of admissions, and led to increased acceptance rates of applicants. The combination of these trends has had important implications for shifts in Japanese university student demographics over time, most notably the likelihood of gradual changes in students' educational backgrounds, academic profiles, and scholastic abilities. Indeed, the observed decline in overall grammar and reading trends, as well as the negative shocks to these series observed in the impact analyses provide some support for the negative influence of factors affecting program outcomes over time.

Interestingly, while the overall grammar and reading proficiency trends experienced gradual decline, the listening proficiency series remained consistent over the 20-year period. Although earlier program cohorts demonstrated slightly higher entering listening levels, the results indicated that most cohorts achieved comparable listening levels upon completion of the program. Considering the overall downward trends observed for grammar and reading, this finding suggests that listening proficiency might develop independently of changes to student demographics. In other words, participation in courses where English is the medium of instruction, regardless of skill focus, might be sufficient to promote the development of listening proficiency. In fact, the program in this study was not only academically demanding, but it also emphasized a target language use policy—meaning that course materials, instruction, required tasks and assignments, and communication with students were predominantly in the target language. For listening development, this meant that students were regularly exposed to and required to engage in English with both teachers and classmates in all courses, regardless of the skill area focus. In stark contrast to the typical Japanese high school English class where use of the target language is minimal, students' engagement in over 330 hours of all-English coursework was likely a dominant factor in promoting listening proficiency growth across all cohorts.

The clear differences found in the emerging proficiency trends provided important practical implications for the program included in this study. While listening development was stable across time, the decline in entering literacy-related proficiencies observed and the limited gains demonstrated by more recent cohorts suggest the need for greater program impact intervention for reading and grammar development. In this case, it might be beneficial for program administrators to consider shifting the allocation of instructional focus from listening skills to an increased emphasis on literacy skill development.

Program Impact on Proficiency Outcomes

The findings demonstrated a clear and positive impact of the two-year program on proficiency gains across cohorts, as captured by the pre-, mid-, and post-program TOEFL ITP administrations. That is, all cohorts experienced significant gains for reading, grammar, and listening as they progressed through and upon completion of the two-year program. This finding has important implications for program evaluation purposes. While it is speculated that listening proficiency development might be facilitated by the intensive nature of the all-English program environment, cohorts also experienced significant reading and grammar gains over the two-year program despite overall downward trends. In this regard, the positive gains observed in each year of the program could demonstrate the additive value of course participation and instruction on development, particularly for the reading and grammar proficiency domains.

Positive program impact on literacy development is further evidenced by the emerging growth trajectories following the start of the relaxed education entrants in 2006. After the initial negative shock to the reading proficiency trend upon their entrance, significant upward trends were captured for both reading and grammar from that point onward. Although students likely started entering the program having attained less literacy ability at the secondary education level than previous cohorts, this finding suggests that the program effectively promoted development in these areas.

The cohort-specific investigation of program impact also highlights the importance for program evaluators and administrators to ensure the realized validity of program outcome measures. In this study, the third and final proficiency exam was found to be somewhat problematic. Visual inspection of the plotted aggregate means for the exams (Figures 7.2–7.4) reveals that the sharpest proficiency increases typically occurred during the first year, from ITP1 to ITP2. However, the second-year gains as measured by ITP3 were characterized by mixed results, including slight gain, no gain, and sometimes a loss. While the first and second administrations of the exam were used for program placement purposes, with likely perceived importance and value to students, the third administration was solely a post-program measure with no bearing on students' academic records or third-year departmental coursework. For this reason, it is likely that most students did not perceive any concrete need to perform well, resulting in a variable decline in mean scores on the final measure. This finding suggests that a lack of student motivation and clearly realized incentives to perform well can confound the results of the program-end exam, which is arguably the most important measure for evaluating program outcomes.

Historical Event Impact on Proficiency Outcomes

Perhaps most importantly, the findings of this extensive longitudinal study emphasize the importance of considering EFL program evaluation within the larger historical context, accounting for both the internal and external events that might impact program performance and outcomes over time. To this end, the time series regression approach was instrumental in identifying emerging patterns of program proficiency outcomes over an extended period. Further, the interrupted time series analyses allowed for specific points in time to be tested to examine the impact of institutional events and larger external influences, which were found to have both immediate and lasting influence on program proficiency outcomes. For example, the introduction of the new undergraduate major altered students' starting proficiency, which inevitably contributed to overall downward literacy trends. Understandably, institutions and departments must evolve, develop, and, in the case of Japanese universities, attempt to compete and survive by attracting more students. However, as the findings of this study suggest, such institutional decisions can sometimes have unexpected consequences on the language programs they house. Moreover, potential influences of forces external to the institution, such as the effects of national education policies or larger population trends, may also contribute to gradual undetected changes to program outcomes. Without considering the historical context of the program in this study, the administrators, or potentially and more consequentially the higher stakeholders such as institutional leadership, might be quick to attribute the observed declining proficiency trends to shortcomings in program effectiveness.

Conclusion

In sum, the time series approach demonstrated in this chapter was successful in capturing changes in proficiency trends over time, program impact on successive cohorts of learners, and the effects of macro- and micro-level factors hypothesized to have influenced program outcomes. This suggests that, as an analytical tool, the time series can play an instrumental role in longitudinal language program evaluation efforts. The cumulative picture that it provides can serve as the basis for a comprehensive understanding of the complexity of language program outcomes, taking into account the influences of the larger historical context in which language programs function.

References

Barkaoui, K. (2014). Quantitative approaches for analyzing longitudinal data in second language research. *Annual Review of Applied Linguistics, 34*, 65–101. doi:10.1017/S0267190514000105

Butler, Y. G., & Iino, M. (2005). Current Japanese reforms in English language education: The 2003 "action plan". *Language Policy, 4*(1), 25–45.

Field, A. (2009). *Discovering statistics using SPSS* (3rd ed.). London: Sage.

Goodman, R. (2010). The rapid redrawing of boundaries in Japanese higher education. *Japan Forum, 22*(1-2), 65–87.

Ministry of Education, Culture, Sports, Science, and Technology. (2012). *Daigaku no nyugaku teiine • nyugakusya suu no suii.* [Changes in university admission capacity and number of entrants.] Retrieved from www.mext.go.jp/b_menu/shingi/chukyo/chukyo4/siryo/attach/__icsFiles/afieldfile/2012/06/28/1322874_2.pdf

Ministry of Education, Culture, Sports, Science, and Technology. (2017). *Koutou kyouiku no syorai kousou ni kansuru kisode-ta.* [Basic data on the future vision of higher education.] Retrieved from www.mext.go.jp/b_menu/shingi/chukyo/chukyo4/gijiroku/__icsFiles/afieldfile/2017/04/13/1384455_02_1.pdf

Mohr, L. (1995). *Impact analysis for program evaluation* (2nd ed.). Thousand Oaks, CA: Sage.

Norris, J. M. (2009). Understanding and improving language education through program evaluation: Introduction to the special issue. *Language Teaching Research, 13*(1), 7–13. doi:10.1177/1362168808095520

Nunnery, J. A., Ross, S. M., & McDonald, A. (2006). A randomized experimental evaluation of the impact of Accelerated Reader/Reading Renaissance implementation on reading achievement in grades 3 to 6. *Journal of Education for Students Placed at Risk, 11*(1), 1–18. doi:10.1207/s15327671espr1101_1

Ono, L. (2018). *Coherence in quantitative longitudinal language program evaluation* [Doctoral dissertation, Temple University]. Temple University Electronic Theses and Dissertations.

Ross, S. J. (2005). The impact of assessment method on foreign language proficiency growth. *Applied Linguistics, 26*(3), 317–342. doi:10.1093/applin/ami011

Schafer, J. L. (1997). *Analysis of incomplete multivariate data.* London: CRC.

Shite, K. (2007). Gakuryoku Saikou: Gakusei no eigoryoku no genjyou to kanrensasete no Ichikousatsu. [A reconsideration of scholastic proficiency: A discussion regarding students' English academic performance.] *Kanagawa University International Management Review, 34*, 109–118.

Singer, J. D., & Willett, J. B. (2003). *Applied longitudinal data analysis: Modeling change and event occurrence.* New York, NY: Oxford University Press.

Tabachnick B. G., & Fidell, L. S. (2013). *Using multivariate statistics* (6th ed.). New York, NY: Pearson.

8

CURRICULAR INNOVATION IMPACT ANALYSIS

Parallel Process Growth Curve Models

Atsuko Nishitani

Background of the Study

The number of colleges and universities in Japan has doubled during the past 50 years, from 389 in 1971 to 795 in 2020 (Obunsha Educational Information Center, 2020). Now more than 50% of high school graduates advance on to four-year universities, and more than 80% go to some kind of higher educational institution, including junior colleges and technical/vocational schools. Reasons for the increase in institutions are complex, given the fact that Japan has been experiencing a low birthrate, and universities, consequently, have been facing a decline in the population of 18-year-olds. Between the years of 2010 and 2018, 21 universities closed down due to a shortage of applicants ("Chihou shidai no heikou aitsugu," 2019). In 2019, more than 30% of private universities had insufficient enrollment (Promotion and Mutual Aid Corporations for Private Schools of Japan, 2019). In order to survive this difficult situation, many universities are attempting new strategies to attract high school graduates: they start new programs, advertise their graduates' employment rates, and lower their standards for admission.

One of the main concerns for prospective students is the number of job opportunities that they would have upon graduation. In Japan, companies hire new graduates in a fixed hiring season, and the new employees uniformly start their jobs on the first day of April, which is the first day of a new fiscal year. This system requires students to find employment while still attending university, as it is more difficult to get full-time employment after graduation. Thus, the employment rate for graduates is an important factor for high school graduates in selecting a university. Indeed, most universities advertise the fact that they maintain a supportive career center to assist their graduates to find employment. It has been said that universities in Japan are more like preparatory schools for employment than

DOI: 10.4324/9781003087939-9

centers of higher learning (McVeigh, 2002). Recently Japanese industry and the government started to call for universities to foster globally competitive human resources, and consequently many colleges and universities have started to reform their English as a foreign language (EFL) curriculum to appeal to both prospective students and to industry (Bradford & Brown, 2018; Hashimoto, 2018).

Japanese universities have had a long-standing research-centered academic culture, even for foreign language instruction (Yamada, 2014). Professors in Japan have for generations tended to see English as literature in translation and placed emphasis on reading and writing so that students could at least read and write academic papers in English. English classes used to be taught by literature professors, and "this legacy continues to some extent with many university EFL classes centered around reading passages" (Jones, 2019, p. 25). The grammar-translation method has been widely used in such courses. Although native speakers of English have often been hired to teach communication courses, many universities have not invested in systematically developing students' communicative skills. As a result, communication courses are often not coordinated program-wide and lack much accountability (McVeigh, 2002). Such a division of labor model between Japanese faculty and native foreign language instructors is commonly seen in EFL programs in Japan, and until recently, universities typically offered conversation courses taught by native speakers of English and reading/grammar courses taught by Japanese teachers "with no specific common goal" for proficiency development (Tokunaga, 2008, p. 270).

The seeds of change were sown in 1979 when the Ministry of Trade and Industry contracted with Educational Testing Service to design an EFL proficiency test in the domain of business English. After decades of gradual adoption, many companies in Japan use the scores of the Test of English for International Communication (TOEIC)[1] as part of their initial hiring decisions, determining promotions, or assigning employees to overseas posts. Consonant with the description of universities as preparation for employment, an increasing number of Japanese universities are offering TOEIC preparation courses to improve students' scores so that they may have a better chance of getting desirable jobs. In this way, universities also intend to set clear foreign language proficiency goals for students and motivate them (Brock, 2006). The test has gained popularity, and in 2019, over 2.2 million people took the TOEIC test, and about 2,900 organizations worldwide used test results for human resources decision making and program monitoring (Institute for International Business Communication, 2020).

The university in this study reformed its two-year compulsory EFL program for non-English majors in 2013 in response to the government's request for universities to foster globally competent human resources. By doing so, the university intended to receive grants from the government, which is often an incentive for many universities to reform their foreign language curriculum. Because the Ministry of Education, Culture, Sports, and Science and Technology (MEXT), the successor of the Ministry of Trade and Industry, called for universities to assure instructional quality with measurable outcome indicators (Bradford & Brown, 2018; Hashimoto, 2018), the university decided to implement TOEIC-based courses so that the TOEIC scores could be used as measures of educational outcomes and students could use the scores in seeking future employment.

Before the curriculum reform, students had a choice of enrolling in: (1) an oral communication course and a reading course; (2) an oral communication or a reading course, and another foreign language course; or (3) foreign language courses other than English – notably, in languages for which no end-of-instruction proficiency indicators were available. In the former English courses (i.e., oral communication and reading), students had to do extensive reading, which was one of the selling points of the program. In the new program, however, students have no choice but to enroll in English courses: Communication and TOEIC preparation courses. The extensive reading program was discontinued because it appeared insufficient for improving both listening and reading proficiencies as measured on the TOEIC test. Students enrolled in the compulsory EFL courses are non-English majors, many of whom are not primarily interested in foreign languages and were found to be less motivated to engage with the graded readers prepared for the extensive reading program, as such materials often appeared childish to college-age students. From the students' perspective, extensive reading in English had less utility than preparation for employment. As a result, the new curriculum was implemented to have the non-English majors be exposed to a syllabus focused on TOEIC-type materials, which use everyday workplace English. Designers of the new curriculum hoped that the TOEIC test could become a motivator for non-English majors to study English.

The TOEIC preparation courses, which are taught by Japanese teachers, are focused on reading in the first and third semesters and listening in the second and fourth semesters. The Communication courses are taught by native speakers of English, which is the same division of labor as in the old curriculum, with a few modifications. In the old curriculum, teachers were allowed to choose from a list of recommended textbooks, and final examinations were listening tests. In the new curriculum, coordinators of the Communication courses choose textbooks for each level, and interview tests are administered as final examinations. Teacher training sessions are conducted once or twice a year, which is the same as in the TOEIC preparation courses. Given the fact that the Institutional version of the TOEIC test has listening and reading/structure subtests, listening is taught in both courses; however, one is TOEIC-focused, and the other is communication-focused. Writing is lightly taught in the Communication courses.

After the curriculum reform, evaluation of the impact became necessary. As mentioned above, the MEXT called for universities to provide quality assurance, and the TOEIC test was introduced into the new curriculum so that it would be easier to evaluate the effects of the program by comparing pre- and post-instruction scores. Actually, many universities have chosen the TOEIC test as the criterion outcome for the measurement of the effects of their English programs.

Oftentimes university administrators show on their websites how much their students' TOEIC scores have improved and claim how effective their English programs are by showing "before" and "after" test outcomes. Such an approach is not enough as the basis for an evaluation of a curricular change such as the one described in this chapter. When evaluating the effectiveness of the curriculum, it is necessary to compare which part of the division of labor aspect of the program (e.g., listening/speaking classes by native speakers or reading/writing classes by Japanese teachers) is relatively effective on the skill domains they address.

Design

The primary goal of the analyses to follow is to assess the impact of the division-of-labor EFL curriculum. Conventionally, a repeated-measures analysis of variance (ANOVA) is used to examine the change over time (Duncan et al., 2011; Schumacker & Lomax, 2016). The shortcoming of the repeated-measures approach is that it is focused exclusively on group means. This study employed latent growth curve modeling, which has the advantage of including variation in individual learners' change trajectories over the repeated measures, as well as group-level predictors of variation in those trajectories. Ross (2005) used latent growth curve modeling to investigate the degree to which changes in achievement co-varied with growth in language proficiency at a Japanese university program. The present study expands on the growth prediction model approach used by Ross to include parallel growth processes. Each component of the curriculum (i.e., Communication and TOEIC preparation) in the new program produces four time-varying course grades, which are achievement indicators in the form of grades given by instructors, and three time-varying proficiency tests, which indicate starting proficiency and growth in proficiency over the course of the two-year program. The four achievement measures and the three proficiency measures are analyzed to examine their relationships on growth in proficiency in reading and listening. More specifically, this study aims to answer the following research questions:

1. Does initial high proficiency in listening and reading lead to a more rapid growth in proficiency over the course of the two-year program?
2. Do students who achieve higher grades in the first semester demonstrate a more rapid growth in achievement over two years?
3. Do initially proficient students achieve higher grades in the first semester?
4. Do initially proficient students demonstrate a more rapid growth in achievement over time?
5. Do students who achieve higher grades in the first semester demonstrate a more rapid growth in proficiency over time?
6. Does growth in achievement lead to a positive change in proficiency over the course of the two-year program?

Participants

Four cohorts of students at a Japanese university participated in this study. The compulsory EFL program that they enrolled in was for freshmen and sophomores, ranging from 18 to 20 years of age. The total number of the participants was 4,673 (3,024 males and 1,649 females). The actual number of students who were enrolled in EFL courses at the university was much larger, but: (1) those who majored in English or International Relations were exempted from the program; (2) those who were placed in the lowest proficiency level progressed through a different curriculum than the other levels and thus were not included in this study; (3) those whose scores on the placement test (i.e., the TOEIC Bridge test) were higher or lower than the scores listed in the TOEIC Bridge–TOEIC conversion table, which will be discussed later, were not included either; and (4) those with missing data were also excluded, for the purpose of this study. In addition, there was a small subset of students who reached a criterion score on the TOEIC test in the middle of the program and were thus exempted from further instruction and testing. In sum, participants of this study were those who stayed in the program for the whole two years, had no missing data, had the initial TOEIC Bridge test scores within the range listed in the TOEIC Bridge–TOEIC conversion table, and were not placed in the lowest proficiency level. They met once (90 minutes) a week for each course (i.e., Communication and TOEIC preparation), 15 weeks per semester, for four semesters for a total of 90 hours of classroom instruction.

Proficiency Measures

The TOEIC Bridge test was administered as a placement test before the two-year program, and students were streamed into four proficiency levels. However, as mentioned above, those who were placed in the lowest level were not included in this study, which means that the participants of this study were placed in three proficiency levels. The Institutional version of the TOEIC test was administered at the end of the first year and also at the end of the second year as a final examination of the TOEIC preparation courses. The TOEIC test is a two-hour, multiple-choice test of English that consists of 100 listening questions and 100 reading questions. Scores for each section (i.e., listening and reading) are presented on a scale of 5–495, and the total scores add up to a scale of 10–990. The TOEIC Bridge test was developed for beginners to lower-intermediate learners and is shorter and easier than the TOEIC test. It is a one-hour, multiple-choice test that consists of 50 listening questions and 50 reading questions. The TOEIC Bridge test was redesigned and launched in June, 2019, but the tests used in this study were old versions, and its maximum score was 180 (90 each on listening and reading). It would have been ideal to administer the TOEIC test as a placement test as well so that the results of the three administrations of the test would be more comparable, but the university decided that the TOEIC Bridge test would be more appropriate for a placement test, since the TOEIC test cannot differentiate lower-level students well. In sum, each participant had a TOEIC Bridge test score as a pre-test indicator and two TOEIC test scores as mid- and post-test indicators.

As mentioned above, the TOEIC Bridge scores were converted into TOEIC scores. Table 8.1 is the conversion table provided by the Educational Testing Service (n.d.), which developed these tests. Because the TOEIC Bridge scores listed here range from 44 to 80, students whose placement test scores were below 44 or above 80 on either section were excluded from the study.

TABLE 8.1 TOEIC Bridge–TOEIC score conversion

Bridge L/R	44	50	56	62	68	74	80
TOEIC L	150	160	180	200	230	270	325
TOEIC R	90	100	110	120	140	180	235

TOEIC = Test of English for International Communication; L = listening; R = reading.

Achievement Measures

Final grades of each course were used as achievement measures. The participants enrolled in both Communication and TOEIC preparation courses for four semesters; thus, each participant had four grades for each course at the end of the two-year program. The maximum score of the Communication courses was 100, but that of the TOEIC preparation courses was 60. The mid- and post-TOEIC tests were used as final examinations for the second and fourth semesters of the TOEIC preparation courses, and they accounted for 40% of the final grades. Because the TOEIC test scores were also used as proficiency measures, they could not be included in achievement measures. Therefore, the remaining 60% of the grades based on homework, quizzes, and class participation was used as an achievement indicator for the TOEIC preparation courses. The TOEIC test was not administered at the end of the first and third semesters, and different multiple-choice tests made by the faculty were used as final examinations; however, their scores were also excluded from the study for consistency so that all four achievement scores for the TOEIC preparation courses would sum to 60. Table 8.2 summarizes the types of data used in this study.

TABLE 8.2 Measures of proficiency and achievement

	Placement	Semester 1	Semester 2	Semester 3	Semester 4
Proficiency	TOEIC Bridge		TOEIC 1		TOEIC 2
Achievement		Grade 1	Grade 2	Grade 3	Grade 4

TOEIC = Test of English for International Communication.

Analyses and Results

One-Way Repeated-Measures ANOVA

First, a one-way repeated measures ANOVA was conducted using IBM SPSS Statistics (Version 27). Table 8.3 shows the means and standard deviations for the listening scores, the reading scores, the Communication course grades, and the TOEIC preparation course grades. As mentioned above, the pre-test was the TOEIC Bridge test, and the scores listed in the table as pre-test scores are converted TOEIC-scale scores.

TABLE 8.3 Means (M) and standard deviations (SD) for proficiency scores and grades

	Listening		Reading	
	M	sd	M	sd
Pre-test	208.01	25.50	153.98	31.10
Mid-test	230.26	39.40	162.33	35.90
Post-test	254.19	43.40	177.62	40.96
	Communication		TOEIC Preparation	
	M	sd	M	sd
First semester	78.00	8.52	47.18	0.13
Second semester	76.58	8.44	46.03	0.14
Third semester	78.02	9.32	45.91	0.14
Fourth semester	77.37	9.85	44.41	0.13

TOEIC = Test of English for International Communication.
The maximum scores for the Communication courses and the TOEIC preparation courses were 100 and 60, respectively.

Both repeated-measures ANOVAs with a Greenhouse–Geisser correction on the listening and reading scores showed a significant main effect (F (2, 6,896) = 2,090.90, p < 0.001, partial η^2 = 0.39; and F (2, 6,896) = 590.48, p < 0.001, partial η^2 = 0.15, respectively), which indicates that there was a steady growth trajectory for both listening and reading proficiency over the course of the two-year program. While listening had a linear trend (F (1, 3,448) = 4,143.44, p < 0.001, partial η^2 = 0.55), reading had both linear and quadratic trends (F (1, 3,448) = 1,108.69, p < 0.001, partial η^2 = 0.24; and F (1, 3,448) = 34.29, p < 0.001, partial η^2 = 0.01, respectively).

Repeated-measures ANOVAs with a Greenhouse–Geisser correction on the Communication course grades and the TOEIC preparation course grades also showed a significant main effect (F (3, 10,347) = 28.40, p < 0.001, partial η^2 = 0.01;

and F (3, 10,347) = 113.43, p < 0.001, η^2 = 0.03, respectively), which also indicates that there was a steady change pattern for both courses. However, the Communication courses had negative quadratic and cubic trends (F (1, 3,449) = 12.93, p < 0.001, partial η^2 = 0.004; and F (1, 3,449) = 91.50, p < 0.001, η^2 = 0.03, respectively), and the TOEIC preparation courses had negative linear and cubic trends (F (1, 3,449) = 247.98, p < 0.001, partial η^2 = 0.07; and F (1, 3,449) = 27.52, p < 0.001, η^2 = 0.01, respectively). Figure 8.1 shows the change trajectories of each course.

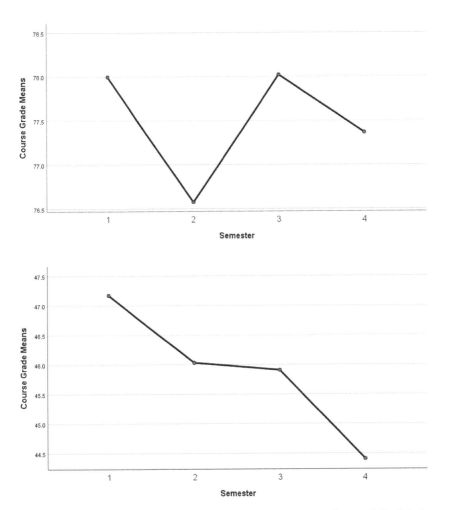

FIGURE 8.1 Means plots of grades of Communication (top) and Test of English for International Communication (TOEIC) preparation (bottom) courses.

It is not surprising to see that course grades tend to go down over time. In Japan, there is a pervasive view that university students lack academic motivation (Manalo et al., 2006). Japanese high school students study extremely hard to pass university entrance examinations, and once they gain admission to a university, they lack incentives for further study. Freshmen often have high motivation in the first semester, but soon they are influenced by numerous campus social opportunities and part-time jobs and eventually lose motivation (Kikuchi, 2015). They also tend to suffer from "May disease," which is a term to describe the onset of apathy a few months after matriculation and a purposeless depressed state of mind that university students experience in May. The fiscal and academic year begins in April in Japan. Not only new students but also newly hired workers feel fresh and motivated at the beginning of April, but they soon face difficulties adjusting to a new environment and are said to lose motivation after Golden Week, which is the longest (5–10-day) national holiday in early May. Many students start skipping classes and plot strategies for getting passing grades with the minimum of effort. As previously mentioned, one of the purposes of the curriculum redesign and inclusion of the TOEIC preparation courses is to keep students motivated because the scores could help them find employment later, but in reality, freshmen and sophomores probably cannot see job hunting as an immediate concern and thus lose motivation for foreign language study easily.

Latent Growth Curve Models

Latent growth curve modeling was carried out using IBM SPSS Amos (Version 27). The growth model approach is often used to investigate individual differences in change over time, and has become a viable alternative to a repeated-measures ANOVA (Tomarken & Waller, 2005). Little (2013) describes growth curve models as follows:

> the focus is on intra-individual (within-person) change; each person typically has an intercept and slope parameter that characterizes his or her growth trend over the course of a study. Growth curve models address questions about the rate of change and the shape of change that characterizes a sample of persons. ... the growth curve model characterizes the set of intercepts and slopes for all participants into a mean intercept with a distribution of intercept values and a mean slope with a distribution of slope values (p. 249).

According to Newsome (2015), growth curve modeling has become the most popular method for analyzing longitudinal data; it is a flexible approach that allows for investigation of both linear and non-linear trends, and it is used to "investigate the relationship between latent predictor variables on growth, the effects of growth on other factors, mediational hypotheses, and modeling of parallel growth curves" (p. 171).

In this study, each indicator (i.e., proficiency in listening and reading; and achievement in the Communication and TOEIC preparation courses) was first applied to a univariate latent growth curve model separately in order to examine its own growth and model fit. Because the results of repeated-measures ANOVAs indicated that the changes in achievement (i.e., course grades) were not linear, the first and last slope parameters were fixed as 0 and 1, respectively, and the second and third slope parameters were left free.

The model fit was measured by three indices: chi-square (χ^2), comparative fit index (CFI), and root mean square error of approximation (RMSEA). The chi-square value represents the discrepancy between the perfect-fit model and the hypothesized model – the bigger the probability value, the better the model fit (Blunch, 2013; Bollen, 1989; Byrne, 2016; Xie & Andrews, 2012). However, the chi-square test is sensitive to sample size, and a hypothesized model tends to get rejected if the sample size is large; therefore, other fit indices such as CFI and RMSEA are commonly used to evaluate the model fit (Blunch, 2013; Newsome, 2015). CFI values larger than 0.95 indicate a good fit. As for RMSEA, values less than 0.05 indicate a good fit, values as high as 0.08 are considered a reasonable fit, and values between 0.8 and 1.0 indicate an acceptable fit. Akaike Information Criterion (AIC) values were also examined to determine a better model. Figure 8.2 shows the final hypothesized models.

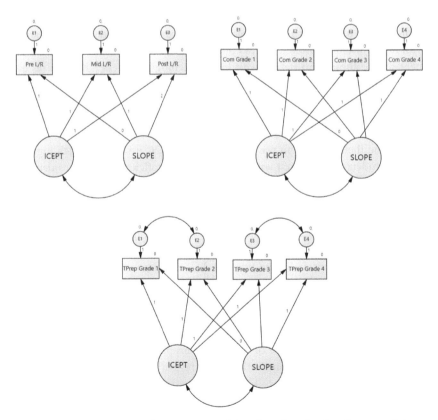

FIGURE 8.2 Latent growth curve models for listening/reading proficiency, Communication achievement, and Test of English for International Communication (TOEIC) preparation achievement.

Except for the listening proficiency model, the χ^2 statistics were significant due to the large sample size. However, the CFI values indicated a good fit in all models, and the RMSEA values indicated a good fit in the proficiency models ($\chi^2 = 0.271$, $df = 1$, $p = 0.603$, CFI $= 1.000$, RMSEA $= 0.000$ for listening; and $\chi^2 = 5.555$, $df = 1$, $p < 0.05$, CFI $= 0.998$, RMSEA $= 0.031$ for reading), and an acceptable fit in the achievement models ($\chi^2 = 109.384$, $df = 3$, $p < 0.001$, CFI $= 0.967$, RMSEA $= 0.087$ for Communication; and $\chi^2 = 20.966$, $df = 1$, $p < 0.001$, CFI $= 0.994$, RMSEA $= 0.065$ for TOEIC preparation).

For listening proficiency, the mean intercept (i.e., the average starting point) was 207.379, and the mean slope (i.e., the average change rate) was 21.879. Both were significant ($p < 0.001$). This indicates that the students started with an average score of 207.379, and their scores increased by an average score of 21.879 for each retest. The variances for both the intercept and slope were statistically significant ($p < 0.001$), which indicates that both the initial listening proficiency and the rate of change over time varied across students. The covariance between the intercept and slope was 22.948, and their correlation was not significant ($r = 0.088$, $p = 0.142$), which suggests that the students' initial listening proficiency and their changes over time were not related. In other words, the students who started with higher listening proficiency did not necessarily demonstrate a higher rate of increase, and those who started with lower listening proficiency did not necessarily demonstrate a slower increase in gains.

For reading proficiency, the mean intercept was 153.255 ($p < 0.001$), and the mean slope was 11.271 ($p < 0.001$). The variances for both the intercept and slope were significant ($p < 0.001$). The covariance between the intercept and slope was 52.101, and their correlation was significant ($r = 0.426$, $p < 0.01$), which suggests that the students who started with higher reading proficiency tended to demonstrate a higher rate of increase, and those who started with lower reading proficiency tended to demonstrate a slower increase.

The model for the Communication courses showed that the mean intercept was 77.846 ($p < 0.001$), and the mean slope was -0.461 ($p < 0.05$). The variances for both the intercept and slope were significant ($p < 0.001$). The covariance between the intercept and slope was -24.297, and their correlation was significant ($r = -0.503$, $p < 0.001$). A negative correlation coupled with a negative slope suggests that higher initial levels are associated with a more rapid decrease (Newsome, 2015), so this result suggests that students who achieved higher grades in the Communication courses in the first semester tended to demonstrate a steeper decline over the course of two years. This phenomenon is often observed in Japanese university programs – those starting with higher proficiency tend to regress to the mean faster.

The model for the TOEIC preparation courses showed that the mean intercept and the mean slope were 48.752 and -4.174, respectively, and both were significant ($p < 0.001$). The variances for the intercept and slope were both significant ($p < 0.001$). The covariance between the intercept and slope was -9.162, and their correlation was significant ($r = -0.404$, $p < 0.001$), which suggests that students who achieved higher grades in the TOEIC preparation courses at the end of the first semester tended to demonstrate a steeper decline over the course of two years, in a pattern similar to the Communication courses.

Parallel-Process Growth Models

After examining each model individually, proficiency growth models and achievement growth models were combined into four parallel process growth models: listening proficiency–Communication achievement, listening proficiency–TOEIC preparation achievement, reading proficiency–Communication achievement, and reading proficiency–TOEIC preparation achievement. A parallel process model analyzes changes across two or more domains when those domains are measured at the same points in time (Kline, 2016). It can examine whether the initial status and the rate of change in one domain influence those in another domain. As seen in Figure 8.3, the parallel process models tested in this study assessed the following four paths: (1) the effect of the initial proficiency status on the initial achievement status; (2) the effect of the initial proficiency status on the achievement growth; (3) the effect of the initial achievement status on the proficiency growth; and (4) the effect of the achievement growth on the proficiency growth.

All four models fit the data well. Although the χ^2 statistics were significant due to the large sample size, other model fit statistics indicated a good or reasonable fit. In the listening proficiency–Communication achievement model, $\chi^2 = 158.79$, $df = 12$, $p < 0.001$, CFI $= 0.975$, and RMSEA $= 0.051$. In the reading proficiency–Communication achievement model, $\chi^2 = 127.874$, $df = 12$, $p < 0.001$, CFI $= 0.978$, and RMSEA $= 0.045$. In the listening proficiency–TOEIC preparation achievement model, $\chi^2 = 119.311$, $df = 10$, $p < 0.001$, CFI $= 0.980$, and RMSEA $= 0.048$. In the reading proficiency–TOEIC preparation achievement model, $\chi^2 = 144.220$, $df = 10$, $p < 0.001$, CFI $= 0.975$, and RMSEA $= 0.054$.

Table 8.4 presents the results of the four parallel process growth models. The listening proficiency–Communication achievement model revealed that three paths were significant: the effect of the initial listening proficiency on the initial achievement (path a in Figure 8.3), the effect of the initial achievement on the listening proficiency growth (path c), and the effect of the achievement growth on the listening proficiency growth (path d). Only the effect of the initial listening proficiency on the growth in achievement was not significant (path b). This suggests that the students with high initial listening proficiency achieved high grades in the first semester of the Communication courses, but the initial listening proficiency had no influence on the growth in achievement. Because the mean of the growth in proficiency was negative, positive paths from the initial achievement and the achievement growth suggest that the students who achieved higher grades in the first semester and those who had greater improvement in their course grades tended to demonstrate less decline in listening proficiency.

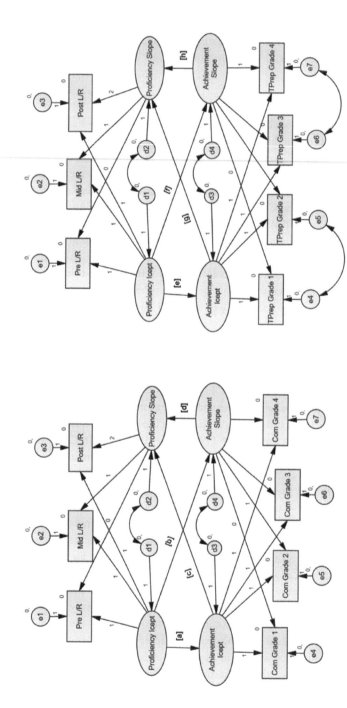

FIGURE 8.3 Parallel process growth model for Communication achievement–proficiency, and Test of English for International Communication (TOEIC) preparation achievement–proficiency.

TABLE 8.4 Means and standardized path coefficients of four parallel process growth models

Predictor		Listening				Reading			
		M	AI	AS	PS	M	AI	AS	PS
Communication	PI	207.382***	0.321***			153.257***	0.228***		
	PS	−21.899**		−0.018		−19.986**		−0.028	
	AI	54.153***			0.273***	66.238***			0.385***
	AS	1.155			0.218***	1.242			0.305***
TOEIC Preparation	PI	207.378***	−0.102***			153.251***	0.089*		
	PS	9.130*		0.011		−16.700***		−0.333***	
	AI	54.780***			0.114***	44.956***			0.623***
	AS	−4.677*			0.136*	6.735***			0.616**

TOEIC = Test of English for International Communication.

PI = proficiency intercept; PS = proficiency slope; AI = achievement intercept; AS = achievement slope. The maximum scores for the Communication courses and the TOEIC-preparation courses were 100 and 60, respectively. * $p < 0.05$; ** $p < 0.01$; *** $p < 0.001$.

Although the Communication courses are not focused on reading, the relationship between reading proficiency and achievement in the Communication courses was also examined. It is often said that the four language skills are interrelated; therefore, it would be beneficial to check if improvement in listening and speaking skills could influence reading proficiency. The findings were similar to those of the listening–Communication model. Three paths were significant: the effect of initial reading proficiency on the initial achievement (path a), the effect of the initial achievement on the reading proficiency growth (path c), and the effect of the achievement growth on the reading proficiency growth (path d). The effect of the initial reading proficiency on the growth in achievement was not significant (path b). This suggests that the students with high initial reading proficiency achieved high grades in the first semester of the Communication courses, but the initial reading proficiency was not associated with the achievement growth. The mean of the growth in reading proficiency was negative, so the positive paths from the initial achievement and the achievement growth suggest that the students who achieved higher grades in the first semester and those who had greater improvement in their course grades tended to demonstrate less decline in reading proficiency as well as listening proficiency.

The listening–TOEIC preparation model also revealed that three paths were significant: the effect of the initial listening proficiency on the initial achievement (path e), the effect of the initial achievement on the listening proficiency growth (path g), and the effect of the achievement growth on the listening proficiency growth (path h). As with the Communication models, the effect of the initial listening proficiency on the growth in achievement was the only insignificant path in this model (path f). The findings suggest that the students with higher initial listening proficiency received lower grades in the first semester of the TOEIC preparation courses ($\beta = -0.102$), but the initial listening proficiency was not associated with the growth (or decrease) in achievement. In contrast, the students who achieved higher grades in the first semester and those who had greater improvement in their course grades demonstrated a more rapid growth in listening proficiency.

The reading–TOEIC preparation model revealed that all four paths were significant. The findings suggest that the students with higher initial reading proficiency achieved higher grades in the first semester of the TOEIC preparation courses; however, the initial high proficiency in reading led to less growth in the course grades over two years ($\beta = -0.333$). The mean growth in reading proficiency was negative, so positive paths from the initial achievement and the achievement growth suggest that the initial high achievers and those who improved the course grades over two years tended to demonstrate less decline in reading proficiency.

Discussion

This study examined the longitudinal co-development of achievement and proficiency among Japanese university students who enrolled in a two-year compulsory

EFL program. The univariate latent growth curve models revealed that the initial proficiency had a positive impact on reading proficiency improvement but no impact on listening proficiency improvement. Because both listening and reading proficiency had a positive slope on average, the findings could suggest that the program improved students' listening proficiency regardless of their initial level, but for the purpose of improving students' reading proficiency, the program was more beneficial to those who were initially more proficient in reading. Although the students were streamed into classes based on their initial proficiency and thus were supposed to receive appropriate level-specific instruction, the findings suggest that the classes for lower-level students were not effective enough to improve their reading proficiency. A number of interpretations are possible – the lingering effects of the "May Disease," a fault in the selection of appropriate teaching materials, or too few hours of instruction to substantively affect proficiency changes.

The findings also revealed that the course grades tended to decline over time in both courses, but higher achievers in the first semester tended to demonstrate a steeper decline. As previously mentioned, Japanese university students may have high motivation initially, but soon they are influenced by part-time jobs, social activities, and other non-academic interests. It should also be mentioned that negative peer pressure often affects serious students. Students often make fun of hard-working peers. If the initial achievers are affected by these social factors and lose motivation, then their drops in grades would appear precipitous in relation to their initial grades. Therefore, this result might simply confirm that even higher achievers in the first semester, who seem to have survived the onset of "May Disease," gradually lose motivation over the course of two years. Although possible explanations for the results of univariate models are presented, the findings also revealed that there were significant increases in students' proficiency trajectories, which suggests that further investigation was necessary. Thus, the growth of achievement and the growth of proficiency were tested in parallel process growth models.

The parallel process growth models revealed that initial high proficiency seems to work as an advantage in the first semester in general. However, the initial listening proficiency had a negative influence on the initial achievement in the TOEIC preparation courses. This result was not so surprising because the TOEIC preparation courses were focused on reading during the first semester, and listening was not taught until the second semester. It is possible that the students with high listening proficiency were not motivated to improve their reading and thus achieved low grades in the courses. In fact, returnee students, those who have studied English in high school while abroad, often struggle with grammar and reading in the courses, but do not seem to care because they are satisfied with their relatively higher listening and speaking abilities compared to their peers. In addition, non-English majors might not perceive the need to prepare for a career that will require English proficiency, and thus may not feel it necessary to study grammar or reading.

In contrast, the initial reading proficiency had a positive influence on the initial achievement in the Communication courses, even though the courses were not focused on reading. In general, university freshmen who have high reading proficiency are those who studied English seriously for six years in junior and senior high schools. They are usually initially motivated to study and have a good grounding in English; therefore, they may have made efforts in the Communication courses in a manner similar to the way they did in high school courses and thus achieved relatively high grades. It is also possible that they enjoyed speaking courses taught by native English speakers after studying seriously with Japanese teachers in high school and thus were motivated to do well in class.

Initial proficiency may work as an advantage, at least in the first semester, if the course content is focused on the same language skill (e.g., students with high listening proficiency in listening courses). However, if the course content is focused on a different skill (e.g., students with high listening proficiency in reading courses), it could be motivation, not initial proficiency, that helps students achieve high grades; as Duckworth et al. (2007) found, university students who were "gritty" (i.e., motivated, passionate, and persistent) earned higher grade point averages (GPAs) than their less gritty peers did, and smarter students tended to be slightly less gritty. The present study also found that initial proficiency generally had no influence on the growth of achievement. As just discussed above, it had some influence in the first semester to a certain extent, but it did not last. In order for students to keep receiving good grades, they have to take coursework seriously and keep studying hard, but it is difficult for non-English majors to stay motivated to study English for the reasons previously mentioned. It is disappointing to find that the students who were initially proficient in reading demonstrated a steeper decline in achievement in the TOEIC preparation courses over time. Again, students who have high reading proficiency are usually those who studied hard in junior and senior high schools in order to pass university entrance examinations. It is possible that such students lose motivation to study for yet another test, the TOEIC test.

The findings also revealed that course grades in the first semester had a positive influence on the proficiency growth. The students who achieved high grades in the first semester of the Communication courses demonstrated less decline in listening or reading proficiency, and the initial low achievers demonstrated a steeper decline in proficiency. In the TOEIC preparation courses, those who achieved high grades in the first semester gained in listening proficiency more, and their reading proficiency declined less over two years, compared to initial low achievers. The findings suggest that the program was more beneficial to the initial high achievers. Because the courses were designed on the assumption that students would successfully complete the previous course(s) before moving on to the next, it is possible that the students who did not do well in the first semester found it difficult to keep up with increasingly difficult classes in the following semesters and thus demonstrated a greater decrease in proficiency.

The main focus of this study was the significant paths from the achievement growth to the proficiency growth, which would indicate the effects of the program. The findings revealed that both Communication and TOEIC preparation courses had a positive impact on both listening and reading proficiency – the more the increase in achievement, the more the sustainment or increase in proficiency. The students who took the coursework seriously and met teachers' expectations over two years outperformed those who did not. In Japan, it is often said that students have the highest academic skills and knowledge when entering university and start losing them soon thereafter. Not only improving but even maintaining students' proficiency is difficult in Japan, especially when there is no immediate practical need for English. The new EFL program seems to have benefited the students who seriously worked on the coursework, which suggests that the course contents per se were effective. Because the TOEIC preparation courses taught both listening and reading, it was expected that the courses would improve both listening and reading proficiency. On the other hand, the Communication courses taught listening but not reading; therefore, they were expected to improve students' listening proficiency but not reading proficiency. However, the findings indicated that the achievement growth in the Communication courses also had a positive influence on the growth in reading proficiency, which could be because the students had to enroll in both Communication and TOEIC preparation courses concurrently, and the two courses may have created a synergistic effect. It is also possible that the high achievers are generally those who are highly motivated and thus study hard in both Communication and TOEIC preparation courses.

In order to investigate the difference in effects of the courses, the coefficients of the paths from the achievement growth to the proficiency growth were compared. The Communication courses show a larger impact on the listening proficiency growth than the TOEIC preparation courses, as might be expected from syllabus content and focus. For the reading proficiency growth, on the other hand, the impact of the TOEIC preparation courses is twice the size of that of the Communication courses. The findings suggest that the courses taught by native speakers of English had a more positive impact on students' listening proficiency than the courses taught by Japanese teachers did, and the courses taught by Japanese teachers had a more positive impact on students' reading proficiency than the courses taught by native English speakers. The division-of-labor curriculum seems to have been working as planned.

Conclusion

This study investigated the effects of a compulsory EFL program by examining the relationship between achievement and proficiency. Parallel process growth curve models indicated that both Communication and TOEIC preparation courses had a positive impact on students' growth in listening and reading proficiency. It was also revealed that the division of labor was generally effective, and the Communication courses taught by native speakers of English influenced students' listening proficiency more positively, while the TOEIC preparation courses taught by Japanese teachers influenced students' reading proficiency more positively. The findings also suggest that motivation could be another important factor. High achievers in class are usually those who stay motivated, and they did outperform the low achievers in terms of proficiency gain. The course contents seem to work effectively for high achievers, so the next issue that the program has to consider would be how to motivate lower-proficiency students.

There are several limitations in this study. First, the pre-test was the TOEIC Bridge test, while the mid- and post-tests were the TOEIC test. Although they were developed by the same testing organization and the official score conversion table is available, the use of converted scores made the results less reliable. This study was not an experimental design, and the data analyzed were from the existing program data archives. Using the TOEIC test for a pre-test was not an available option. Future research should use the same test for all pre-, mid-, and post-tests, if it is allowed, so that more reliable results would be yielded. Still, this study demonstrated how to make the most of what was available.

Second, the use of the TOEIC Bridge test created other disadvantages in this study. Again, the use of converted scores makes the results less reliable, and thus other factors that could further cloud the results had to be addressed. More specifically, the students whose TOEIC Bridge scores were below or above the scores listed in the official conversion table and those who had missing data were excluded from the study. High-proficiency students who tested out in the middle of the program were also excluded. Kline (2016) states that missing values that are less than 5% in the total data need not be a concern, but the number of students who were excluded from this study was 39% of the data. As Ross (2005) pointed out, list-wise deletion may omit crucial data and could lead to biased conclusions, making it difficult to evaluate the program properly. The use of the same test for all pre-, mid-, and post-tests would have mitigated the problem. It is also recommended that data imputation be performed for missing values in future research.

Third, this study used the TOEIC test scores as proficiency measures because of the reasons explained at the beginning, but the pros and cons of incorporating the TOEIC test into English programs in universities have been debated in higher education circles. It is often argued that the TOEIC test is designed to measure listening and reading skills for the workplace and thus is not suitable for university students. Some also argue that the TOEIC test's standard error of measurement is too large to measure students' progress (McCrostie, 2006). According to the Educational Testing Service (2019), the standard error of measurement of the TOEIC test is about 25 points for each of the listening and reading sections. Again, this study was not an experimental design and had to use what was available, which must be the case for most researchers or program administrators. It is hoped that this study could be of help for those who need to evaluate programs in similar situations.

Finally, course grades were used as achievement indicators, and teachers' differences in grading could have affected the results. About 30 teachers were involved in each TOEIC preparation and communication course. Although they all agreed on the common grading standards/rubrics, there can be variation between more lenient and strict grading standards across teachers, which is a factor that is difficult to control. Students might have a lenient teacher during the first year and a strict teacher during the second year, or vice versa. Investigations of inter- and intra-teacher consistency in grading would be beneficial, especially for program administrators, so that they could better improve their programs. In any case, the use of parallel process growth curve models such as those shown in this study could be beneficial for assessing curricular changes and program impacts.

Note

1 The TOEIC tests have two types now: the Listening and Reading test (TOEIC LR) and the Speaking and Writing test (TOEIC SW). In this study, the TOEIC test refers to the TOEIC LR.

References

Brock, R. (2006). Why is the TOEIC so popular? *On Cue, 14*(2), 33–34.

Blunch, N. J. (2013). *Introduction to Structural Education Modeling Using IBM SPSS Statistics and AMOS* (2nd ed.). Los Angeles, CA: Sage.

Bollen, K.A. (1989). *Structural Equation Models with Latent Variables.* New York: John Wiley.

Bradford, A., & Brown, H. (2018). Road-mapping English medium instruction in Japan. In A. Bradford & H. Brown (Eds.), *English-Medium Instruction in Japanese Higher Education: Policy, Challenges, and Outcomes* (pp. 3–13). Bristol: Multilingual Matters.

Byrne, B. M. (2016). *Structural Equation Modeling with Amos: Basic Concepts, Applications, and Programming* (3rd ed.). New York: Routledge.

Chihou shidai no heikou aitsugu: Jichitai ga yuuchi, keikaku no amasa ukiborini – susumu touta. [Private universities in rural areas close down one after another: Local governments invited universities to their areas too optimistically and a shakeout is going on.] (2019, May 15). *The Nishinippon Shimbun.* www.nishinippon.co.jp/item/n/510113/

Duckworth, A. L., Peterson, C., Matthews, M. D., & Kelly, D. R. (2007). Grit: Perseverance and passion for long-term-goals. *Journal of Personality and Social Psychology, 92*(6), 1087–1101. https://doi.org/10.1037/0022-3514.92.6.1087.

Duncan, T. E., Duncan, S. C., & Strycker, L. A. (2011). *An Introduction to Latent Variable Growth Curve Modeling* (2nd ed.). New York: Lawrence Erlbaum.

Educational Testing Service (n.d.). *TOEIC Bridge and TOEIC Score Comparisons.* www.ets.org/s/toeic/pdf/bridge-score-comparisons.pdf.

Educational Testing Service (2019). *Score User Guide: TOEIC Listening & Reading Test.* www.ets.org/s/toeic/pdf/ toeic-listening-reading-test-user-guide.pdf.

Hashimoto, H. (2018). Government policy driving English-medium instruction at Japanese universities: Responding to a competitiveness crisis in a globalizing world. In A. Bradford & H. Brown (Eds.), *English-Medium Instruction in Japanese Higher Education: Policy, Challenges, and Outcomes* (pp. 14–31). Bristol: Multilingual Matters.

Institute for International Business Communication (2020). *TOEIC Program Data & Analysis 2020*. www.iibc-global.org/library/default/toeic/official_data/pdf/DAA.pdf.

Jones, B. A. (2019). The role of English education in Japan. *Memoirs of Learning Utility Center for Konan University Students, 4*, 21–31.

Kikuchi, K. (2015). *Demotivation in Second Language Acquisition: Insights from Japan*. Bristol: Multilingual Matters.

Kline, R. B. (2016). *Principles and Practice of Structural Equation Modeling* (4th ed.). New York: Guilford Press.

Little, T. D. (2013). *Longitudinal Structural Equation Modeling*. New York: Guilford Press.

Manalo, E., Koyasu, M., Hashimoto, K., & Miyauchi, T. (2006). Factors that impact on the academic motivation of Japanese university students in Japan and in New Zealand. *Psychologia, 49*, 114–131. https://doi.org/10.2117/psysoc.2006.114.

McCrostie, J. (2006). Why are universities abandoning English teaching for TOEIC training? *On Cue, 14*(2), 30–32.

McVeigh, B. (2002). *Japanese Higher Education as Myth*. New York: Routledge.

Newsom, J. T. (2015). *Longitudinal Structural Equation Modeling: A Comprehensive Introduction*. New York: Routledge.

Obunsha Educational Information Center (2020). *50nenkan de daigakusuu gakuseisuu tomo baizou!* [The numbers of universities and university students have doubled during the past 50 years.] http://eic.obunsha.co.jp/resource/viewpoint-pdf/202011.pdf.

Promotion and Mutual Aid Corporations for Private Schools of Japan (2019). *Heisei 31 (2019) nendo shiritsu daigaku tanki daigaku tou nyuugaku shigan doukou* [Trends in application to private universities and junior colleges in 2019.] www.shigaku.go.jp/files/shigandoukouH31.pdf.

Ross, S. J. (2005). The impact of assessment method on foreign language proficiency growth. *Applied Linguistics. 26*(3), 317–342. https://doi.org/10/1093/applin/ami011.

Schumacker, R. E., & Lomax, R. G. (2016). *A Beginner's Guide to Structural Equation Modeling* (4th ed.). New York, NY: Routledge.

Tokunaga, M. (2008). Students' assumptions for TOEIC classes. In K. Bradford-Watts, T. Muller, & M. Swanson (Eds). *JALT 2007 Conference Proceedings*. Tokyo: JALT.

Tomarken, A. J., & Waller, N. G. (2005). Structural equation modeling. *Annual Review of Clinical Psychology, 1*, 31–65. https://doi.org/10.1146/annurev.clinpsy.1.102803.144239.

Xie, Q., & Andrews, S. (2012). Do test design and uses influence test preparation? Testing a model of washback with structural equation modeling. *Language Testing, 30*(1), 49–70. https://doi.org/10.1177/0265532212442634.

Yamada, R. (2014). Japanese higher education: Policies and future issues. In R. Yamada (Ed.), *Measuring Quality of Undergraduate Education in Japan* (pp. 17–33). Singapore: Springer.

9

VALIDATING TASK-CENTERED SELF-ASSESSMENT ON SECOND LANGUAGE PROFICIENCY GROWTH

A Cross-Lagged Panel Analysis

Qi Zheng

Introduction

Self-assessment is a low-cost, but effective, alternative to standard measurements in assessing one's ability in a given construct. Using self-assessment enjoys a lot of benefits: it's easy to monitor, less time consuming, and can provide external evidence in combination with other tests in facilitating the understanding of the construct being assessed. In second language (L2) learning and testing, self-assessment is frequently used as an alternative placement test in assessing learners' ability in general or in a specific domain, and it could also be used to determine criterion-referenced interpretations for other proficiency measures (e.g., oral proficiency interview, standardized and computerized proficiency tests, etc.).

Self-efficacy, often referred to as one's perceived competency level of completing certain tasks within a given construct, has been widely investigated since its first appearance (Bandura, 1977). Task-centered self-assessment, in particular, is considered a reliable indicator of self-efficacy and has been widely used in measuring self-efficacy in the past (Caprara et al., 2008; Garavalia & Gredler, 2002; Usher & Pajares, 2008; Zimmerman & Kitsantas, 2005). Self-efficacy and language learning success are also closely related, as researchers suggest that the procedure of assessing one's self-efficacy includes careful examination of specific tasks, which in turn regulate perceived sense of fulfillment and mediate the performance in practice (Paris & Paris, 2001).

The purpose of the current study is to examine the predictive validity of a task-centered self-assessment as it relates to the influence of language learning self-efficacy on language learning proficiency. In the self-efficacy literature, the number of studies on self-efficacy gains and its association with language learning success is limited, and the use of cross-lagged panel analysis in the current study

DOI: 10.4324/9781003087939-10

will potentially provide insightful discussions on how self-efficacy and success in language learning are connected.

Background

The TOEIC Bridge Test

The Test of English for International Communication (TOEIC) Bridge test is a simplified version of the TOEIC test. It is developed by the Educational Testing Service (ETS) and is used to assess the English proficiency of beginning to intermediate-level English learners. The TOEIC Bridge test serves as a reliable, but shortened, TOEIC test with 100 items and a scaled score from 20 to 180. It is therefore widely used in different areas and industries (e.g., ETS, 2016; Jarrell, 2003; Miller, 2004; Saida & Hattori, 2004). Table 9.1 briefly displays the TOEIC Bridge test composition.

TABLE 9.1 Test of English for International Communication (TOEIC) Bridge test composition

Comprehensive listening (appx. 25 min)	Reading skills (appx. 35 min)
Photographs (15 items, 4-choice) Question–response (20 items, 3-choice) Short conversation/talks (15 items, 4-choice)	Incomplete sentences (30 items, 4-choice) Reading comprehension (20 items, 4-choice)

A number of validation studies have been conducted on the TOEIC Bridge test in understanding how the test scores are related to the constructs being measured (Powers & Yan, 2013; Powers, Mercadante, & Yan, 2013; Sinharay et al., 2008; Tannenbaum & Wylie, 2013). For example, Sinharay and colleagues compared the TOEIC Bridge test scores against local English proficiency test scores, teacher ratings, and students' self-assessment using factor analysis. The authors concluded that all the proficiency measures maintained a general consistency with the score interpretation provided by the TOEIC Bridge test. Another study conducted in China (Powers et al., 2013) found moderate consistency between aggregated teacher ratings against overall proficiency measured by the TOEIC Bridge test. In Japan and Korea, Powers and Yan (2013) validated the TOEIC Bridge test against self-assessment among young participants (with a median age of 13 for Japanese participants and a median age of 18 for Korean participants). Their results indicated that, through cross-validation against self-evaluation of proficiency, the TOEIC Bridge test was found to be a valid indicator of English proficiency. Other than traditional validation studies using self-assessment and teacher rating as references, the TOEIC Bridge score was also mapped against an international language standard: the Central European Framework of Reference for Languages (CEFR;

Tannenbaum & Wylie, 2013). In the study, 22 experts representing ten different countries discussed how to map certain TOEIC Bridge scores to the standards provided by the CEFR, which extended the application of the TOEIC Bridge test.

Self-Assessment

Self-assessment refers to one's evaluation or reflection of their ability or placement within a given construct. Generally, self-assessment could be considered as "feedback for oneself from oneself" (Andrade & Du, 2007, p. 160). Self-assessment in the field of second language acquisition (SLA) has been widely applied as the measurement of self-monitored L2 proficiency and can also serve as criterion-referenced interpretations of L2 competence (Ross, 1998).

Self-assessment enjoys several positive features: the design procedure is easy, the administration of the assessment is simple, concerns around cheating can be eliminated, and the assessment data are easy to record and analyze (Brindley, 1993; LeBlanc & Painchaud, 1985; Reuland et al., 2009; Strong-Krause, 2000). Research has also found that learners self-assessing themselves have enhanced motivation (Goto Butler & Lee, 2010; LeBlanc & Painchaud, 1985; Oscarson, 1997; Ross, 1998, 2006; Strong-Krause, 2000), clearer reflective learning of weaknesses and strengths (Blue, 1994; Segers & Dochy, 2001; Thompson, Pilgrim, & Oliver, 2005), and, in turn, better learning performances (Andrade, 1999; Andrade & Boulay, 2003; Andrade & Valtcheva, 2009; Gregory, Cameron, & Davies, 2000; Naeini, 2011; Strong, Davis, & Hawks, 2004).

Still, an overwhelming amount of literature in SLA has pointed out that learners are often inaccurate in self-assessment. First, the accuracy of self-assessment is likely to be subject to the variability of the test population when sample competency level, first language background, and acquisition history are mixed (Ehrlinger, Johnson, Banner, Dunning, & Kruger, 2008; Tomoschuk, Ferreira, & Gollan, 2019). Self-assessment is also reported to be inconsistent in estimating one's true performance: low-ability learners tend to overestimate their ability in self-assessment, while high-ability learners tend to underestimate their true ability (Ehrlinger et al., 2008; Reuland et al., 2009). Also, self-assessment is vulnerable to how the scale of rating is being set, and how the questions and statements in the assessment are framed. As a result, learners may lack the confidence or training required to accurately use the self-assessment instrument and may inaccurately and inconsistently assess their true performance (Cassidy, 2007; Leach, 2012).

Psychometric Properties of Self-Assessment: Reliability and Validity

Psychometric properties of self-assessments were discussed as supporting evidence of how reliable and how valid self-assessment can be and can help researchers to understand the use and design of self-assessments in many ways.

Reliability regarding can–do self-assessment was examined in many ways, and most studies have found that the internal consistency of self-assessment is high (e.g., Ross, 2006; Ross, Rolheiser, & Hogaboam-Gray, 1999; Salehi & Masoule, 2017; Summers, Cox, McMurry, & Dewey, 2019). For example, Summers and colleagues (2019) investigated the reliability of the American Council on the Teaching of Foreign Languages (ACTFL) can-do self-assessment and concluded that learners' perceptions of their ability were reliability-separated ($r = 0.92$), and items were different from each other in different difficulty levels ($r = 0.92$ for reading and $r = 0.95$ for writing). Salehi and Masoule (2017) also addressed the high test–retest reliability ($r = 0.84$) of a task-centered English as a foreign language (EFL) self-assessment used in their study.

To investigate the external validity of self-assessment as an alternative to more objective measures, such as standardized tests or teacher evaluations, researchers analyzed correlations between self-assessments and other objective measures. Most studies agreed that the validity of self-assessment is limited (e.g., Carter & Dunning, 2008; Dunn & Tree, 2009; Grosjean, 1998; Kruger & Dunning, 1999; Reuland et al., 2009; Ross, 1998; Schwarz, 1999; Zell & Krizan, 2014). Most studies also reported moderate correlations, ranging from 0.2 to 0.6, depending on the task and the skills being tested (e.g., Brantmeier, Vanderplank, & Strube, 2012; Brown, Dewey, & Cox, 2014; Edele, Seuring, Kristen, & Stanat, 2015; Ross, 1998; Summers et al., 2019; Suzuki, 2015). Ross (1998) reported that self-assessed speaking skills are less accurate than that of reading and listening skills. Salehi and Masoule (2017) compared the validity of peer evaluation and self-assessment with teacher evaluation in writing and oral tasks, and their results supported a higher accuracy in self-assessed writing than oral tasks. Self-assessment accuracy is also reported to be population-dependent (Earley, 1999; Edele et al., 2015; Salili, Chiu, & Lai, 2001; Scholz, Doña, Sud, & Schwarzer, 2002; Tomoschuk et al., 2019), rubric, objective, and context-driven (Brantmeier et al., 2012; Kruger & Dunning, 1999; Mabe & West, 1982; Wang, 2004; Wang, Kim, Bong, & Ahn, 2013). Overall, previous research provides evidence in support of the conclusion that the eternal validity regarding self-assessment could be skill- and task-dependent across different domains.

Self-Efficacy and the Task-Centered Can-Do Self-Assessment

Self-efficacy, "the conviction that one can successfully execute the behavior required to produce outcomes" (Bandura, 1977, p. 193), was first introduced by Bandura in 1977 as an explanatory cognitive mechanism accounting for psychological changes resulting from different modes of treatment. Bandura (1986) posited self-efficacy as an important component in social cognitive theory as it was proposed to explain and predict how individuals are guided by their belief on their knowledge and skill proficiency in a certain context.

Self-efficacy has been particularly interesting to researchers in the field of language learning, since learners' belief in their capability is an indispensable variable in understanding learning as a human function (Urdan & Pajares, 2006). Indeed, much research has shown that self-efficacy appears to play a vital role in explaining and predicting language learners' performance (e.g., Hsieh & Kang, 2010; Lane, Lane, & Kyprianou, 2004; Linnenbrink & Pintrich, 2003; Mills, Pajares, & Herron, 2007; Pajares, 2003; Rahimi & Abedini, 2009; Schunk, 2003; Schunk & Zimmerman, 2007; Wang, Spencer, & Xing, 2009).

The assessment of self-efficacy needs to be both task-specific and context-specific (Bandura, 1986). Traditionally, self-efficacy measurements are mostly carried out using structured interviews and/or questionnaires in which self-perceived scales regarding accomplishing context-specific tasks were rated by levels of capability (i.e., Likert scale from 1 *not well at all* to 7 *very well*; e.g., Caprara et al., 2008; Usher & Pajares, 2008; Zimmerman & Martinez-Pons, 1986; Zimmerman, Bandura, & Martinez-Pons, 1992), by levels of confidence (i.e., Likert scale from 1 *very little confidence* to 5 *quite a lot of confidence*; e.g., Garavalia & Gredler, 2002; Gredler & Schwartz, 1997), or by levels of can-do (i.e., Likert scale 0 *definitely cannot do it* to 100 *definitely can do it*; e.g., Zimmerman & Kitsantas, 2005).

In language testing research specifically, the task-centered can-do self-assessment is one of the typically used self-assessments, since "the goal of [language] testing … is to see what someone 'can do' with the language" (Mendelsohn, 1989, p. 96). The task-centered can-do self-assessment could be considered as self-efficacy in language learning, since it is designed to provide information about how well the learner can use their language skills to achieve certain language-using activities. Similar to self-efficacy measures employed within related contexts, language learners are usually asked to rate their levels of self-confidence from "cannot do" to "can do with difficulty" to "can do" and sometimes to "can do well," according to the Likert scale descriptions offered.

The task-centered can-do self-efficacy measure has a number of attractive features when used within the language learning context. First, language learners' attention will be focused on the *uses of* language rather than *knowledge about* the language (Brindley, 1993; Shohamy, 1992). Second, explicit criteria in the "can-do" statements can provide specified guidelines or goals for learners to check and follow for further improvements (Brindley, 1989; Griffin & McKay, 1992). Additionally, mapping can-do self-assessment information with other proficiency measurements such as Test of English as a Foreign Language (TOEFL), TOEIC, Oral Proficiency Interview (OPI), and teacher evaluation can provide external validity evidence and reflect criterion-based interpretations of these test scores (ETS, 2013; Powers & Powers, 2015; Salehi & Masoule, 2017; Summers et al., 2019).

Validating Self-Efficacy Growth and the Current Study

Other than traditional validity discussions concerning the correlation between a one-time self-efficacy followed by a one-time proficiency measurement, few studies have discussed issues such as the predictive validity of self-assessment in measuring linguistic gains over time (e.g., Meara, 1994; Maiworm, 1997) related to the evaluation of immersion programs such as internship overseas or study abroad. Brown, Dewey, and Cox (2014) matched language learners' can-do self-efficacy with OPI performance from pre-test to post-test, and their conclusion was that, although significant gains were found from pre- to post-test for both measures, the correlations between the gains were only moderate ($r = 0.21$). One constraint of their study is that the OPI measures were rater-dependent and could be more variable than standardized proficiency tests on domains such as listening and reading. Whether such variability introduced more consistency or more chaoticity, and how that might affect the relationship between the gains, remains to be explored.

Researchers have also investigated the predictive validity of standardized proficiency measures on self-assessment. Powers and colleagues discussed the incremental contribution of TOEIC subtests for predicting self-assessed English language skills in authentic learning contexts across four skill domains: listening, reading, speaking, and writing (Powers & Powers, 2015). The authors found 5 that correlations between the TOEIC score and self-assessed skills across different domains were significant. For example, the correlation between the can-do self-assessment of speaking and TOEIC speaking was $r = 0.51$, while its correlations with TOEIC listening, reading, and writing were established at $r = 0.42$, 0.34, and 0.40, respectively. The authors therefore concluded that, after controlling for the TOEIC speaking score, variations in self-assessed skills were still significantly associated with the proficiency of other domains.

Overall, very little research has been conducted on evaluating the predictive validity for self-assessment and self-efficacy change over time on L2 proficiency growth. The current study was therefore designed to focus on EFL learners' self-assessed can-do self-efficacy and to collect validity evidence by linking self-efficacy change to standardized proficiency measures. The following research questions (RQs) are investigated in the current study:

> RQ1: Are there any subscales that constitute the proficiency construct assessed by the current task-centered self-assessment? What is the reliability of the task-centered can-do self-assessment instrument used in this study?
>
> RQ2: Is the change in self-assessed confidence as instructional consequences in any way systematically related to the post-tested proficiency controlling for the pre-tested covariance?

Methodology

Context

Since the 1990s, the demand for the globalization of the Japanese automobile industry has resulted in an increasing need for selling cars and products not only in Japan, but also in other foreign countries. Instead of assembling the car in Japan and selling the entire car overseas, the more efficient and tariff-saving way of exporting cars is to send the manufactured parts of the cars overseas and to have the local factory assemble the cars. As a result, car companies need to train local workers overseas, mainly in Southeast Asian countries, to assemble the cars.

Japanese automobile companies are typically faced with two options: (1) train local employees overseas using the Japanese language and send Japanese workers overseas to teach local employees how to assemble the car; or (2) train Japanese workers in English, having the Japanese workers and the local workers communicate in English. Training overseas workers using Japanese has been found to be a relatively time-consuming option, since local workers in Southeast Asian countries typically do not have any previous knowledge of Japanese and training them using Japanese would be costly.

The alternative option utilizes workers' existing knowledge of English in local countries, such as Malaysia, Indonesia, and Thailand, and is therefore found to be preferable for most Japanese automobile companies. The problem with this choice was that in the 1990s, assembly workers did not have to finish high school to be able to work in Japanese automobile companies. The companies only required a minimum of eighth- or ninth-grade educational background for their employees, and many companies would hire people out of junior high school and train them in special technical schools to gain the requisite manufacturing and assembling skills. Therefore, Japanese workers familiar with specialized knowledge of car assembly were not equipped with enough English proficiency to enable them to teach the Southeast Asian local workers how to assemble automobiles. The car companies, therefore, opted to send technology-experienced workers to intensive English for specific purpose (ESP) programs to learn English skills to instruct their counterparts in Southeast Asia to assemble the automobiles on site.

The TOEIC and TOEIC Bridge test have been widely utilized under this need-based industry background since the 1990s. In Japan, companies like Honda, Toyota, and Nissan all required TOEIC (or TOEIC Bridge) scores for both their present and future employees (Templer, 2004). In the case discussed in the current study, the TOEIC Bridge scores were used to evaluate whether skills needed were fulfilled by the specialized English training, and the TOEIC Bridge scores also served as a selection criterion for nominating workers with the English skills to be sent overseas to conduct technology transfer tasks in the car-assembling process.

Participants

The sampled population used in the current study was from an automobile company that required their employees, mostly beginning to intermediate level English learners, to have English language training for work purposes. In this study, 239 responses of employees from an automobile company in Japan were analyzed, and all participants were beginning to lower intermediate level learners of English who were required to participate in an English training program for work purposes.

Instruments

Proficiency Test

The TOEIC Bridge test (listening and reading) was used as the measure of general English proficiency in this study. The test has 50 listening items, and 50 structure and vocabulary items.

Self-Assessment

The task-centered can-do self-assessment used in this study is composed of 60 task-centered statements about different language use situations. Participants were asked to rate their level of confidence in the can-do self-assessment using an eight-point Likert-type scale ranging from 1 (*not at all*) to 8 (*very well*). Before the start of the training, some employees had no knowledge of English, and the target test population was mostly within the low to intermediate-level English proficiency level. The can-do self-assessment was therefore designed to be conducted in Japanese, not in English (see interpretations of the 60 can-do self-assessment statements in Appendix 9.1).

Procedures

The data were collected following a typical longitudinal pre-test, intervention, post-test design. At the pre-test stage, all employees first finished both the TOEIC Bridge test and the can-do self-assessment. After the pre-test, instruction of English (i.e., intervention) was monitored in the training stage. During the training stage, employees were given one to two hours of English instruction per day as part of their daily work assignments at the assembly plants. After accumulating 80–100 hours of English training, the employees were then required to take the TOEIC Bridge test and the can-do self-assessment once again.

Statistical Procedures

Rasch Modeling: Diagnostics and Reliability

To assess the reliability of the can-do self-assessment, the self-assessment data were analyzed using the Rasch scaling analysis (Andrich, 1978; Rasch, 1960) with Winsteps software (Bond & Fox, 2007; Linacre, 2018). The software was used to complete the Rasch principal component analysis (PCA) to check the dimensionality of the self-assessment followed by a Rasch rating-scale analysis in evaluating other psychometric properties.

Predictive Validity Measure: Cross-Lagged Panel Analysis

Together with dimensionality diagnostics and decisions based on dimensionality diagnostics by Rasch PCA, cross-lagged panel analyses (e.g., Huck, Cormier,

& Bounds, 1974) were used to investigate the association between the can-do self-efficacy growth and the proficiency growth. Cross-lagged panel analysis compares the relationship between two (or more) variables measured at two (or more) time points to examine the stability and associations between the variables longitudinally. Mplus 7.0 (Muthén & Muthén, 2012) was used to analyze the model(s).

Figure 9.1 shows the model structure of cross-lagged panel analysis. The latent construct of English proficiency is indicated by two measured variables: TOEIC reading and TOEIC listening, and the latent construct self-efficacy is composed of test takers' performance in task-centered can-do items. The two horizontal single-arrowed lines, labeled as β_{SE1SE2} and β_{P1P2} in Figure 9.1, are path coefficients between the same variables (i.e., self-efficacy and proficiency), measured before and after EFL instruction (i.e., time 1 and time 2). The two double-arrowed lines, labeled as r_{SE1P1} and r_{SE2P2}, are synchronous correlations because the two corresponding measures ocurred at the same time. The two diagonal single-arrowed lines, labeled as β_{SE1P2} and β_{P1SE2}, are the path coefficients between self-efficacy at time 1 and proficiency at time 2 and between proficiency at time 1 and self-efficacy at time 2. β_{SE1P2} and β_{P1SE2} are also called the cross-lagged relationships.

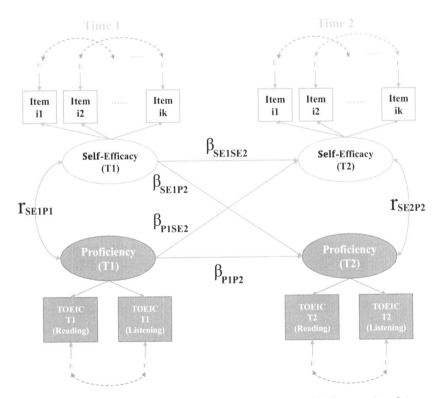

FIGURE 9.1 Hypothesized cross-lagged relationships between self-efficacy and proficiency.

Results

Descriptive Statistics: Pre-to-Post Self-Efficacy and Proficiency Changes

Figures 9.2 and 9.3 display the pre-to-post self-efficacy (measured by can-do self-assessment) and language learning proficiency (measured by the TOEIC Bridge test) changes. The average can-do self-assessment at the pre-test stage (time 1) is 2.52 and 4.20 at the post-test stage (time 2). For the TOEIC Bridge test, the mean score of both listening and reading sub-test increased over time, with a mean increase of 7.52 points for listening from pre-test to post-test, and a 5.08-point mean increase for the reading skills – a total of 12.60 points change.

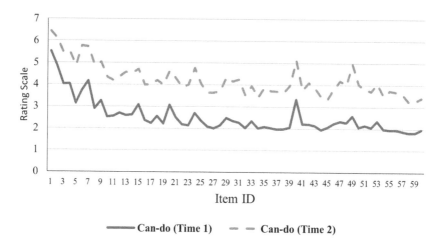

FIGURE 9.2 Can-do self assessment pre- and post-scores.

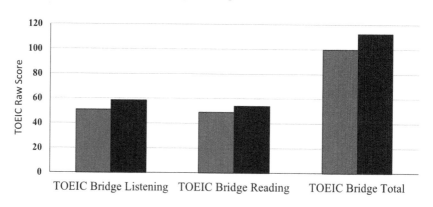

FIGURE 9.3 Language learning proficiency pre- and post-scores. TOEIC = Test of English for International Communication.

The Can-Do Self-Assessment: Dimensionality and Reliability

The Rasch PCA generated dimensionality diagnostics for the can-do self-assessment, in which contrastive residual patterns (items with standardized residual loadings larger than 0.4 or smaller than –0.4) were detected. To guarantee the extra dimensions (e.g., subscales) are theoretically meaningful, the contrastive patterns were examined together with the infit statistics and the contents of the can-do statements. Three theoretically meaningful subscales that constituted large enough residual contrasts were detected: (1) basic English skills self-efficacy: statements 1–7; (2) intermediate English skills self-efficacy: statements 8–25; 29–33; 40; 46–49; 53; and (3) job-specific English skills self-efficacy: statements 26–28, 34–39, 41–45, 50–52, and 54–60 (see Appendix 9.1 for the self-assessment statements).

The Rasch rating scale analysis was then conducted to obtain measure statistics, reliability, separation indexes, as well as infit statistics for the can-do self-assessment.

The *measure statistics* is the Rasch calibration of the span of examinee ability and item difficulty. Measure statistics above 0 indicate the item has a higher-than-average difficulty, and vice versa. Figure 9.4 displays the person and item distribution map (also called the "ruler" graph) with measure statistic positions: from pre-test (left) to post-test (right), a decrease in the item difficulty was observed, displaying a perceived increase in self-efficacy.

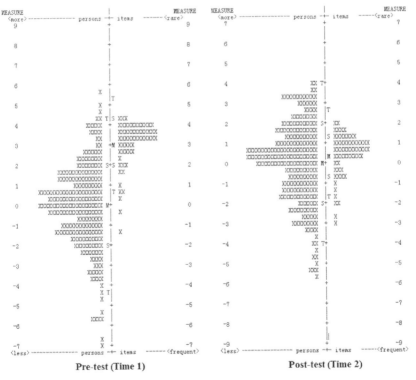

Pre-test (Time 1)   **Post-test (Time 2)**

FIGURE 9.4 Person and item measure statistics distribution map (the "ruler" graph).

The *reliability statistics* reports the Spearman reliability (i.e., the ratio of true variance to observed variance; Spearman, 1904). The reported item reliability of the can-do self-assessment of the current study is 0.99. The *infit mean-square statistics* presents how each individual fits or misfits the Rasch model by comparing the observed data with the expected data. Infit values over or below the range between 0.7 and 1.3 suggest a data–model misfit of being too consistent (below 0.7) or too chaotic (above 1.3). Interestingly, before dividing the entire can-do self-assessment into three subscales, item performance was relatively chaotic, with frequent infit statistics below 0.7 or over 1.3; however, the infit statistics for extracted subscales functioned well.

The Cross-Lagged Panel Analysis

The previous section presented the statistical evidence to extract three subscales from the self-efficacy measure used in the current study. In the following section, cross-lagged panel analyses were conducted to these three subscales to investigate the relative salience of pre-test self-efficacy and proficiency in predicting post-test self-efficacy and proficiency. Table 9.2 reports the estimates of the model coefficients and data–model fit indices of these three models.

TABLE 9.2 Standardized model parameter estimates and fit statistics (see Figure 9.1 for coefficient reference)

Coefficients	Basic English skills		Intermediate English skills		Job-specific English skills	
	Estimate	se	Estimate	se	Estimates	se
β_{P1P2}	0.565***	0.048	0.572***	0.045	0.557***	0.045
β_{SE1SE2}	0.963***	0.029	0.960***	0.030	0.963***	0.029
r_{SE1P1}	0.071	0.082	0.085	0.071	0.036	0.065
r_{SE2P2}	−0.145	0.180	−0.178	0.185	−0.113	0.187
β_{SE1P2}	0.019	0.046	0.059	0.045	0.059	0.043
β_{P1SE2}	−0.088	0.062	−0.030	0.073	0.024	0.043
Fit statistics						
RMSEA	0.064		0.076		0.066	
CFI	0.967		0.884		0.947	
SRMR	0.040		0.046		0.029	

***p <0.001.
RMSEA = root mean square error of approximation; CFI = comparative fit index;
SRMR = standardized root mean squared residual.

Data–model fit refers to the ability of a designed model to reproduce the data collected (for most occasions, reproducing the variance–covariance matrix of the data). Data–model fit indices indicate how well a model fits the data by examining to what extent the model could explain the variances and covariances in the data.

Three fit indices were examined in the current study: (1) the standardized root mean squared residual (SRMR) is an absolute measure of fit comparing observed against model-implied variance–covariance matrix; (2) the root mean square error of approximation (RMSEA) is a parsimonious measure of fit that adjusts for model complexity; and (3) the comparative fit index (CFI) is an incremental measure of fit comparing the target model versus the baseline (null) model. Suggested fit index values to retain a model are: SRMR ≤ 0.08, RMSEA ≤ 0.06, or CFI ≥ 0.95 (Hu & Bentler, 1999). According to Table 9.2, all three models yield satisfactory data–model fit in terms of SRMR, indicating that very little variance in all three subscale models was left unexplained in the data. The RSMEA and CFI statistics showed the models generated for the basic English skill subscale and the job-specific English skill subscale were good-fitting models, while the intermediate English skill subscale had relatively unsatisfying RSMEA and CFI.

All three models showed consistent patterns of path coefficient significance. Path coefficients between the same variables (i.e., self-efficacy and proficiency) measured before and after EFL instruction, β_{SE1SE2} and β_{P1P2} are the only significant parameters in all three models: (1) proficiency before training is a significant and positive predictor of the proficiency tested in the post-TOEIC Bridge test (basic English skills: $\beta_{P1P2} = 0.963$, $p < .001$; (2) intermediate English skills: $\beta_{P1P2} = 0.960$, $p < 0.001$; and (3) job-specific English skills: $\beta_{P1P2} = 0.963$, $p < 0.001$). Self-efficacy before training is also a significant predictor of that after the training (basic English skills: $\beta_{SE1SE2} = 0.565, p < 0.001$; intermediate English skills: $\beta_{SE1SE2} = 0.572, p < 0.001$; job-specific English skills: $\beta_{SE1SE2} = 0.557, p < 0.001$). Secondly, none of the cross-lagged path coefficients are statistically significant: over and above the variance explained by pre-test proficiency, self-efficacy measured at pre-test was not a significant predictor of post-test proficiency; over and about the variance explained by pre-test self-efficacy, proficiency measured at pre-test was also not a significant predictor of post-test self-efficacy. Lastly, two synchronous correlations, r_{SE1P1} and r_{SE2P2}, were not significant either.

Discussion

RQ1: Are there any subscales that constitute the proficiency construct assessed by the current task-centered self-assessment? What is the reliability of the task-centered can-do self-assessment instrument used in this study?

The PCA of Rasch residuals showed that there is potential multidimensionality in the current task-centered self-assessment which is designed to measure self-efficacy, indicating independent analyses on additional dimensions (i.e., subscales of the self-assessment) might be necessary to further investigate the psychometric property of the self-assessment (Linacre, 2014). In fact, measuring language proficiency as a unidimensional construct might be difficult, and previous research has suggested that it would not be surprising to observe a complex construct like language proficiency, tested by self-assessment, to have multiple subconstructs (Buck, 1994; Nunan, 1989). After screening the contents of the items, three subscales of self-efficacy were created: (1) the basic English skill subscale; (2) the intermediate level English skill subscale; and (3) the job-specific English skill subscale. After splitting the entire self-assessment into three subscales, the infit statistics became less chaotic (or more variate for items being too consistent), and the follow-up Rasch residual analyses of the remaining residuals did not detect any secondary contrast within each subscale – no additional psychometric meaningful dimension was diagnosed by the Rasch measurement model. In fact, can-do statements about basic English skills, intermediate level English skills, or about job-related performances, are all can-do aspects of general English skills and treating the entire test as one construct is defensible provided that the purpose of the self-assessment is to focus on the union of the three sets of skills tested as a whole.

To determine the reliability of the can-do self-assessment used in this study, the Rasch rating scale analysis was applied to the data collected and infit reliability statistics showed that the self-assessment was a reliable measure. Additionally, a decrease of item difficulty – an increase in can-do self-rating – was observed in the Rasch analyses for all subscales. Together with descriptive statistics reported in the results section, it, therefore, leads to our discussion of the next research question: since an observable pre-test-to-post-test increase in both self-assessed self-efficacy and proficiency was observed, are changes in self-efficacy systematically associated with changes in proficiency?

>   RQ2: Is the change in self-assessed confidence as instructional consequences systematically related to the post-tested proficiency controlling for the pre-tested covariance?

The cross-lagged panel analysis was designed to describe the lagged relationships between self-efficacy and proficiency measured on two sequential occasions (i.e., pre-test, post-test) to better understand how self-efficacy and proficiency influence each other over time. Specifically, in order to minimize the bias while estimating the cross-legged effects, the cross-lagged panel analysis in the current study allows the control for correlations between self-efficacy and proficiency measured at the same time, as well as the autoregressive effect (i.e., the stability of individual differences) within self-efficacy and proficiency across time when estimating the cross-lagged effects between the two constructs.

None of the cross-lagged relationships were significant in our study. That is, the change in self-efficacy was not a significant predictor of the change in proficiency over time. In fact, even the synchronous correlations between self-efficacy and proficiency measured at the same time point were not significant, indicating that no systematic association between self-efficacy and actual proficiency before and after instruction was found. Significant autoregressive effects within both self-efficacy and proficiency were observed for all three subscales, indicating both constructs have small variance over time, and the pre-to-post influence within the same construct was strong.

Given that the population being tested in the current study were mostly beginning to lower intermediate level learners of English, the findings that synchronous correlations between self-efficacy and proficiency were not significant is consistent with previous research in support of the idea that lower-ability level learners are less accurate in self-evaluating their actual ability as compared with high-ability learners (Ehrlinger et al., 2008; Reuland et al., 2009; Ross, 1998). It is plausible to expect that lower-level ability learners tend to select extreme answers since they are less aware and confident to place themselves in a proper position without knowing their true ability scales. This might also indicate that self-assessment may not function well if the test takers are relatively new to the construct being assessed.

Importantly, although improvements in both self-efficacy and proficiency were observed after instruction, self-efficacy increase was not systematically associated with proficiency growth over time once the initial proficiency and initial self-efficacy were controlled. The following are potential explanations.

Firstly, the self-assessed can-do skills in the current study are spoken skills required by the automobile company, while the proficiency measure used, although required by the automobile company as well, contained only listening and reading tasks. The use of an unmatched self-assessment and proficiency measure was due to empirical restrictions: the TOEIC Bridge test was an easily accessible English proficiency measure that is not only used in selecting employees for overseas working purposes but is also an important reference for industry decision makers to refer to in recruitment, placement, and promotion decision making. Unfortunately, there were no speaking sessions in the TOEIC Bridge test and finding an instrument to evaluate beginning to lower intermediate speaking ability precisely was relatively difficult – not much person separation could be found using OPI or other oral proficiency measures (Brown et al., 2014; Salehi & Masoule, 2017). Although previous research indicated that domains like speaking, listening, and reading are linked by basic processes such as phonology, morphology, syntax, etc., cross-domain prediction of growth across time might fade away through the process of cross-domain validation (Powers & Powers, 2015).

Second, the growth of self-efficacy, as an indirect measure, might be less reliable in many ways. For example, examinees might have experienced a perspective shift after the training, because their self-rating criteria might be different from that at the pre-test session due to increased skills and familiarity with the self-assessment. Learners with no knowledge of the skills might be able to rate their ability easily, but as they start to gain experience and knowledge of the skills, their confidence level tends to drop (Gilovich, Kerr, & Medvec, 1993). It is therefore plausible to argue that the self-assessed self-efficacy growth in the current study might not be able to accurately reflect actual self-efficacy improvement. In recent years, rather than indirectly calculating the growth of self-efficacy, direct rating of self-efficacy changes (i.e., self-assessment on whether and to what extent a specific skill has improved) was recommended as an alternative to avoid perspective shift issues in self-efficacy research (Brown et al., 2014).

Conclusion

The current study investigated the use of task-centered can-do self-assessment from several perspectives. The dimensionality diagnoses of the self-assessment, and the PCA of Rasch residuals showed that potential subdimensions might exist within the self-efficacy construct measured by the self-assessment: basic English skills self-efficacy, intermediate English skills self-efficacy, and job-specific English skills self-efficacy. Furthermore, a cross-lagged panel analysis was applied to investigate the interrelationships between self-efficacy and proficiency measured across time. Self-efficacy was not reflective of proficiency measured at the same time point, either at the pre-test or the post-test session. Additionally, the pre-to-post change in self-efficacy is not systematically associated with the change in proficiency, although both measures showed a clear pattern of improvement from the pre-test to post-test. The findings of the current study helped us to better understand the empirical use as well as the psychometric property of the task-centered self-assessment, and in turn, provided insightful messages about challenges in the use of self-assessment in language learning and testing.

References

Andrade, H. G. (1999). Student self-assessment: at the intersection of metacognition and authentic assessment, *ERIC Doküman no: ED431030*. Retrieved from: https://files.eric.ed.gov/fulltext/ED431030.pdf

Andrade, H. G., & Boulay, B. A. (2003). Role of rubric-referenced self-assessment in learning to write. *The Journal of Educational Research*, 97(1), 21–30.

Andrade, H., & Du, Y. (2007). Student responses to criteria-referenced self-assessment. *Assessment & Evaluation in Higher Education*, 32(2), 159–181.

Andrade, H., & Valtcheva, A. (2009). Promoting learning and achievement through self-assessment. *Theory into Practice*, 48(1), 12–19.

Andrich, D. (1978). Application of a psychometric rating model to ordered categories which are scored with successive integers. *Applied Psychological Measurement*, 2(4), 581–594.

Bandura, A. (1977). Self-efficacy: Toward a unifying theory of behavioral change. *Psychological Review*, 84(2), 191.

Bandura, A. (1986). Social foundations of thought and action. *Englewood Cliffs*, NJ, 1986(23-28).

Blue, G. M. (1994). Self-assessment of foreign language skills: Does it work?. *CLE Working Papers*, 3, 18–35.

Bond, T. G., & Fox, C. M. (2007). *Applying the Rasch Model: Fundamental Measurement in the Human Sciences*. Mahwah, NJ, US.

Brantmeier, C., Vanderplank, R., & Strube, M. (2012). What about me?: Individual self-assessment by skill and level of language instruction. *System, 40*(1), 144–160.

Brindley, G. (1989). The role of needs analysis in adult ESL programme design. *The Second Language Curriculum*, 63–78.

Brindley, G. (1993). 1994: Task-centred assessment in language learning: The promise and the challenge. In Bird, N., Falvey, P., Tsui, A., Allison, D. and McNeill, A., editors, *Language and Learning: Papers Presented at the Annual International Language in Education Conference*.

Brown, N. A., Dewey, D. P., & Cox, T. L. (2014). Assessing the validity of can-do statements in retrospective (then-now) self-assessment. *Foreign Language Annals, 47*(2), 261–285.

Buck, G. (1994). The appropriacy of psychometric measurement models for testing second language listening comprehension. *Language Testing, 11*(2), 145–170.

Caprara, G. V., Fida, R., Vecchione, M., Del Bove, G., Vecchio, G. M., Barbaranelli, C., & Bandura, A. (2008). Longitudinal analysis of the role of perceived self-efficacy for self-regulated learning in academic continuance and achievement. *Journal of Educational Psychology, 100*(3), 525.

Carter, T. J., & Dunning, D. (2008). Faulty self-assessment: Why evaluating one's own competence is an intrinsically difficult task. *Social and Personality Psychology Compass, 2*(1), 346–360.

Cassidy, S. (2007). Assessing 'inexperienced' students' ability to self-assess: Exploring links with learning style and academic personal control. *Assessment & Evaluation in Higher Education, 32*(3), 313–330.

Dunn, A. L., & Tree, J. E. F. (2009). A quick, gradient bilingual dominance scale. *Bilingualism: Language and Cognition, 12*(3), 273–289.

Earley, P. C. (1999). Playing follow the leader: Status-determining traits in relation to collective efficacy across cultures. *Organizational Behavior and Human Decision Processes, 80*(3), 192–212.

Edele, A., Seuring, J., Kristen, C., & Stanat, P. (2015). Why bother with testing? The validity of immigrants' self-assessed language proficiency. *Social Science Research, 52*, 99–123.

Ehrlinger, J., Johnson, K., Banner, M., Dunning, D., & Kruger, J. (2008). Why the unskilled are unaware: Further explorations of (absent) self-insight among the incompetent. *Organizational Behavior and Human Decision Processes, 105*(1), 98–121.

ETS. (2013). *Can-Do Guide Executive Summary TOEIC Bridge Test*. Retrieved from: www.ets.org/s/toeic/pdf/bridge-can-do-guide.pdf

ETS. (2016). *TOEIC Bridge Examinee Handbook*. Retrieved from: www.ets.org/s/toeic/pdf/toeic-bridge-exam.pdf

Garavalia, L. S., & Gredler, M. E. (2002). An exploratory study of academic goal setting, achievement calibration and self-regulated learning. *Journal of Instructional Psychology, 29*(4), 221–231.

Gilovich, T., Kerr, M., & Medvec, V. H. (1993). Effect of temporal perspective on subjective confidence. *Journal of Personality and Social Psychology, 64*(4), 552.

Goto Butler, Y., & Lee, J. (2010). The effects of self-assessment among young learners of English. *Language Testing, 27*(1), 5–31.

Gredler, M. E., & Schwartz, L. S. (1997). Factorial structure of the self-efficacy for self-regulated learning scale. *Psychological Reports, 81*(1), 51–57.

Gregory, K., Cameron, C., & Davies, A. (2000). *Knowing What Counts: Self-Assessment and Goal Setting*. Merville, BC: Connections.

Griffin, P., & McKay, P. (1992). Assessment and reporting in the ESL language and literacy in schools project. *National Languages and Literacy Institute of Australia, ESL Development: Language and Literacy in Schools Project, 2*, 9–28.

Grosjean, F. (1998). Studying bilinguals: Methodological and conceptual issues. *Bilingualism: Language and Cognition, 1*(2), 131–149.

Hsieh, P. P. H., & Kang, H. S. (2010). Attribution and self-efficacy and their interrelationship in the Korean EFL context. *Language Learning, 60*(3), 606–627.

Hu, L. T., & Bentler, P. M. (1999). Cutoff criteria for fit indexes in covariance structure analysis: Conventional criteria versus new alternatives. *Structural Equation Modeling: A Multidisciplinary Journal, 6*(1), 1–55.

Huck, S. W., Cormier, W. H., & Bounds, W. G. (1974). *Reading Statistics and Research* (pp. 74–102). New York, NY: Harper & Row.

Jarrell, D. S. (2003). Extensive reading for weak readers. *Nagoya Joshi Daigaku Kiyou, 49*, 199–205.

Kruger, J., & Dunning, D. (1999). Unskilled and unaware of it: How difficulties in recognizing one's own incompetence lead to inflated self-assessments. *Journal of Personality and Social Psychology, 77*(6), 1121.

Lane, J., Lane, A. M., & Kyprianou, A. (2004). Self-efficacy, self-esteem and their impact on academic performance. *Social Behavior and Personality: An International Journal, 32*(3), 247–256.

Leach, L. (2012). Optional self-assessment: Some tensions and dilemmas. *Assessment & Evaluation in Higher Education, 37*(2), 137–147.

LeBlanc, R., & Painchaud, G. (1985). Self-assessment as a second language placement instrument. *TESOL Quarterly, 19*(4), 673–687.

Linacre, J. M. (2014). Dimensionality: contrasts & variances. *A user's guide to Winsteps Ministep Rasch-model computer programs (version 3.81. 0)*. Retrieved from: www. winsteps. com/winman/principalcomponents.htm.

Linacre, J. M. (2018) *Facets Computer Program for Many-Facet Rasch Measurement, Version 3.81.0*. Beaverton, Oregon: Winsteps.com.

Linnenbrink, E. A., & Pintrich, P. R. (2003). The role of self-efficacy beliefs in student engagement and learning in the classroom. *Reading & Writing Quarterly, 19*(2), 119–137.

Mabe, P. A., & West, S. G. (1982). Validity of self-evaluation of ability: A review and meta-analysis. *Journal of Applied Psychology, 67*(3), 280.

Maiworm, F. (1997). *The ERASMUS Experience: Major Findings of the ERASMUS Evaluation Research Project*. Luxembourg: Office for official publications of the European communities.

Meara, P. (1994). The year abroad and its effects. *Language Learning Journal, 10*(1), 32–38.

Mendelsohn, D. J. (1989). Testing should reflect teaching. *TESL Canada Journal, 7*(1), 95–108.

Mills, N., Pajares, F., & Herron, C. (2007). Self-efficacy of college intermediate French students: Relation to achievement and motivation. *Language Learning, 57*(3), 417–442.

Miller, J. C. (2004). An overview of standardized English tests in Japan. *Practical English Studies, 2004*(11), 31–42.

Muthén, L. K., & Muthén, B. O. (2012). Mplus. *Statistical Analysis with Latent Variables. User's Guide, 7*. Los Angeles, CA: Muthén & Muthén.

Naeini, J. (2011). Self-assessment and the impact on language skills. *Educational Research, 2*(6), 1225–1231.

Nunan, D. (1989). Item response theory and second language proficiency assessment. *Prospect, 4*(3), 81–93.

Oscarson, M. (1997). Self-assessment of foreign and second language proficiency. *Encyclopedia of Language and Education*, 7, 175–187.

Pajares, F. (2003). Self-efficacy beliefs, motivation, and achievement in writing: A review of the literature. *Reading & Writing Quarterly*, *19*(2), 139–158.

Paris, S. G., & Paris, A. H. (2001). Classroom applications of research on self-regulated learning. *Educational Psychologist*, *36*(2), 89–101.

Powers, D. E., & Powers, A. (2015). The incremental contribution of TOEIC listening, reading, speaking, and writing tests to predicting performance on real-life English language tasks. *Language Testing*, *32*(2), 151–167.

Powers, D. E., & Yan, F. (2013). TOEIC Bridge scores: Validity evidence from Korea and Japan. In Powers, D. E. (Ed.) *The Research Foundation for the TOEIC Tests: A Compendium of Studies: Vol. II*, pp. 5.1–5.10. Princeton, NJ: Educational Testing Service. Retrieved from: www.ets.org/Media/Research/pdf/TC2-05.pdf

Powers, D. E., Mercadante, R., & Yan, F. (2013). Validating TOEIC Bridge scores against teacher ratings for vocational students in China. In Powers, D. E. (Ed.) *The Research Foundation for the TOEIC Tests: A Compendium of Studies: Vol. II,* pp. 4.1–4.11. Princeton, NJ: Educational Testing Service. Retrieved from: www.ets.org/Media/Research/pdf/TC2-04.pdf

Rahimi, A., & Abedini, A. (2009). The interface between EFL learners' self-efficacy concerning listening comprehension and listening proficiency. *Novitas-Royal*, *3*(1).

Rasch, G. (1960). *Probabilistic Models for Some Intelligence and Attainment Tests*. Chicago, IL: University of Chicago Press.

Reuland, D. S., Frasier, P. Y., Olson, M. D., Slatt, L. M., Aleman, M. A., & Fernandez, A. (2009). Accuracy of self-assessed Spanish fluency in medical students. *Teaching and Learning in Medicine*, *21*(4), 305–309.

Ross, S. J. (1998). Self-assessment in second language testing: A meta-analysis and analysis of experiential factors. *Language Testing*, *15*(1), 1–20.

Ross, J. A., Rolheiser, C., & Hogaboam-Gray, A. (1999). Effects of self-evaluation training on narrative writing. *Assessing Writing, 6*(1), 107–132.

Ross, J. A. (2006). The reliability, validity, and utility of self-assessment. *Practical Assessment Research & Evaluation*, *11*(10), 2.

Salili, F., Chiu, C. Y., & Lai, S. (2001). The influence of culture and context on students' achievement orientations. *Student Motivation: The Culture and Context of Learning*, 221–247.

Saida, C., & Hattori, T. (2004). The development of an item bank for English testing and a computer program for estimating ability. *ARELE: Annual Review of English Language Education in Japan*, *15*, 209–218.

Salehi, M., & Masoule, Z. S. (2017). An investigation of the reliability and validity of peer, self-, and teacher assessment. *Southern African Linguistics and Applied Language Studies*, *35*(1), 1–15.

Scholz, U., Doña, B. G., Sud, S., & Schwarzer, R. (2002). Is general self-efficacy a universal construct? Psychometric findings from 25 countries. *European Journal of Psychological Assessment*, *18*(3), 242.

Schunk, D. H. (2003). Self-efficacy for reading and writing: Influence of modeling, goal setting, and self-evaluation. *Reading & Writing Quarterly*, *19*(2), 159–172.

Schunk, D. H., & Zimmerman, B. J. (2007). Influencing children's self-efficacy and self-regulation of reading and writing through modeling. *Reading & Writing Quarterly*, *23*(1), 7–25.

Schwarz, N. (1999). Self-reports: How the questions shape the answers. *American Psychologist, 54*(2), 93.

Segers, M., & Dochy, F. (2001). New assessment forms in problem-based learning: The value-added of the students' perspective. *Studies in Higher Education, 26*(3), 327–343.

Sinharay, S., Feng, Y., Saldivia, L., Powers, D. E., Ginuta, A., Simpson, A., & Weng, V. (2008). Establishing the validity of TOEIC Bridge test scores for students in Colombia, Chile, and Ecuador. *ETS Research Report Series, 2008*(2), i-31.

Shohamy, E. (1992). Beyond proficiency testing: A diagnostic feedback testing model for assessing foreign language learning. *The Modern Language Journal, 76*(4), 513–521.

Spearman, C. (1904). "General Intelligence," objectively determined and measured. *The American Journal of Psychology, 15*(2), 201–292.

Strong-Krause, D. (2000). Exploring the effectiveness of self-assessment strategies in ESL placement. *Learner-Directed Assessment in ESL*, 49–73.

Strong, B., Davis, M., & Hawks, V. (2004). Self-grading in large general education classes: A case study. *College Teaching, 52*(2), 52–57.

Summers, M. M., Cox, T. L., McMurry, B. L., & Dewey, D. P. (2019). Investigating the use of the ACTFL can-do statements in a self-assessment for student placement in an Intensive English Program. *System, 80*, 269–287.

Suzuki, Y. (2015). Self-assessment of Japanese as a second language: The role of experiences in the naturalistic acquisition. *Language Testing, 32*(1), 63–81.

Tannenbaum, R. J., & Wylie, E. C. (2013). Mapping TOEIC and TOEIC Bridge test scores to the Common European Framework of Reference. *The Research Foundation for the TOEIC Tests: A Compendium of Studies, 2*, 6–1. Retrieved from: www.ets.org/Media/Research/pdf/TC2-06.pdf

Templer, B. (2004). High-stakes testing at high fees: Notes and queries on the international English proficiency assessment market. *Journal for Critical Education Policy Studies, 2*(1), 1–8.

Thompson, G., Pilgrim, A., & Oliver, K. (2005). Self-assessment and reflective learning for first-year university geography students: A simple guide or simply misguided? *Journal of Geography in Higher Education, 29*(3), 403–420.

Tomoschuk, B., Ferreira, V. S., & Gollan, T. H. (2019). When a seven is not a seven: Self-ratings of bilingual language proficiency differ between and within language populations. *Bilingualism: Language and Cognition, 22*(3), 516–536.

Urdan, T., & Pajares, F. (Eds.). (2006). *Self-efficacy Beliefs of Adolescents*. Greenwich, CT: IAP.

Usher, E. L., & Pajares, F. (2008). Self-efficacy for self-regulated learning: A validation study. *Educational and Psychological Measurement, 68*(3), 443–463.

Wang, C. (2004). *Self-Regulated Learning Strategies and Self-Efficacy Beliefs of Children Learning English as a Second Language*. Doctoral dissertation, The Ohio State University.

Wang, C., Kim, D. H., Bong, M., & Ahn, H. S. (2013). Examining measurement properties of an English self-efficacy scale for English language learners in Korea. *International Journal of Educational Research, 59*, 24–34.

Wang, J., Spencer, K., & Xing, M. (2009). Metacognitive beliefs and strategies in learning Chinese as a foreign language. *System, 37*(1), 46–56.

Zimmerman, B. J., & Martinez-Pons, M. (1986). Development of a structured interview for assessing student use of self-regulated learning strategies. *American Educational Research Journal, 23*(4), 614–628.

Zimmerman, B. J., Bandura, A., & Martinez-Pons, M. (1992). Self-motivation for academic attainment: The role of self-efficacy beliefs and personal goal setting. *American Educational Research Journal, 29*(3), 663–676.

Zimmerman, B. J., & Kitsantas, A. (2005). Homework practices and academic achievement: The mediating role of self-efficacy and perceived responsibility beliefs. *Contemporary Educational Psychology, 30*(4), 397–417.

Zell, E., & Krizan, Z. (2014). Do people have insight into their abilities? A metasynthesis. *Perspectives on Psychological Science, 9*(2), 111–125.

Appendix 9.1 Can-Do Self-Assessment

Instructions: Read each language use situation and rate your ability to use English successfully. Circle the number that best matches your level of confidence.

Example:

"I can introduce myself in English"

Not at all							Very well
1	2	3	4	5	6	7	8

		Not at all							Very well
1	I can count numbers in English	1	2	3	4	5	6	7	8
2	I can state possession of objects	1	2	3	4	5	6	7	8
3	I can tell time and dates	1	2	3	4	5	6	7	8
4	I can express likes and dislikes	1	2	3	4	5	6	7	8
5	I can talk about past events	1	2	3	4	5	6	7	8
6	I can ask where people are from	1	2	3	4	5	6	7	8
7	I can ask for object identification	1	2	3	4	5	6	7	8
8	I can describe clothes	1	2	3	4	5	6	7	8
9	I can describe my family	1	2	3	4	5	6	7	8
10	I can describe my weekly schedule	1	2	3	4	5	6	7	8
11	I can describe my home	1	2	3	4	5	6	7	8
12	I can describe my job	1	2	3	4	5	6	7	8
13	I can express basic needs	1	2	3	4	5	6	7	8
14	I can ask for assistance	1	2	3	4	5	6	7	8
15	I can ask for objects	1	2	3	4	5	6	7	8
16	I can describe abilities	1	2	3	4	5	6	7	8
17	I can ask for permission	1	2	3	4	5	6	7	8
18	I can offer objects	1	2	3	4	5	6	7	8
19	I can state obligations	1	2	3	4	5	6	7	8
20	I can describe quantities	1	2	3	4	5	6	7	8
21	I can describe volume	1	2	3	4	5	6	7	8
22	I can advise co-workers	1	2	3	4	5	6	7	8
23	I can state future plans	1	2	3	4	5	6	7	8
24	I can express time duration	1	2	3	4	5	6	7	8
25	I can give confirmations	1	2	3	4	5	6	7	8
26	I can remind co-workers of events and duties	1	2	3	4	5	6	7	8
27	I can ask for instructions	1	2	3	4	5	6	7	8
28	I can give instructions	1	2	3	4	5	6	7	8
29	I can make comparisons	1	2	3	4	5	6	7	8
30	I can ask for reasons	1	2	3	4	5	6	7	8
31	I can give warnings	1	2	3	4	5	6	7	8
32	I can describe present and past conditions	1	2	3	4	5	6	7	8
33	I can ask simple questions	1	2	3	4	5	6	7	8
34	I can describe event sequences	1	2	3	4	5	6	7	8

		Not at all							Very well
35	I can give step-by-step instructions	1	2	3	4	5	6	7	8
36	I can give reasons for actions	1	2	3	4	5	6	7	8
37	I can give instructions on how to attach an armrest	1	2	3	4	5	6	7	8
38	I can install the trunk garnish	1	2	3	4	5	6	7	8
39	I can give instructions on how to jack up a vehicle	1	2	3	4	5	6	7	8
40	I can make a self-introduction	1	2	3	4	5	6	7	8
41	I can give a job explanation	1	2	3	4	5	6	7	8
42	I can explain the steps in a process	1	2	3	4	5	6	7	8
43	I can describe the functions of workplace tools	1	2	3	4	5	6	7	8
44	I can express event possibilities	1	2	3	4	5	6	7	8
45	I can describe required accuracy levels	1	2	3	4	5	6	7	8
46	I can identify workplace people and objects	1	2	3	4	5	6	7	8
47	I can describe continuous action	1	2	3	4	5	6	7	8
48	I can describe event frequencies	1	2	3	4	5	6	7	8
49	I can describe the location of objects	1	2	3	4	5	6	7	8
50	I can explain steps in a process	1	2	3	4	5	6	7	8
51	I can explain key points in a process	1	2	3	4	5	6	7	8
52	I can direct trainees to attempt a task	1	2	3	4	5	6	7	8
53	I can introduce others to a trainee	1	2	3	4	5	6	7	8
54	I can inquire about workplace problems	1	2	3	4	5	6	7	8
55	I can identify workplace problems	1	2	3	4	5	6	7	8
56	I can express my opinion about a problem	1	2	3	4	5	6	7	8
57	I can make suggestions about a problem	1	2	3	4	5	6	7	8
58	I can express concerns about events or people	1	2	3	4	5	6	7	8
59	I can express worries about events or people	1	2	3	4	5	6	7	8
60	I can express work goals	1	2	3	4	5	6	7	8

10

STUDENT PROFICIENCY DEVELOPMENT IN UNIVERSITY FOREIGN LANGUAGE PROGRAMS

Daniel R. Isbell and Xiaowan Zhang

Introduction

The proficiency outcomes of foreign language programs in the United States have long been of interest to stakeholders in higher education. In this context, the American Council on the Teaching of Foreign Languages' (2012) *ACTFL Proficiency Guidelines 2012* ('*Guidelines*') are used as a common framework of reference in both setting and evaluating curricular goals. The American Council on the Teaching of Foreign Languages (ACTFL) framework distinguishes five major levels of proficiency: Novice, Intermediate, Advanced, Superior, and Distinguished, with the first three levels further divided into three sublevels, Low, Mid, and High. While language proficiency in communicative skills at the end of foreign language programs has long been of interest to those involved in tertiary language education (Carroll, 1967; Winke et al., 2018; Winke, Zhang, et al., 2020), such outcomes have also attracted the attention of stakeholders in the government and military who wish to take stock of the language skills of potential employees.

Although exit outcomes receive a great deal of (warranted) attention, examining the longitudinal growth of language proficiency can lead to additional insights for language programs and other policy makers. While end-of-program outcomes are ultimately critical for what graduates can be expected to be able to do next, they can raise many questions, such as:

- What factors contribute to students achieving higher levels of proficiency?
- What are appropriate pre-graduation targets for students in language programs?

One way of answering these questions is through cross-sectional studies. For example, by comparing the test scores of students at the end of their second year

DOI: 10.4324/9781003087939-11

and those at the end of their fourth year, some insights can be gleaned related to pre-graduate proficiency targets. Previous studies have shown that students in commonly taught European languages (e.g., French, German, and Spanish) typically attain Intermediate-Low to Intermediate-Mid in speaking at the end of the second year (Goertler et al., 2016; Hernández, 2006; Magnan, 1986; Norris & Pfeiffer, 2003; Tschirner, 1992) and Advanced-Low at the end of the fourth year (Glisan et al., 2013; Magnan, 1986), whereas students in less commonly taught language programs (e.g., Russian) on average lag behind their peers' learning by around two ACTFL sublevels in the first two years (Thompson, 1996). Some evidence suggests that the gap between commonly and less commonly taught language learners narrows in the third and fourth years (Glisan et al., 2013; Thompson, 1996). However useful cross-sectional analyses of test data may be, they are nonetheless limited by cohort effects (Little, 2013). As college language programs are built to guide students towards advanced proficiency levels and use placement tests to assign new students (and sometimes study-abroad returners) to courses appropriate for their proficiency levels, proficiency and program level can be confounded. For example, a cohort of "second-year" Spanish 201 students may be a mixture of students who began with Spanish 101 and students placed in Spanish 201 upon program entry due to proficiency developed in high school or as heritage speakers.

Previous longitudinal research in college foreign language programs by Isbell et al. (2019) and Zhang et al. (2020) has revealed several insights about oral proficiency development across languages. Isbell et al. (2019) examined two years of oral proficiency data, measured by the ACTFL Oral Proficiency Interview – computer (OPIc, reviewed by Isbell & Winke, 2019), across Chinese, French, Russian, and Spanish. Data included students with at least two test scores across all program levels. While overall higher levels of proficiency were found among French and Spanish learners, Isbell et al. found little difference in rates of growth across languages. Other factors (K-12 learning experience, heritage language status, number of university language courses taken, and motivation) explained a considerable portion of learners' initial proficiency levels and accounted for some of the difference in growth rates, with growth slowing down as learners accumulated more instruction. This latter finding was interpreted as commensurate with the *Guidelines*, in which higher levels of proficiency are characterized as larger, broader swaths of communicative competence.

Focusing on the first two years of Chinese, French, Russian, and Spanish language programs at the same university as Isbell et al. and using a program-referenced time scale (i.e., time 0 = 102; time 1 = 201, etc.), Zhang et al. (2020) found support for differences in both initial proficiency and growth rates. Matched for instructional level at the various waves of data collection, Chinese and Russian students progressed at roughly a third of an ACTFL sublevel slower each semester compared to their peers in French and Spanish programs. Thus, at least at earlier levels of instruction and proficiency, it appears that language proficiency may develop at different rates, which in turn brings important considerations for setting pre-graduation proficiency targets in different language programs (cf. Liskin-Gasparro, 1982, which reported substantially different learning rates across languages studied at the Defense Language Institute).

While both Isbell et al. (2019) and Zhang et al. (2020) have contributed to a better understanding of proficiency development in college foreign language programs, there is still much more to be learned. For one, skills beyond speaking are also worth investigation. Second, the languages covered by Isbell et al. and Zhang et al. are diverse (including commonly and less commonly taught languages), but expanding the scope of investigation to additional languages is also needed. Finally, the Isbell et al. and Zhang et al. studies both drew on data collected from the same university language programs, and as such the generalizability of their findings could be probed by including data from other sites.

The Current Study

This present study draws on a large longitudinal dataset that features ACTFL speaking, listening, and reading scores collected at two large public universities in the United States over the course of three years (Winke, Gass, et al., 2020). The study expands on previous analyses conducted by Isbell et al. (2019) and Zhang et al. (2020), which both focused solely on speaking proficiency growth across four foreign languages (Chinese, French, Russian, and Spanish) at one university. The following research questions (RQs) guided the study:

RQ1: How does student proficiency change over time in speaking, listening, and reading?
RQ2: How do student variables explain differences in initial proficiency and growth for speaking, listening, and reading?

Methods

Data

Data in this study include archived proficiency test data and background information collected by Winke, Gass et al. (2020). This dataset includes 22,979 proficiency test scores in speaking, listening, and reading collected from students studying ten languages at three US universities over the course of three academic years from fall 2014 through spring 2017. The dataset also includes background information for students who were tested in spring 2017. According to Winke, Gass et al., proficiency in all three skills was assessed using computer-delivered tests administered by Language Testing International, an official testing subsidiary for ACTFL. Specifically, the OPIc, the Reading Proficiency Test (RPT), and the

Listening Proficiency Test (LPT) were used to assess speaking, reading, and listening skills, respectively. Whereas the OPIc was rated by ACTFL-certified raters, the multiple-choice listening and reading tests were automatically and objectively scored. Scores from two universities were reported on the ACTFL scale, whereas those from the other university were reported out on the Interagency Language Roundtable (ILR) scale.

For this study, three longitudinal datasets were constructed, one for each skill, to investigate the relationship between proficiency growth and background characteristics for undergraduate students learning Arabic, Chinese, French, Russian, and Spanish. For each skill, data were gathered from students who had complete background information and were tested in that skill more than one time over the three-year data collection span. As most students obtained scores on the ACTFL scale, those students with ILR scores were excluded due to the lack of a one-to-one correspondence with the ACTFL scale. This resulted in one of the three universities being excluded. Students must have obtained viable ACTFL test scores to be included in this study, which means that non-scored tests with a rating of below range, above range, or unratable were excluded. This yielded a speaking dataset with 452 cases, a reading dataset with 336 cases, and a listening dataset with 296 cases. Arabic learners were excluded from the listening dataset due to scarcity ($n = 2$). For each skill, time 0 is defined as a student's first test score. Subsequent time points indicate the number of semesters that had elapsed since the first test (ranging from one to five semesters). This definition of time resulted in six time points in each dataset, namely time 0 through time 5. In each dataset, students had at least two scores and up to five scores. Most students had two speaking, listening, or reading scores, while a few had five test scores in a particular skill. Full details on missing data are provided in Table 10A1 in the e-companion/online materials.

Outcome variables of interest included speaking, reading, and listening proficiency scores, all on the ACTFL scale. To facilitate data analyses, the ACTFL scores were numerically coded as integers following Kenyon and Malabonga (2001), with 1 representing Novice Low and 10 representing Superior. Every one-point increment represented a one-sublevel increase on the ACTFL scale. Background variables included target language (Spanish, the largest group, chosen as the reference category), initial level of instruction at time 0 (three categories indicating enrollment in first-year, second-year, or third/fourth-year courses, with first-year courses as the reference category), total number of years of K-12 language instruction (ranging from 1 to 13, with 13 indicating that the student had studied the target language for 13 years from kindergarten through twelfth grade), heritage learner status (0 = non-heritage learner, 1 = heritage learner), language major and minor status (0 = non-major/minor, 1 = language major/minor), and school (school A and B, with the larger A as reference). Only major and minor status were treated as time-varying variables; all remaining background characteristics of interest were time-invariant.

Analyses

The data were first examined from a descriptive standpoint, including visualization. To answer the first and second RQs, three separate growth curve analyses (one analysis for each skill) were performed using a mixed-effects modeling approach (Mirman, 2014). All analyses were conducted using *lme4* (version 1.1-23, Bates, Maechler, Bolker, & Walker, 2015) and *lmerTest* (version 3.1-2, Kuznetsova, Brockhoff, & Christensen, 2017) packages in R 4.0.2. (R Core Team, 2020). For each skill, a series of two-level models were fitted to predict proficiency growth in that skill as a function of time (as measured in semester) and background variables. Given that repeated measures of proficiency were nested within individual subjects, Level 1 models were used to predict *within-subject* change over time, and Level 2 models were used to explain *between-subject* differences in initial status and change over time (Singer & Willet, 2003). The same model-building and testing procedure was used for the analysis for each skill (described below):

1. First, an unconditional means model (i.e., a model without covariates) with a random intercept term (Model 1a) was fitted to delineate the amount of within- and between-subject variance in proficiency scores. Model 1a provided a useful baseline for evaluating subsequent models and allowed us to assess whether there was significant within- and between-subject variance to be explained by predictors.
2. Next, time was entered into Model 1a as the only covariate to determine the shape of students' proficiency growth. Two alternative unconditional growth models were fitted, one *linear* model (Model 1b) and one *quadratic* model (Model 1c). Both models included a linear fixed effect for time and a random intercept, and Model 1c also included a quadratic fixed effect for time. Models 1a and 1b were first compared to determine if the linear time effect was significant; if so, Models 1b and 1c would be further compared to test the significance of the quadratic term. Models that failed to converge were not considered further. The model selected in this step was the most parsimonious model that provided best goodness of fit to the data.
3. Then, random effects for time slopes were included in the model selected in step 2 to test whether the effect of time varied significantly across subjects. All random effects were allowed to correlate with each other. The model selected in step 2 was first compared with a random-*linear*-slope model, Model 1d (i.e., a model with a random linear slope for time and a random intercept). If Model 1d provided a significantly better fit to the data and had a quadratic term, it would be further compared with a random-*quadratic*-slope model, Model 1e (i.e., a model with a random linear slope and a random quadratic slope for time and a random intercept). Models that did not converge or were not identified were not considered further. Again, the most parsimonious model that provided best fit to the data was selected in this step.

4. After the best-fitting unconditional growth model was determined, the following background variables were entered into the model as fixed-effects covariates for the intercept and linear time slope: language, program level, heritage learner status, K-12 language experience, major and minor status, and school (Model 2). Background variables were only allowed to interact with the linear time slope in cases where the linear time slope had a significant random effect.

Alternative models were compared via log-likelihood ratio tests (LRTs). Inferences about specific fixed-effects predictors are based on coefficient estimates and associated p values (with alpha level set to $p < 0.05$). For model diagnosis, model residuals were examined via QQ-plots, histograms of residuals, and residual plots. These plots are available from the authors upon request.

Results

The results are presented in two parts: descriptive statistics of test scores over time, which address RQ1, and growth models, which primarily address RQ2.

Descriptive Statistics

Table 10.1 presents a summary of test scores for each skill across the six time points, aggregated across learners and languages. For speaking, the average initial proficiency was approximately Intermediate Low and the average proficiency five semesters later was about Intermediate Mid. For listening, an initial average ability somewhere between Novice High and Intermediate Low was observed while the average five semesters later was close to Intermediate High. Reading proficiency was highest overall, with an initial average of Intermediate High and an average of Advanced Low five semesters later. It should be noted that there were markedly fewer observations at later time points, and that these aggregate summary statistics do not account for differences across languages nor do they clearly reflect growth within individuals.

TABLE 10.1 Test summary statistics by measurement occasion

Time	Speaking				Listening				Reading			
	n	M	sd	Med.	n	M	sd	Med.	n	M	sd	Med.
0	452	4.03	1.44	4	298	3.54	1.93	4	336	4.06	1.95	4
1	123	4.33	1.36	4	97	3.56	1.69	4	105	3.92	1.80	4
2	278	4.46	1.38	4	153	3.87	2.03	4	182	4.53	2.07	4
3	116	4.74	1.26	5	69	4.94	1.46	5	66	5.77	1.75	6
4	63	4.89	1.49	5	25	5.76	1.20	6	30	6.43	1.33	7
5	87	5.18	1.35	5	32	5.81	1.49	6	34	6.97	1.45	7

Tables 10A2, 10A3, and 10A4 in the e-companion/online materials contain summary statistics for speaking, listening, and reading scores broken down by language at each time point. Importantly, these tables illustrate some language-specific gaps and points of scarcity in the data. In speaking and reading, Arabic data are missing at time 1, 3, and 5 and only two observations were available for time 4. Similarly, no Chinese learner data are present at time 4 or 5 in listening or reading. In terms of mean/median scores, some variability across languages at the initial observation and later observations was apparent. For example, in speaking Chinese and Russian learners were a whole sublevel lower, on average, compared to learners of other languages (Novice High vs. Intermediate Low), and this also held five semesters later (roughly Intermediate Low vs. Intermediate Mid). French learners had visibly higher listening scores across all time points, and French and Spanish learners achieved impressive proficiency levels at later time points, with an average of Advanced Low five semesters later. The impressive average speaking scores of Arabic learners is notable (Intermediate High/Advanced Low at time 4), but as mentioned the average found at the fourth retest is based on only two learners.

The language breakdown of average scores at different time points was interesting, but still does not account for within-learner growth. Figure 10.1 illustrates the average growth trends (black, triangle-studded lines) and individual linear growth trajectories of individual learners in speaking, listening, and reading skills, with students sorted by initial proficiency level (panels). Presenting the data in this way usefully illustrates differing growth trends across (up to) five semesters of instruction. Across all three skills, average growth appears greater at lower initial proficiency levels. This initially rapid rate of growth appears to taper off sooner for speaking but is sustained for longer for receptive skills: speaking growth tends to slow down after crossing the intermediate threshold, while listening and reading do not flatten until the advanced threshold. Another visible trend is that the proportion of learners showing overall positive growth, from their first to last test scores, seems to be higher among learners with lower initial proficiencies.

Speaking

An unconditional growth model was selected that included a linear and quadratic fixed effect for time and correlated random effects for subject intercepts and linear time slopes. Background variables and their interactions with linear time were entered as fixed-effect covariates (Table 10.2). The conditional model provided a statistically significant superior fit to the data compared to the unconditional model according to an LRT, $\chi^2 (22) = 484.36, p < 0.001$. In this conditional model, a significant quadratic time effect was not obtained. The covariates accounted for approximately 71% of the intercept variance and 65% of the slope variance compared to the unconditional model (model marginal $R^2 = 0.54$,

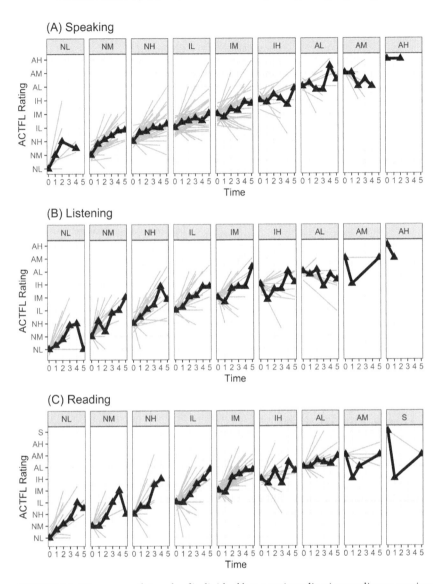

FIGURE 10.1 Linear growth trends of individual learners (gray lines) according to starting proficiency, with group means at each time point represented by triangle-studded black lines. ACTFL = American Council on the Teaching of Foreign Languages.

conditional $R^2 = 0.81$). While the unconditional model yielded a non-trivial negative correlation between subject intercepts and slope ($r = -0.36$), indicating that growth was slower for students with higher initial proficiency, inclusion of the covariates substantially changed this relationship ($r = 0.10$). Most covariates significantly predicted subject intercepts, except for academic status (major/minor),

TABLE 10.2 Growth curve model results – speaking

	Unconditional growth model	Conditional growth model	
Random effects			
Intercept	1.67	0.50	
Slope (time)	0.02	0.01	
Correlation	−0.36	0.10	
Fixed effects	B (SE)	B (SE)	
Intercept	4.04 (0.07)★★★	2.31 (0.12)★★★	
Time	0.31 (0.04)★★★	0.45 (0.05)★★★	
Time^2	−0.02 (0.01)★	−0.01 (0.01)	
		Intercept	*Slope*
Arabic		0.43 (0.25)	0.26 (0.09)★★
Chinese		−0.12 (0.14)	−0.11 (0.04)★
French		0.54 (0.11)★★★	0.01 (0.04)
Russian		0.10 (0.18)	−0.09 (0.06)
200-level		0.77 (0.12)★★★	−0.12 (0.04)★★
> 200-level		1.88 (0.14)★★★	−0.21 (0.05)★★★
Heritage		1.32 (0.16)★★★	−0.14 (0.05)★
K-12		0.08 (0.02)★★★	−0.02 (0.01)★★
School B		1.25 (0.15)★★★	−0.09 (0.05)
Major		0.20 (0.11)	0.13 (0.04)★★
Minor		0.07 (0.10)	−0.01 (0.04)

★$p < 0.05$; ★★$p < 0.01$; ★★★$p < 0.001$.

with French students starting off about half a level higher than Spanish students. Focusing on time covariates, growth rates significantly slowed at higher program levels, for heritage learners, and for those with more K-12 learning experience, and for Chinese learners, but increased for academic majors and, notably, Arabic learners.

Figure 10.2 (first column) compares empirical averages (points with error bars) and model predictions (lines) for speaking proficiency development over time across several relevant subgroupings (language, initial course level, and heritage status). Lines that come close to points indicate a reasonably good match-up between model predictions and actual proficiency levels. On average, speaking ability predictions followed empirical observations for the various subgroup breakdowns. Readers are advised that fluctuations in the trends visible in Figure 10.2 are largely reflective of the sampling of learners (and conversely, missing data) at each time point; *individual* Chinese learners do not generally regress in speaking proficiency four semesters after their initial tests.

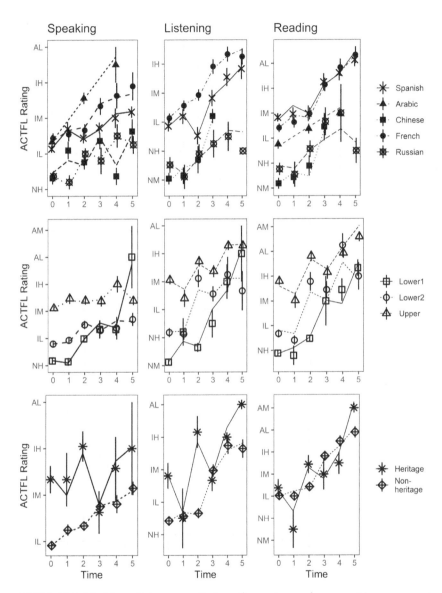

FIGURE 10.2 Model proficiency predictions for various subgroups. Lines represent the mean of conditional growth model predictions while points with standard error bars correspond to empirical values. ACTFL = American Council on the Teaching of Foreign Languages.

Listening

For listening growth, an unconditional model was selected that included a linear fixed effect of time and random effects including intercepts and linear time slopes. In this model, random intercepts and slopes were non-trivially and negatively correlated ($r = -0.35$). A conditional model with the addition of all fixed-effect covariates (Table 10.3) was able to explain 77% of intercept variation and 83% of slope variation (model marginal $R^2 = 0.67$, conditional $R^2 = 0.85$). It is worth noting that there was initially relatively little random-slope variation (variance = 0.04) in the unconditional model, but nonetheless the conditional model was able to explain a considerable proportion of it. Interestingly, the correlation between random intercepts and slopes became more strongly negative in the conditional model ($r = -0.47$).

The fixed-effects covariates of program level, heritage status, K-12 experience, and school all had positive effects on the intercept. For languages, Chinese had a large negative effect on the intercept while French had a moderate positive effect (both compared to Spanish). Turning to time interactions, growth slowed down in

TABLE 10.3 Growth curve model results – listening

	Unconditional growth model	Conditional growth model	
Random effects			
Intercept	3.21	0.74	
Slope (time)	0.04	0.01	
Correlation	−0.35	−0.47	
Fixed effects	B (SE)	B (SE)	
Intercept	3.51 (0.11)★★★	1.71 (0.17)★★★	
Time	0.32 (0.03)★★★	0.26 (0.07)★★★	
		Intercept	*Slope*
Chinese		−1.75 (0.22)★★★	0.24 (0.09)★★
French		0.59 (0.15)★★★	0.23 (0.05)★★★
Russian		−0.21 (0.26)	−0.18 (0.10)
200-level		1.19 (0.18)★★★	−0.01 (0.07)
> 200-level		2.66 (0.21)★★★	−0.22 (0.08)★★
Heritage		1.09 (0.24)★★★	0.03 (0.08)
K-12		0.07 (0.03)★★	0.00 (0.01)
School B		1.53 (0.20)★★★	−0.06 (0.07)
Major		−0.07 (0.18)	0.10 (0.07)
Minor		−0.09 (0.15)	0.08 (0.07)

★$p < 0.05$; ★★$p < 0.01$; ★★★$p < 0.001$.

upper-division courses while increased growth, compared to Spanish, was found for Chinese and French. No other covariates had significant effects associated with growth rates. Like the speaking model predictions, listening model predictions largely aligned with empirical observations (Figure 10.2, second column).

Reading

For reading, an unconditional growth model was selected that included a linear time fixed effect and a random intercept, but no random time slope (Table 10.4). Adding fixed-effect covariates in a conditional model explained approximately 74% of intercept variation (model marginal $R^2 = 0.63$, conditional $R^2 = 0.83$). The fixed effects of program level, heritage status, K-12 experience, and school all had positive effects on the intercept. Among languages, Chinese, Russian, and Arabic had lower initial reading test scores compared to Spanish and French. With little variation in reading growth (time slopes) across participants, interactions between covariates and time were not included. Like the speaking and listening model predictions, reading model predictions tracked well with empirical observations (Figure 10.2, third column).

TABLE 10.4 Growth curve model results – reading

	Unconditional growth model	Conditional growth model
Random effects		
Intercept	3.07	0.86
Fixed effects	B (SE)	B (SE)
Intercept	4.02 (0.10)★★★	2.76 (0.16)★★★
Time	0.38 (0.02)★★★	0.37 (0.03)★★★
		Intercept
Arabic		−0.69 (0.32)★
Chinese		−2.24 (0.21)★★★
French		0.03 (0.15)
Russian		−1.01 (0.24)★★★
200-level		1.21 (0.17)★★★
> 200-level		2.56 (0.20)★★★
Heritage		0.46 (0.22)★
K-12		0.05 (0.03)★
School B		1.40 (0.19)★★★
Major		0.02 (0.15)
Minor		0.04 (0.12)

★$p < 0.05$; ★★$p < 0.01$; ★★★$p < 0.001$.

Discussion

In several ways, the findings related to growth of speaking proficiency are similar to those of Isbell et al. (2019). In both studies, the average initial proficiency level was around Intermediate Low, and after three semesters the average was around Intermediate Mid. Growth rates were greater in the present study (0.31 sublevel per semester compared to 0.23 for unconditional models in each study). This faster growth may be partially explained by the addition of another language (Arabic) and another university. While the growth modeling approach in this study is most similar to Isbell et al., the speaking levels and growth rates observed in this study are also comparable to those reported in Zhang et al. (2020). In the unconditional growth models, listening growth (0.32 sublevel/semester) was similar to speaking while reading (0.38) was slightly higher.

Growth in reading differed from speaking and listening. Namely, there was such little variation in growth rates that it was unnecessary to model a random time slope or include interactions between time and other covariates. This finding was somewhat surprising given the non-trivial variation found in growth rates for the other skills. The lack of random variation in reading proficiency growth rates could simply be an artefact of the sample. With this caveat in mind, some speculatory interpretation of these results will be offered. Unlike the other skills, reading comprehension is less speeded, and learners featured in the present study, all university students, had advanced literacy skills in at least one other language that they could potentially transfer to their second language. Reading comprehension is generally well explained by language knowledge (grammar and vocabulary) and decoding skills (i.e., the Simple View of Reading, Hoover & Gough, 1990; see also Kremmel et al., 2017). It may be that because decoding can be mastered relatively quickly by adult learners, similar rates of growth in grammar knowledge and vocabulary size among learners within and across foreign language programs in turn lead to highly similar rates of reading comprehension improvement. Reasonable objections might be made to this interpretation along the lines of (1) greater difficulty in acquiring effective decoding of non-alphabetic scripts for Arabic and Chinese learners or (2) fewer lexical cognates available for Arabic, Chinese, and Russian learners. Further longitudinal research on reading ability using standardized tests would be well complemented by repeated measurements of decoding ability and lexical knowledge.

Contrary to Isbell et al. (2019), but in line with Zhang et al. (2020), the present study found appreciable differences in speaking growth rates across languages. While this study adopted the statistical approach of Isbell et al. (i.e., growth curve analysis in a linear mixed-effect modeling framework), it also adopted the inclusion of initial program level as a time-invariant covariate, similar to Zhang et al. (but note that Zhang et al. included program level as a time-varying covariate that defined time scores). Doing so accounts for much of the observed differences in growth rate that are attributable to the differences in program level at time 0, and in turn allows the remaining differences across languages to be detected. There is some conflation between student proficiency and course level, as curricula (and initial student placements) are generally designed with target proficiency levels in mind, but clearly there are different rates of growth at different levels of proficiency. One particularly striking finding was the superior speaking growth rates for learners of Arabic. Although this finding should be taken in moderation due to the small number of Arabic learners (33 in the speaking data), it runs counter to widely touted claims that Arabic is an incredibly difficult language for (English-speaking) American students, and in turn slower to be learned (Liskin-Gasparro, 1982). As it turns out, all Arabic learners were from one school (School B). It may be worth investigating the Arabic program at School B to find out what seems to be working so well for oral proficiency development. Of course, future research would benefit from including more Arabic learners and learners from other universities.

Speaking was not the only skill in which differences in growth rates across languages were observed. In fact, the differences appeared to be even greater for listening ability. Here, compared to Spanish, French and Chinese listening proficiency developed at faster rates (nearly double). This contrasts with Tschirner's (2016) finding that listening proficiency was lower in French than in Spanish at almost all levels of instruction. The discrepancy between the two studies may be attributed to different research designs: while a longitudinal approach was used in this study, Tschirner relied on cross-sectional analyses, which may have led to compromised results due to cohort effects (Little, 2013). With respect to oft-cited difficulty in rankings of languages, the Chinese listening proficiency growth is surprising, as Chinese is considered among the most difficult languages for American students to learn. One possible explanation is that Spanish is commonly taken by students seeking to satisfy minimum foreign language coursework requirements, meaning they may be less motivated and invest less time and effort into their learning compared to students who select languages like French or Chinese, especially given the perceived difficulty and fewer opportunities to study the latter before university. While the present study included several covariates like initial course level, K-12 learning experience, and major/minor status which partially accounted for these potential differences in initial proficiency and investment, a self-selection effect could nonetheless be at play.

Alternatively, in the case of Chinese, these findings may also be an artefact of the data available. No observations of Chinese listening proficiency were available at the final two time points (four and five semesters after the initial test), and although initial program level was included as a covariate to account for differences in initial proficiency, Chinese students nonetheless had a substantially lower intercept (initial proficiency) in the listening model. Given what is known about slower rates of growth at higher proficiency levels (i.e., Figure 10.1 and the -0.47 correlation between slopes and intercepts in the listening model), the deck may be stacked when comparing to the growth rates of Chinese learners.

Implications

Across all skills, prior learning in K-12 contributed to higher initial proficiency ratings. Despite proficiency growth slowing down at higher ACTFL levels, learners with higher initial proficiency levels nonetheless tended to maintain an absolute advantage in subsequent semesters (see Figure 10.1 and the middle row of Figure 10.2). This trend is also seen in the average proficiency levels of students studying the same language: learners of Spanish and French, widely taught in K-12 settings, tend to start higher and finish higher. In other words, students with lower proficiency levels advance quickly but are mostly unable to catch up to their more proficient peers over the course of several years of college foreign language learning. These findings speak to the efficacy of K-12 foreign language education and the unique contribution it makes towards developing highly proficient adult language users (Bernhardt & Leffell, 2020; Winke, Zhang et al., 2020).

Similarly, heritage language learners also had a leg up on their peers, with an average initial proficiency level over one sublevel higher in speaking and listening and half a sublevel higher in reading. Like K-12 learning experience, exposure to the target language in the home/community is clearly beneficial and contributes to achieving higher levels of proficiency in university. Language programs should be encouraged to cater specifically to heritage learners in recruitment and course offerings, such as accelerated tracks. Further, the results of this study also reflect a common phenomenon in which heritage learners possess stronger oral than written language skills. This might motivate language programs to offer heritage-oriented courses dedicated to foundational literacy and intensive reading.

On a methodological note, there are some challenges in using ACTFL ratings. As mentioned, the sublevels of the *ACTFL Guidelines* are not units of uniform quantity. Nonetheless, this study treated all sublevels as representative of equal intervals, as has been done in several other studies. Doing so allows the use of easier-to-estimate linear models which yield parameter estimates in the same metric as the dependent variable, i.e., ACTFL sublevels, rather than less intuitive metrics such as odds ratios. While this choice should not fundamentally distort the findings of this study, given the clearly observable differences in growth rates at different proficiency levels, it may become useful, if not necessary, for researchers to appropriately treat the relations among ACTFL ratings as ordinal. Related to this point, for the reading and listening tests interval-scaled test scores are converted to the coarser ACTFL sublevel rating, potentially masking subtler trends in growth. That said, the ACTFL ratings are meaningful in real-world decision making and program development, and thus researchers should not shy away from some of the technical challenges the ratings may present from an analytical perspective.

Last, and with the previous points in mind, this study may call into question the comparability of test scores across languages. The accelerated Arabic speaking and Chinese listening growth defy common expectations. Possible explanations have been discussed in terms of different learner profiles and learning contexts, but to some extent misalignment of test scores across languages could partially account for these findings (Isbell et al., 2019; Isbell & Winke, 2019). Does a Novice High in Chinese mean the same thing, in terms of functional language ability, as a Novice High in Spanish? Similarly, is the difference between Novice Mid and

Novice High equivalent for French and Arabic? The present study cannot answer these questions, but the analyses and interpretations of this data would be better informed if these questions were answered by rigorous empirical research.

Conclusion

This chapter reported on growth curve analyses of foreign language proficiency test scores spanning hundreds of learners across three skills, five languages, and two universities in the United States. Reinforcing the findings of Zhang et al. (2020), this study provided further evidence of differences in speaking growth rates across languages when program level (and by proxy, initial proficiency) are accounted for. Building on previous work that has focused on speaking ability, the present study expanded the scope of investigation to receptive skills and facilitated comparisons of growth in listening and reading ability. Perhaps most striking in these comparisons is the higher levels of overall attainment in reading and minimal variation in reading growth rates. Future research that involves other contexts, longer time spans, and well-measured background characteristics and individual differences is needed to continue to refine the understanding of how foreign language learners develop their skills over time.

References

American Council on the Teaching of Foreign Languages. (2012). *ACTFL proficiency guidelines 2012*. Retrieved from www.actfl.org/sites/default/files/pdfs/ACTFLProficiencyGuidelines2012_FINAL.pdf

Bates, D., Maechler, M., Bolker, B., & Walker, S. (2015). Fitting linear mixed-effects models using lme4. *Journal of Statistical Software, 67*(1), 1–48. https://doi.org/10.18637/jss.v067.i01

Bernhardt, E. B., & Leffell, C. M. (2020). Oral proficiency levels of first-year entering college students with and without Advanced Placement scores. *Foreign Language Annals, 53*, 401–415. https://doi.org/10.1111/flan.12484

Carroll, J. B. (1967). Foreign language proficiency levels attained by language majors near graduation from college. *Foreign Language Annals, 1*(2), 131–151.

Glisan, E. W., Swender, E., & Surface, E. A. (2013). Oral proficiency standards and foreign language teacher candidates: Current findings and future research directions. *Foreign Language Annals, 46*(2), 264–289. https://doi.org/10.1111/flan.12030

Goertler, S., Kramer, A., & Schenker, T. (2016). Setting evidence-based language goals. *Foreign Language Annals, 49*(3), 434–454. https://doi.org/10.1111/flan.12214

Hernández, T. A. (2006). Integrative motivation as a predictor of achievement in the foreign language classroom. *Foreign Language Annals, 39*, 605–617. https://doi.org/10.1111/j.1944-9720.2006.tb02279.x

Hoover, W. A., & Gough, P. B. (1990). The simple view of reading. *Reading and Writing: An Interdisciplinary Journal, 2*, 127–160.

Isbell, D. R., & Winke, P. (2019). ACTFL Oral Proficiency Interview–computer (OPIc). *Language Testing, 36*, 467–477. https://doi.org/10.1177/0265532219828253

Isbell, D. R., Winke, P., & Gass, S. M. (2019). Using the ACTFL OPIc to assess proficiency and monitor progress in a tertiary foreign languages program. *Language Testing, 36*(3), 439–465. https://doi.org/10.1177/0265532218798139

Kenyon, D. M., & Malabonga, V. (2001). Comparing examinee attitudes toward computer-assisted and other oral proficiency assessments. *Language Learning & Technology, 5*(2), 60–83.

Kremmel, B., Brunfaut, T., & Alderson, J. C. (2017). Exploring the role of phraseological knowledge in foreign language reading. *Applied Linguistics, 38*(6), 848–870. https://doi.org/10.1093/applin/amv070

Kuznetsova, A., Brockhoff, P. B., & Christensen, R. H. B. (2017). lmerTest package: Tests in linear mixed effects models. *Journal of Statistical Software, 82*(13), 1–26. https://doi.org/10.18637/jss.v082.i13

Liskin-Gasparro, J. E. (1982). *ETS oral proficiency testing manual.* Princeton, NJ: Educational Testing Service.

Little, T. D. (2013). *Longitudinal structural equation modeling.* New York: Guilford Press.

Magnan, S. S. (1986). Assessing speaking proficiency in the undergraduate curriculum: Data from French. *Foreign Language Annals, 19,* 429–438. https://doi.org/10.1111/j.1944-9720.1986.tb01031.x

Mirman, D. (2014). *Growth curve analysis and visualization using R.* New York, NY: CRC Press.

Norris, J. M., & Pfeiffer, P. C. (2003). Exploring the usefulness of ACTFL oral proficiency ratings and standards in college foreign language departments. *Foreign Language Annals, 36,* 572–581. https://doi.org/10.1111/j.1944-9720.2003.tb02147.x

R Core Team. (2020). R: A language and environment for statistical computing. Vienna, Austria: R Foundation for Statistical Computing. www.R-project.org/.

Singer, J. D., & Willet, J. B. (2003). *Applied longitudinal data analysis: Modeling change and event occurrence.* Oxford: Oxford University Press.

Thompson, I. (1996). Assessing foreign language skills: Data from Russian. *The Modern Language Journal, 80,* 47–65.

Tschirner, E. (1992). Oral proficiency base lines for first- and second-year college German. *Die Unterrichtspraxis/Teaching German, 25*(1), 10–14.

Tschirner, E. (2016). Listening and reading proficiency levels of college students. *Foreign Language Annals, 49*(2), 201–223. https://doi.org/10.1111/flan.12198

Winke, P., Gass, S. M., & Heidrich, E. S. (2018). Modern-day foreign language majors: Their goals, attainment, and fit within a twenty-first century curriculum. In P. Winke & S. M. Gass (Eds.), *Foreign Language Proficiency in Higher Education* (pp. 93–113). Cham: Springer.

Winke, P. M., Gass, S. M., Soneson, D., Rubio, F., & Hacking, J. F. (2020). Foreign language proficiency test data from three American universities, 2014–2017. Inter-university Consortium for Political and Social Research, 2020-03-10. https://doi.org/10.3886/ICPSR37499.v1

Winke, P., Zhang, X., Rubio, F., Gass, S., Soneson, D., & Hacking, J. (2020). The proficiency profile of language students: Implications for programs. *Second Language Research & Practice, 1*(1), 25–64.

Zhang, X., Winke, P., & Clark, S. (2020). Background characteristics and oral proficiency development over time in lower-division college foreign language programs. *Language Learning, 70*(3), 807–847. https://doi.org/10.1111/lang.12396

INDEX